The Many Faces of Islam

Florida A&M University, Tallahassee
Florida Atlantic University, Boca Raton
Florida Gulf Coast University, Ft. Myers
Florida International University, Miami
Florida State University, Tallahassee
University of Central Florida, Orlando
University of Florida, Gainesville
University of North Florida, Jacksonville
University of South Florida, Tampa
University of West Florida, Pensacola

The Many Faces of Islam

Perspectives on a
Resurgent Civilization

Nissim Rejwan

University Press of Florida

Gainesville Tallahassee·Tampa Boca Raton
Pensacola Orlando Miami Jacksonville Ft. Myers

05 04 03 02 01 00 6 5 4 3 2 1

Library of Congress Cataloging-in-Publication Data
The Many faces of Islam / Nissim Rejwan [editor].
p. cm.
ISBN 0-8130-1807-2 (cloth: alk. paper)
1. Islam—Appreciation. 2. Islam—Essence, genius, nature. 3. Islam and
world politics. 4. Islam—20th century. 5. Islamic countries—politics and
government. I. Rejwan, Nissim.
BP163.M363   2000
297—dc21   00-032587

The University Press of Florida is the scholarly publishing agency for the
State University System of Florida, comprising Florida A&M University,
Florida Atlantic University, Florida Gulf Coast University, Florida
International University, Florida State University, University of Central
Florida, University of Florida, University of North Florida, University of
South Florida, and University of West Florida.

University Press of Florida
15 Northwest 15th Street
Gainesville, FL 32611–2079
http://www.upf.com

God does not charge a soul with more than it can bear.

It shall be requited for whatever good or whatever evil it had done.

The Qur'an, trans. N. J. Dawood

Contents

Preface

With the rise and continued growth of what has been variously called Islamic fundamentalism, Islamism, radical Islam, and Islamic extremism, it has become customary to identify Islam generally with these movements, their teachings, and their practices. This of course is fundamentally wrong both theologically and historically, and has led to distorting and maligning Islam as religion, as culture, and as a way of life.

Not that this distorted image of Islam and the Muslims is new in the non-Muslim world, especially the West; it has just been made more widespread by recent developments in countries like Algeria, the Sudan, Iran, Egypt, and Jordan.

Nor have these misconceptions remained unchallenged; a number of commentators and specialists in the field, Muslims and non-Muslims alike, have written extensively about the subject, warning against generalizations of this kind—generalizations to which, to be sure, Muslim extremists themselves continue to lend credence by their own often mindless utterances and actions.

Sometime in the mid-1970s, London hosted an Islamic exhibition of considerable proportions called the World of Islam Festival. In the spate of books, pamphlets, brochures, and reviews which descended from everywhere and sundry, one was liable to lose sight of the forest for the trees. But the declared aim of the event was clear enough. It was to correct the distorted picture of Islam said to have been accepted in the West and to have prevailed there for too long. The organizers of the festival believed that such a rectification could best be achieved by providing Westerners with the opportunity of seeing Islam and Islamic civilization as the Muslims themselves saw them.

The underlying assumption—namely that Islam and the Muslims have for centuries been misunderstood in the West and their image distorted—is fairly valid even though much of what the West and the world now know about Islam as religion and as civilization was made possible largely thanks to that branch of Western scholarship that we have come to know as Oriental studies. (One indeed is constantly struck by the amount of borrowing many Muslim and Arab students of Islam allow themselves to make from these studies, otherwise much maligned and condemned as at best ill conceived and inaccurate, at worst ill intentioned, condescending, and a tool in the hands of missionaries and imperialists.)

And yet there is a good deal of justice in the claim that the West's overall image of Islam, and the East generally, is considerably distorted. Lord Macaulay claimed over a century ago never to have met any student of Eastern languages who could convince him that the whole of Oriental literature was worth a single shelf of the classics of Europe. This verdict was dismissed by the late Arthur J. Arberry as "a partly malicious and wholly ignorant misrepresentation of the facts."

In undertaking this brief survey of Islam and of the variegated ways in which it is viewed by the non-Muslim world, and in collating the short reading selections appended to each of the ten chapters, my aim has been to make a modest contribution toward rectifying such widespread misconceptions.

This work is aimed at the enlightened general reader, as well as the interested specialist, and it is written in what the author hopes is an easily accessible style; the selected readings, too, are meant to inform and instruct rather than to break new ground. However, while no pretense is made here to make any special contribution to the literature available in the field, I hope that the authenticity and accessibility of the presentation, and its wide-ranging coverage, will justify the basic thrust of the book's title—namely, that viewing Islam as being uniform and monolithic can result in confusion and miscomprehensions and, ultimately, in conflict.

Credits for permissions to use passages excerpted in Readings are listed at the end of the book. My thanks are due also to the directors and staff of the Harry S. Truman Institute for the Advancement of Peace, Hebrew University, Jerusalem, where as a Research Fellow I continue to enjoy their hospitality, encouragement, and help.

1

The Uniqueness of Islam

In at least three Arab states—Algeria in the West (*Maghrib*), Jordan in the East (*Mashriq*), and Sudan in the Nile Valley—Islamic fundamentalism has been gaining in strength. In Algeria, especially, the Islamic Salvation Front remains a serious contender for power with the ruling National Liberation Front, while in Jordan the Muslim Brotherhood has nearly a third of the seats in Parliament. Both movements call for the establishment of an Islamic state run and administered according to the rules of the *shariᶜa* (religious law). However, while these calls are not new, there is no unanimity of opinion on the subject among Muslim theologians. There are, in fact, two leading schools of thought, two answers to the question of how a Muslim community should conduct its affairs in the modern world.

There is, first, the answer provided by leading Muslim thinkers in Egypt of the late nineteenth and early twentieth centuries, from Jamal al-Din al-Afghani and Muhammad ᶜAbduh, through Rashid Rida, to the leaders of the Muslim Brotherhood, who demanded an out-and-out Islamic state based strictly on the precepts of the shariᶜa.

There is, second, the answer offered by Muslim religious savants (*ᶜulema*) such as ᶜAli Abdel-Raziq and, later, Khalid Muhammad Khalid—both again Egyptians. These two respected theologians and their followers envisaged a lay state in which Islam is either the "official religion" of the state or the private concern of the individual Muslim citizen. In somewhat simpler terms, the alternative here is one between understanding Islam as both creed (*ᶜaqida*) and law (shariᶜa) as fundamental tenets embodied in a religious state law, or as ᶜaqida alone, with a state law that is modern, independent of religious origin or sanction, but in conformity with the ᶜaqida.

Both of these stands, however, pose difficulties which are likely to remain unresolved. The fundamentalists, who advocate an Islamic state run strictly in accordance with the shariᶜa, face the difficulty that as members

2 / The Many Faces of Islam

of the comity of nations and as signatories of the United Nations Charter, Muslim states must take due note of the fact that this cannot be reconciled with Islam's division of the world into two realms—the realm of Islam (*dar al-Islam*) and the realm of war (*dar al-harb*)—which latter must be conquered and incorporated into the Islamic state in order to make Islam prevail the world over.

The modernizers, on the other hand—those who would be satisfied with a lay state in which Islam is the private concern of the Muslim individual—run the risk of being accused of repudiating, if only by implication, Islam's claim to encompass the world as well as the hereafter, to be both a faith and a way of life and government, and to regulate economic affairs in its own way.

These difficulties and contradictions, by their very nature, are not given to simple solutions, as recent developments and controversies in Algeria, Jordan, Sudan, Egypt, and elsewhere in the Arab-Muslim world show. Hundreds of books and pamphlets, mostly polemical in character, have been written on the subject in Arabic in recent years, as well as scores of treatises in Western languages. A number of these latter works are surveyed briefly here.

On the specific subject of Islam's basic political stance, the late London University professor P. J. Vatikiotis provides, in *Islam and the State,* a brief but concise examination of the theoretical problems to which the adoption by Muslim societies of the modern European ideology of nationalism and of the nation-state gave rise. In the book's six chapters he explains and interprets the relation between religion and politics in Islam in general, and Islam's relation to the state and to the nation-state in particular. As he is careful to point out, however, in Islam content and approach are based not on a strictly theoretical examination of ideas, but "on the relation of these ideas to political events—to the historical experience of Moslem society, and the evolution of Islamic belief and practice in the crucible of actual practice."[1]

One particular question about the Islamic world has preoccupied Vatikiotis: "Whatever else it may or may not do, can an Islamic political order create a new society, one . . . with common shared values, a common attitude of mind, even its own morality, and one that can cope reasonably with the problems . . . of modernity?" The reason why this question has been bothering him, he adds, is that "with historical hindsight it may be asserted that religious faith (any religious faith) is both the foundation of society and the rock on which it can be shipwrecked, and the nation perish. . . ."[2]

Viewing Islam in political terms, Vatikiotis poses more specific questions: Can the nation-state system fulfill the politico-religious demands of Islam? "Does Islam, quiescent, pacific, militant or otherwise, constitute an international political movement with definite goals that can and have been articulated?" Assuming that such an international movement does exist, moreover, "are its goals capable of political solution by anyone, or are they primarily emotive and symbolic and therefore unsatisfiable and never-ending?" Finally, is the current Islamic militant movement a passing phenomenon or a threat both to the established nation-state regimes and to the international order of nation-states?

Vatikiotis's answers to these and many other related questions can only be hinted at here. Nationalism itself as an ideology, he writes, is not only incompatible with Islam but is its greatest, perhaps its deadliest, enemy, since "it represents an attempt to separate Islam from politics and isolate it from the resolution of temporal matters." It also "denies Islam its central role in the regulation of Moslem earthly political affairs."[3]

On the central issue of the role of Muslim religious law, Vatikiotis writes: "The debate among Moslems over the role of the *shariʿa* in the state continues. In short, the question of religion and state remains open. Actually the *umma*, the community of believers, itself lacks consensus over major political issues; nation-states within the *umma* have broken ranks with the community of the faithful following their respective secularly perceived national state interest. A recent example of this is the conclusion of a peace treaty in 1979 between Israel (for long proclaimed as the single greatest enemy of the Moslem community) and Egypt, home of al-Azhar and centre of the study of the religious sciences of Islam."

Concerning the even more crucial subject of church and state in Islam, Vatikiotis sums up the problem by drawing an analogy with the situation in medieval Christendom: "Serious problems arise when one realizes that Islam is indissolubly religion *and* community, or nation, and it demands that this combination or duality be inscribed in temporal structures. As a religion, it is not a private affair; it is rather closer to the medieval conception: it determines man's whole being, his identity and status."

Nor is the umma a church; it is a society of believers, comprising those who profess Islam, pray to the *qibla* (direction of the Kaʿba), observe the shariʿa and preferably live in dar al-Islam. "Its unity is and is not strictly political. Its law is a decision of divine will; there is no other source of law, including Nature and Reason. Religious and social ethics are equated, so that there is no dichotomy between man the individual in relation to family and society—or the member of a political organization—on the one hand, and man expressing himself in religious terms about God on the other. God is the Lord of the Universe and the earth is His lawful realm; a kind of secular and eschatological notion simultaneously. The purpose of Islam . . . is to make it dominant in every sphere of life."[4]

In his concluding chapter, "Islam and Europe: Conflict or Cooperation?" Vatikiotis identifies more clearly what separates the Islamic from the non-Islamic historical-political experience of Europe. He is aware that in doing so, in underlining "certain contradictions of attitude and/or behaviour on the part of my Moslem contemporaries, and [reminding] them uncomfortably of the less attractive aspects of their history," he may displease many of his Muslim friends.

On the nature of the shariᶜa and its characteristics, Joseph Schacht reminds us of one distinctive feature of Islamic law. An important criterion of the sociology of law, he writes, is the degree to which the legal subject matters are distinguished and differentiated from one another. "There is no such distinction in Islamic law," he adds. "Even a systematic arrangement of the legal subject-matters is lacking. Public powers are, as a rule, reduced to private rights and duties, for instance the right to give a valid safe-conduct, the duty to pay the alms-tax, the rights and duties of the persons who appoint an individual as Imam or Caliph, and the rights and duties of this last."[5]

In the field of what, in modern terminology, is called penal law, Schacht adds, "Islamic law distinguishes between the rights of God and the rights of humans. Only the rights of God have the character of a penal law proper, of a law which imposes penal sanctions on the guilty. Even here, in the centre of penal law, the idea of a claim on the part of God predominates, just as if it were a claim on the part of a human plaintiff. This real penal law is derived exclusively from the Koran and the 'traditions,' the alleged reports of the acts and sayings of the Prophet and of his Companions."[6]

Islamic law represents an extreme case of a "jurists' law," Schacht writes; "it was created and developed by private pious specialists. Islamic jurisprudence or fiqh did not grow out of an existing law, it itself created the law; and the formation of Islamic law took place neither under the impetus of the needs of practice nor under that of juridical technique, but under that of religious and ethical ideas. At the very time that Islamic law came into existence, its perpetual problem, the contrast between theory and practice, was already posed. "Because Islamic law is a jurists' law, legal science is amply documented, whereas the realities of legal life are much less well known and must be laboriously reconstructed from occasional evidence."[7]

Duncan MacDonald and the Unity of Islam

Another prominent Orientalist of the old generation, Duncan Black Mac-Donald, speaks at length of Islam's uniqueness. His book *Development of Muslim Theology, Jurisprudence and Constitutional Theory*, written over a hundred years ago, has lost little of its relevance, its readability or its sound scholarship—and reading it in the late 1990s tends to show how certain problems and issues persist.

MacDonald wrote his book considerably before the dismemberment of the Ottoman Empire and decades before any of the modern Muslim nation-states had to come to grips with the problem of building modern, Western-type state apparatus without formally breaking with their religious tradition. Yet the roots of that particular problem are all indirectly surveyed and explained in the book, lucidly expounded by the author in his introduction and subsequently developed in the book's three parts and the useful selections from original Muslim authors given in translation in the appendixes.

Islam's true dilemma resides in its very uniqueness. Considering that it is generally seldom possible, and even less advisable, to divide civilizations into departments and to attempt to trace their separate courses of development, MacDonald rightly points out that this is emphatically true of the civilization of Islam, whose intellectual unity, for good or for evil, is its one outstanding quality. "It may have solved the problem of faith and science, as some hold; it may have crushed all thought which is not of faith, as many others hold. However that may be, its life and thought is a unity."[8]

This is the case also with Islam's institutions—and here the contrast with Europe's experience and development is complete. "In Europe, the State may rule the Church, or the Church may rule the State; or they may stand side by side in somewhat dubious amity, supposedly taking no account each of the other. But in the Muslim countries, church and state are one indissolubly, and until the very essence of Islam passes away, that unity cannot be relaxed."

Thus in Islam, MacDonald continues, it is never possible to say, "He is a great lawyer; he, a great theologian; he, a great statesman." One man may be all three, almost he *must* be all three, if he is to be any one. "The statesman may not practise theology or law, but his training, in great part, will be that of a theologian and a legist. The theologian-legist may not be a man of action, but he will be a court of ultimate appeal on the theory of the state. He will pass upon treaties, decide disputed successions, assign to each his due rank and title. He will tell the Commander of the Faithful himself what he may do and what, by law, lies beyond his reach."[9]

This is the essence of Islamic government, in theory at least, and to try to preserve even a semblance of it at the beginning of the twenty-first century is an enterprise that is obviously fraught with difficulties and even dangers. That the dilemma has not changed materially since MacDonald's book was published in 1903 is a fact amply borne out by further research made more recently into the problems confronting Islam and the Muslims today in building a modern, Western-type nation-state.

To be sure, MacDonald himself was fully aware of the persistent character of the problem. His "sketch," he wrote, is incomplete "because the development of Islam is not yet over." "If," he added, "as some say, the faith of Muhammad is a *cul-de-sac,* it is certainly a very long one; off it, many courts and doors open; down it, many people are still wandering. . . ."[10]

More recently, in his book *Islam in the Modern National State,* written more than sixty years after MacDonald's classic work, the Cambridge Orientalist E. I. J. Rosenthal—who is the author of a standard work on political theory in medieval Islam—guides us through many subways and byways of this huge cul-de-sac while setting out to appraise Islam's reactions and its attempts at adjustment in face of the challenges posed by the need to establish the modern nation-state. He deals with the situation in such Muslim countries as Pakistan, Malaysia, Iran, Turkey, Tunisia, and Morocco—which he visited in the 1960s while doing research into Islamic constitutional theory and law. The aim of the research was to try and determine the role Islam was to play in the modern Muslim national state.

Not unfamiliar with the complex theoretical aspects of his investigation, Rosenthal was soon in a position to put his finger on the heart of the problem of modern Islam: not only was there the difficulty of adjusting an essentially medieval culture and civilization to an outlook and to institutions that had been molded in the West and that have come to define contemporary state and society; there was also the hurdle that modern Muslims feel a great need to preserve their Islamic identity, both as individuals and as nations. In other words, the problem is one of creating states that are to be both modern-national and fundamentally Islamic.

The question, then, is what part Islam is to play in these modern states. It is obvious that, as far as the administration and the political-economic organization of his state are concerned, the modern Muslim simply must look to the West—a West "which only yesterday was his enemy and today is not only his teacher but also, to his mind, the cause of his inner conflicts and the source of many difficulties, cultural, social and economic."[11]

Thus, unless Muslims are to attain complete secularization—a highly unlikely development—and since it is either religion or humanism which must provide modern man with a spiritual center, there appears to be no way for resolving the difficulty other than by building Islam somehow into the individual and group identity of the modern Muslim.

"Some accommodation," Rosenthal explains, "will have to be made if the emotional attachment to traditional Islam and the intellectual orientation towards the West are to be integrated into a whole personality—one that is conscious of its heritage and at the same time determined to belong to this age and to build a future world which is one economically, yet differentiated politically, socially and culturally." He realizes, he adds, that to achieve such a balanced personality, both on the individual and the collective levels, modern man in general and the modern Muslim in particular must preserve historical continuity.[12]

This, of course, is easier formulated in theory than realized in practice. In the case of the modern Muslim, the problem ultimately leads to the inescapable question: What is Islam? Is it personal faith, piety, and devotion, or is it a religious and political community of believers? If the former, then Islam has no role to play in the public life of a modern Muslim state. But if Islam is both a system of beliefs and practices and a law for the community of believers, then its relevance to the modern Muslim state and society becomes self-evident.

It is precisely because Islam is rather more than mere personal observance and piety that things seem to have become so intractable in the contemporary Arab-Muslim world, and an endeavor made over the past hundred years or so to attain that measure of compromise that would ensure the twin goals of a balanced personality and historical continuity, which Rosenthal envisaged has come to so little.

Khalid Muhammad Khalid's Alternative

There is, however, an alternative to the fundamentalist stand—an alternative which, though seldom expounded in writing, is the one that may prevail ultimately. Of the few Muslim thinkers after ʿAli Abdel Raziq who have found the courage actually to give expression to this alternative in public is Khalid Muhammad Khalid, who in his well-known book *Min huna nabda* (From here we start) advocates the separation of religion and state. On this issue, Khalid cites Rousseau's argument against the religious scholars of the past for their support of unjust rulers, maintaining that the separation of church and state would prevent collusion between religion and politics and is the only way to rid the people of unjust government. Khalid also intimates that his socialism is Western, not Islamic, thus rather surprisingly repudiating, even if only by implication, Islam's claim to encompass the world as well as the hereafter and to regulate economic affairs in its own way.

But it is by no means certain that such arguments, logical and realistic though they sound, can be effective when addressed to the masses of ordinary Muslims unaffected by Western concepts. Men like Sayyid Qutb and Muhammad al-Ghazzali—Khalid's two most vocal critics—write what they write from a deep sense of vocation. Belonging to an activist religious movement, the Muslim Brotherhood, they, unlike Khalid and the secularizing modernists, have something positive to offer their coreligionists: the true and pure Islam of the Prophet with its message of justice, equality, and brotherhood. In an age of bewildering change and great social and economic stresses it would be a mistake to underrate the force of such an appeal. Rosenthal rightly feels that, by contrasting pure Islam with the "corrupt West" the ideologist of the brotherhood "diverts [the ordinary Muslim's] sense of frustration outwards, so that on psychological grounds alone his revivalist fervour cannot fail to produce a feeling of superiority and a social cohesion which can have a stabilizing effect if contained by disciplined obedience to authority. . . ."[13]

Still, though one may readily agree that these Muslim fundamentalists give expression to widespread popular attitudes and represent the predominant Islamic views on state and society, one cannot help reflecting that, while the liberal Khalid enjoyed a high position as member of the National Assembly, both Qutb and Ghazzali stood trial for their lives, accused of plotting an uprising against the fast-secularizing regime of Gamal Abdel Nasser, himself famously combining almost ideally personal piety and a highly modernist approach in practical politics.

What direction will politico-religious developments take in Islamic lands? Will the approach now prevailing in Egypt, Pakistan, Tunisia, Iraq, Indonesia, and Syria—an approach marked by various degrees of "modernity"— prove lasting, or will the opposing approach of Islamic fundamentalism take its place? It is, of course, rather difficult to say. Rosenthal's searching investigations in such lands as Pakistan, Malaysia, Turkey, and the countries of the Maghrib produce no conclusive answers to such questions. Yet one has a feeling that he has little faith in the power of Western-educated and Western-oriented Muslim intellectuals to prove equal to the test. An Islamic revival, if it comes, is more likely to come from the fundamentalists of the Muslim Brotherhood school, which Rosenthal, for one, believes is more representative of the true spirit of Islam.

However, as Rosenthal asserts, while the very complexity of the problem favors the taking up of radical positions, these can only increase confusion and contradictions. Goodwill and mutual understanding are needed, he writes, "in order to create a public opinion which is well-informed, rooted in the Islamic past and determined to support a truly national effort to establish a modern society on the pattern of the Good Society."[14]

Akbar Ahmed, an anthropologist and himself a Muslim, also offers an alternative interpretation:

> Islam is not really about bombs and book-burning. This is a media image, one which has almost become a self-fulfilling prophecy, and the Islamic injunctions for balance, compassion and tolerance are blotted out by it. The holy Quran has emphasized, "Your religion for you and mine for me" (1989; Sura 109:6) and "There shall be no compulsion in religion" (Sura 2:256). For Muslims, God's two most important and most cited titles are the Beneficent and the Merciful. This is not only forgotten by those who dislike Islam but, more importantly, it is forgotten by Muslims themselves. Chaining and blindfolding "hostages"—however compelling the reasons—do not reflect compassion or mercy; nor does the murder of innocent Armenians in the USSR or Christians in the Sudan; nor does the brutality of despotic Muslim leaders, mercilessly killing their own citizens.[15]

According to Ahmed, there is a danger of conveying the impression that there is a unity in Muslim perception and a totality in Muslim endeavor. This is manifestly not so, he maintains:

> Bengalis, for instance, viewed the Pakistan army as a violent instrument of oppression; many Afghans accused the *jihad* of their compatriots of being funded and organized by the U.S. Central Intelligence Agency; many in Ayatollah Khomeini's Iran, including the Ayatollah himself, criticized General Zia's Islamization efforts in Pakistan as inadequate; in turn, many Muslims in the Middle East and South Asia condemned the Ayatollah's revolution in Iran as excessive. Critics were quick to point out the connection between military regimes and the use of Islam; to them Islam in Numeiri's Sudan and Zia's Pakistan was reduced to the chopping off of hands and whipping of

petty criminals. Some scholars were cynical of colleagues who attempted to "Islamize" knowledge, since merely appending the label "Islamic" was no guarantee of academic quality. Sectarian champions, Shia or Sunni, denounced their rivals and proclaimed their exclusive owner- ship of the truth; smaller groups, like the Ismaili, Ahmadi and Baha'i, were dismissed as heretics and sometimes physically persecuted. At- tempted suppression of multiple interpretations of the truth further exacerbated conflict within Islam, which emphasizes unity. The dy- namics of the tensions in society are provided by people sometimes failing, sometimes succeeding in attempting to live according to the Islamic ideal-type.[16]

While apparently there seems to be little or nothing to add to these de- tailed and learned appraisals, a number of more recent studies and reports offer more valuable insights into the subject. In *Islam in the Modern World,* Elie Kedourie sets out to explore the fortunes of Islam in the region in the modern era, and the ways in which it has tried "to come to terms with, assimilate, or challenge the categories of modernity, particularly in those areas where politics and religion meet and intermingle."[17]

In the course of his analysis, Kedourie takes issue with those who de- scribe Europe's expansion into the Muslim world as imperialism, pointing out that the term's origins lie in European political and intellectual history. "Muslims," he adds, "certainly would not have understood it or found it of much use in explaining their predicament. In their own traditional cat- egories, the conflict with Europe, which issued in such a dismal series of political and military reverses, would have been seen as a clash between Islam and Christendom—as the latest phase of a conflict which, over many centuries, two worlds, two militant faiths, had confronted and defied one another."[18]

The loss of self-confidence which Islam suffered, "the failure of nerve which a long series of setbacks and defeats induced," took quite long to manifest itself. However, despite the West's technical and military superior- ity, opposition to European encroachments was in many cases "remark- ably stout-hearted, resourceful and tenacious."

Kedourie then turns to some of the pronouncements made by leading Muslims since the turn of the century and, after citing the work of Muham- mad Ali Jinnah (1876–1948), writes:

It is apparent from Jinnah's language that he considered Islam more a "civilization" and a "social order" than a faith. In this of course he was not alone, for Westernized Muslims (and Jinnah was one of them) had long learned to transform Islam from an eternally true divine revelation independent of temporal changes and vicissitudes into a product and agent of historical change, or into a social cement. In other words, one was a Muslim not because Islam was true, but because it served, by means of the solidarity which it instilled, to keep together and thus endow with political power the societies in which Islam had hitherto held sway. This in fact is the political doctrine of [Jamal al-Din al-]Afghani who, so we have seen, was a religious sceptic.[19]

Two of the papers collected in *Islam in the Modern World*—"Ibn Saud on the Jews" and "Great Britain and Palestine: The Turning Point"—are based on research into recently released British Foreign Office papers and documents relating to the years 1936 through 1939, the period of the disorders in the Holy Land and the Peel Commission's report. Whether or not it shed light on the attitudes of modern Islam or the modern Muslim, the piece on Ibn Saud and the Jews is interesting in itself.

The pronouncements quoted by Kedourie are reproduced from a report submitted to the Foreign Office in the autumn of 1937 by Colonel Dickson, who had retired the previous year as Political Agent in Kuwait. For close to an hour and a half, it seems, the Saudi monarch delivered himself of a monologue "on the subject obviously close to his heart, namely the Palestine tangle," as Dickson put it.

Apart from some atypical railings—"Verily the word of God teaches us, and we implicitly believe this, O Dickson, that for a Moslem to kill a Jew, or for him to be killed by a Jew, ensures him an immediate entry into Heaven and into the august presence of God Almighty"—Ibn Saud was obviously attempting to establish common ground for Arab and British opposition to "the Jews." Thus: "Our hatred for the Jews dates from God's condemnation of them for their persecution and rejection of Isa [Jesus Christ], and their subsequent rejection later of His Chosen Prophet [Muhammad]. It is beyond our understanding how your Government, representing the first Christian power in the world today, can wish to assist and reward these very same Jews who maltreated your Isa." Again, "The Jews are of course your enemies as well as ours though they are cleverly making use of you now. . . ." Or, "The Jews of Palestine are even now straining every nerve to cause a permanent split between the English people and the Arabs. . . ."[20]

And so on. If these and other similar pronouncements of Ibn Saud's can be said to prove anything concerning the subject at hand, they can only be cited as an example of the ways in which a certain category of modern Muslims are capable of using and manipulating their religious faith to attain political ends. A phenomenon, one ventures to add, not entirely unique to Islam and to its followers.

Readings

The Religious Foundation—Piety—Prayer

Islam aims at comprehending life in its totality. It posits the ideal of a life in which, from the cradle to the grave, not a single moment is spent out of tune with or merely unprovided for by religious ruling. The distinction between important actions and unimportant detail of daily routine loses much of its meaning when every step is thought of as prescribed by divine ordinance. Profane and sacred no longer denote the area withdrawn from, and the area subject to, religious supervision. No sphere is left in which our doings are inconsequential for our fate in the hereafter. The relevancy of our failings will vary according to their moral and social significance, but nowhere shall we find a no-man's-land to which religion does not lay claim. The Prophet had been charged with revealing not merely the great metaphysical truths but the rules of daily conduct as well. The Lord wanted the faithful to organize their commonwealth in a certain manner, he enjoined them to follow a certain code of law, and he selected for them a certain way of life. Thus, by accepting Islam, the believer accepted a ready-made set of mandatory answers to any question of conduct that could possibly arise. As long as he obeyed sacred custom, the Muslim's life was hallowed down to its irksome and repulsive episodes, and he would be fortified by the assurance of his righteousness.

The model to follow is the Prophet. Where the Koran fails to supply the necessary information, his *sunna,* his personal custom or the custom practiced by his community in the earliest times of Islam, fills the lacuna. Mohammed's *sunna* is usually recorded in a *hadith,* a saying of his or about him which directly or by implication describes his usage or else contains a statement touching the present or future condition of his community.

The pagan Arab had endeavored, though to a much smaller extent, to follow the *sunna* of his ancestors; now pre-Islamic custom was replaced by the precedent set or the tradition approved by the Prophet. What could be proved to have been practiced by Mohammed was thereby admitted as normative. At the time of ʿUmar II (717–20) doubt prevailed as to when a youth would come of age. The question was solved when somebody found a *hadith* telling of a boy being rejected for military service by the Prophet at fourteen but accepted at fifteen.

To convince, an opinion had to issue from the Prophet. Innovation, even change in small matters, when based on personal reasoning was to be rejected. Every thesis that cannot be traced in the age of the Prophet, every custom not authorized by the example of his times, is abomination. It is maintained by some that those mentioned in the first sura of the Koran "upon whom anger falls" have incurred God's wrath by *bidᶜa,* innovation, and those "that go astray" are straying off the beaten tracks of the *sunna.*

The tendency to canonize the usage, supposed or actual, of the Prophet's day—a tendency which, thanks to the lack of historical perspective, in many ways aimed at the canonization of the status quo of the recorder's time—led as early as the eighth century to preference being accorded the *sunna* in case it conflicted with the Koran. . . .

The extreme rigidity of the *sunna* concept was mitigated by a variety of factors. Obviously, absolute faithfulness to the mores of the past was an ideal for which the theologians might fight but which was by no means acceptable to everyone. One could perhaps say that a number of *sunna*s strove for supremacy. Pagan ethos, on the one hand, and Persian manners, on the other, offered precedents that would differ from those set by the early believers and prove more attractive to some circles. Neither tradition was, however, sufficiently complete to displace the *sunna* of the Prophet even had there been general readiness to yield it. But the Prophet's *usus* [foundations] did not cover every contingency either, or, if [they] did, much evidence had slipped the memories of his companions or their heirs.

Piety

The very urge to have every detail covered by prophetic precedent forced a certain amount of forgery. Modern practices had to be justified or combated, and a *hadith* was a convenient means of Islamizing such Christian or Jewish matter as was felt to be attractive and spiritually akin to the Muslim faith. It was not too difficult for the experienced traditionalist to construct a convincing chain of authorities who were supposed to have transmitted any particular saying of the Prophet to the theologian's own day. It is freely admitted that the pious are only too ready to lie when it comes to *hadith.*

Mohammed's prophetic powers made it possible for him to have enounced the most detailed predictions as to events and problems, mostly aberrations from the true *sunna* or the true doctrine, that were to trouble his community many centuries after his death. There was nothing improbable in his describing the setting and the virtues of towns to be founded long after he had departed this life. The growing strength of the popular belief in Mohammed's miraculous gifts made it difficult for internal criticism of his reputed sayings to be generally admitted. Instead, criticism of the enormous mass of traditions had to concentrate on the formal correctness of the *isnad*, the chain of witnesses. Once it was established that all the links in this chain had been God-fearing and upright men who at least could have been in personal contact so as to hear the tradition in question one from another, nothing was to be done to invalidate it except perhaps to launch an equally well-authenticated *hadith* of different impact.

To reduce the flood of forgeries the Prophet was—in invented *hadith*—quoted as inveighing against such invention. "Whoso deliberately lies about me, let him enter unto his place in hell-fire." Mohammed predicts: "At the end of the times there will arise forgers and liars who will bring you traditions neither you nor your forebears ever heard. Beware of them lest they lead you into error and temptation."

Such warnings were as appropriate as they were ineffective.

The traditionist, thus, held the keys to the correct arrangement of all human activities; his knowledge of the *sunna* guarded the integrity of the faith, and his authority made him an indispensable instrument of organized power, legitimate or usurped. He administered the treasures bequeathed by the Prophet to his community, and he saw to it that those treasures, which had a way of increasing under his hands, were properly used. Hard was his task but great his glory.

Prayer

The prayer, *salat,* which is obligatory for every believer to perform five times a day, is not so much an effort to achieve personal communication with Allah as a set of ceremonies expressing the Muslim's obedience, worship, and devotion. These prayers are preferably said in common with other faithful, lined up in well-ordered rows behind a prayer-leader, *imam.* Nothing in the service is left to the initiative of the individual. From the ablution preceding the beginning of the ceremony to its very conclusion every act and every utterance are minutely regulated. Inadequate performance voids the validity of the *salat.* The services are of different length, the morning service consisting of two, sunset, of three, noon, midafternoon, and evening, of four *rak'a* each, where *rak'a* means the main part of the *salat,* a sequence of mostly koranic formulas pronounced in various positions of the body (standing, bowing, prostrate).

Al-Ghazali (d. 1111), when describing the *salat*, has this to say of the prostration.

> Next he (the believer) goes down for the Prostration, saying the *takbir* (the formula: *Allahu akbar*, God is greatest), and then places his knees on the ground and places his forehead, nose and palms (on the ground), uncovered. He says the *takbir* while lowering himself, but he does not raise his hands in anything but the Bowing. It is fitting that his knees should be the first to be placed on the ground, and after them his hands, and after them his face; and that he should place his forehead and his nose on the ground; and that he should turn his elbows away from his sides (but a woman should not do that); and that he should keep his feet apart (but a woman should not do that); and that in his Prostration he should leave an open space on the ground (but a woman should not leave a space);—"leaving a space" means raising the stomach from the thighs and separating the knees;—and that he should place his hands on the ground opposite the shoulders, without separating the fingers but rather joining them and joining the thumb to them (but, if he were not to join his thumb, it would not matter); and without extending his arms on the ground, as a dog does, since that is forbidden, and that he should say, "O the praise of my Most High Lord!" three times (but if he increases the number, it is well, unless he is acting as *imam*). . . .

The spiritual significance of this elaborate procedure is suggested by ʿIkrima (d. 724) when he proposed "the tying (of man to God)" as etymology of *salat*. A *hadith* depicts its cleansing power. "The *salat* is like a stream of sweet water which flows past the door of each one of ye; into it he plunges five times a day; do ye think that anything remains of his uncleanness after that?" Al-Ghazali discusses the six "inner realities" which "bring the life of the *salat* to perfection" as the presence of the heart, understanding, respect, reverence, hope, and humility. The heart is to the Muslim not the seat of emotions but the seat of the mind, the receptacle of the "inmost, most secret and genuine thoughts, the very basis of man's intellectual nature." The obstacle to achieving the presence of the heart is distraction, *ghafla*, that *ameleia* which for St. Afrem is the typical state of the impious. External causes of distraction can be removed with comparative ease; the internal causes are more stubborn. They are anchored in earthly cares, preoccupations, desires. Meditation on the future world will counteract them most effectively. The "inner realities" give their true meaning to each phase of the prayer. The physical prostration acquires significance as "the highest degree of submission, for the dearest of your members, which is your face, gets hold of the humblest thing, which is the dust. . . . Whenever you place yourself in the place of lowliness, know that you have placed it in its proper place, and have returned the branch to the trunk, for of the dust you were formed and to it you return. . . ."

The *salat,* however, did not suffice as either vantage point or culmination of devotion. The ritual allows for personal conversation (*munajat*) of the believer with his God at the end of the service, and pious prayer or pious request (*du'a*) is recognized and recommended when the believer feels the need to supplement the *salat.*

It seems that such people as were not, so to speak, professionally concerned with religion or in whose life religion was not the dominant interest were rather slow in making their devotional attitude articulate. More often than not early poetical utterances that sound a religious note are actually expressions of a political program whose slogans happen to be of a more or less doctrinal character. Sayings of the Prophet, scraps from the Koran, are versified. Sometimes the believer declares his allegiance not without naivete.

Gustave E. von Grunebaum, *Medieval Islam* (Chicago: University of Chicago Press, 1961), 108–109, 110–111, 112, 113, 114–115, 116–117.

Dogmas

In Islam five dogmas specify ritual obligations: the profession of faith, or *shahada;* prayer; the giving of alms according to legal standards; the fast of Ramadan; and the pilgrimage to Mecca.

Dogmas are defined by the Qur'an and then elaborated and reinvoked by "orthodox" authorities each time it is necessary to refute opinions deemed to be heterodox. That is why there exists a catechistic literature (*'aqida*) that synthesizes Qur'anic pronouncements into concise propositions. Sura 112 defines the basic dogma of the Islamic faith: "Recite: it is He, God, One, the impenetrable Absolute. He does not procreate; He is not procreated; nothing is equal to him."

All other dogmas flow from the attestation of God, one, absolute transcendent and from his decision to choose Muhammad as His Messenger to reveal the Qur'an. That is the object of the *shahada,* which includes two parts: "There is no divinity other than Allah; and Muhammad is the Messenger of Allah." Jews and Christians accept the first proposition but reject the second. "Allah" is the proper name God takes for Himself in Arabic.

It would take too long to enumerate all the articles in the profession defining the faith of a Muslim. The last judgment, the resurrection of the body, eternal recompense, paradise and hell, angels, jinn, prophets—all are points that require the validation of the faith, *iman*.

The acceptance of dogmas must be translated into good works (*a*ᶜ*mal*): compliance with prescribed rituals and application of the regulations (*ahkam*) defined by the law, *al-shari*ᶜ*a*. The link to dogmas reinforces the previously mentioned sacralization of law and of all conduct to which it is applied.

For certain schools of theology such as the Muᶜtazili, dogmas became the object of rational speculation in the interest of discovering a measure of coherence acceptable at least to the elites (*al-khassa*). A famous example is the theory of the created Qurʾan, which the caliphs Al-Maʾmun (813–833), Al-Muᶜtasim (833–842), and Al-Wathiq (842–847) decided to prescribe as official dogma, thereby arousing the opposition of Ibn Hanbal (d. 855). The caliph Al-Qaʾim (d. 1031) later ordered the famous profession of faith called *al-qadiriyya* to be read in the mosques of Baghdad, forbidding specifically any reference to the dogma of the created Qurʾan.

Mohammed Arkoun, *Rethinking Islam: Common Questions, Uncommon Answers* (Boulder: Westview Press, 1994), 64–65.

Virtues

It might well be thought that after professing the religious beliefs of Islam and performing the various duties of a Muslim the circle of religion had been completed. In addition, however, the Koran imposes upon all a course of right living, thus giving a religious character to private and public morality. From the virtues extolled Muhammad emerges as a moralist and something of a puritan. The Koran limits the number of wives to four, and then adds: "But if you fear that you will act unjustly among them, then marry only one." There are many other commandments which raised the status of women in Arabian society. Settlements are required to be made upon a woman if she is divorced; a widow can marry whomever she wishes; and the burying alive of daughters is prohibited.

Murderers are promised burning in Hell; and earthly penalties are imposed for homicide, stealing, fraud, perjury, and libel. Injunctions are delivered against gambling, usury, and monopolistic practices. The use of wine and the eating of pork are forbidden. An interdiction is imposed upon making statues, pictures, puppets, and any representation of animate objects, because God is the creator of all things and man should not try to imitate His works. Moreover, idolatry is most sinful and the making of images is only one step removed from worshipping other gods. Most of these declarations of right living are injunctions against practices that were common in the pagan and hedonistic society of Mecca.

In view of the comprehensive scope of Islam with respect to religious beliefs, religious duties, and virtues, Muhammad can only be regarded as a very successful prophet and reformer. Muhammad found Mecca, as one writer has well expressed it, a "materialistic commercial" city "where lust of gain and usury reigned supreme, where women, wine, and gambling filled up the leisure time, where might was right, and widows, orphans, and the feeble were treated as superfluous ballast." Muhammad, practically a nobody in so many of the things that counted in Mecca, brought to his people and those of Mecca a knowledge of God and a way of salvation that changed the life and philosophy of all Arabia. Since Islam required individual belief and morality, the tribal and family morality of pre-Islamic Arabia was replaced by the personal responsibilities of the individual Muslim as a member of the universal Muslim brotherhood.

Sydney Nettleton Fisher, *The Middle East: A History* (New York: Knopf, 1969), 66–67.

Khilafah: The Trust of Vicegerency

Khilafah has two meanings, one of which is Qurʾanic and refers to the vicegerency of man as the trustee of Allah on earth. *Khilafah* also refers to the institution of caliphate which was established under the four rightly-guided caliphs (*khulafa rashidun*) and continued down the centuries until its abolition by Attaturk in Turkey in early 1924. Initially, Abu Bakar and Umar, the first two caliphs of Islam, laid emphasis on the legitimacy of their leadership by resorting to *shura* (consultation), *aqd* (the contract between ruler and ruled), and *bayʿah* (an oath of allegiance).

This same method was used in the appointment of their successor, Othman, and the juristic elaboration of the caliphate continued to emphasise *bayʿah* and *shura*, notwithstanding the fact that in actual practice these principles were largely overlooked with the onset of a hereditary monarchy under the Ummayyads. The classical writing of al-Mawardi, Abu Yala al-Farra and Ibn Hazm are mainly concerned with the election, qualifications and duties of the caliph. The theory of caliphate also discusses the rights of the caliph and the citizen's duty of obedience to him. It speaks little of public or political rights, and discussion of the basic rights of individuals is scanty and incidental. None of these works contains a separate chapter, for example, on the fundamental rights of the citizen.

The vast majority of *ulama* have held that electing an *imam* is *wajib* (obligatory) by virtue of the *ijma* (general consensus) of the Prophet's companions (*sahaba*) and of succeeding generations of Muslims across the centuries. Upon the death of the Prophet the companions considered electing a successor to him as leader as a matter of urgency, even greater than attending to his burial. But to say that there must be a leader and that this is an Islamic obligation is not the same, of course, as saying that political leadership must be in conformity with any particular model.

The idea has prevailed among Muslims that there could be but one form of Islamic state, namely the form manifested under the rightly-guided caliphs. This is a common error or misconception. The truth is that Islam does not require conformity to any particular form of political structure. The Islamic state has existed historically not only in one form but many, and it is for the Muslims of every period to discover the form most suitable for their needs. There is nothing in the *shariʿa* to specify any particular type of political organisation. *Khilafah* and *imamah* have developed certain characteristic attributes which are generally regarded as being manifested in the Islamic concept of political leadership. However, this association is not intrinsic but historical, arising mainly as a result of the interplay of juristic doctrine and historical precedents. The political ideas and practices to which this historical association gave rise do not constitute an obligation under the *shariʿa*.

Mohammad Hashim Kamali, "The Islamic State and Its Constitution," in *Shariʿa Law and the Modern Nation-State*, ed. Norani Othman (Kuala Lumpur: Sisters in Islam Forum [Malaysia] Berhad, 1994), 51–52.

Islamic Law

To Muslims, the *Qurʾan* as the word of god is the absolute authority from which spring the very conception of legality and every legal obligation. Said Ramadan, in his book *Islamic Law*, admits that the *Qurʾan*, being basically a book of religious guidance, is not an easy reference for legal studies. It is more an appeal to faith and the human soul than a classification of legal prescriptions. Such prescriptions are comparatively limited and few. Those concerning family law, they are laid down in 70 injunctions; civil in another 70; penal law in 30; jurisdiction and procedure in 13; constitutional law in 10; international relations in 25; and economic and financial order in 10. (Such an enumeration can of course only be approximate.)

According to Ramadan, a thorough study of the *Qur'an* and the *sunna* would bring out the following characteristics in their philosophy of legislation:

1. They are basically inclined towards establishing general rules without indulging in much detail.

   a) In civil law: the *Qur'an* urges, "O ye who believe! Appropriate not one another's wealth among yourselves in falsehood, except it be as a trade by mutual consent" (*an-Nisa* 4:29).

   b) In criminal law: the *Qur'an* declares that "every soul is held in pledge for its own deeds" (*al-Muddaththir* 74:38), and that "each soul earneth only on its own account, nor doth any laden bear another's load" (*Fatir* 35:18). These injunctions state a basic principle in criminal law, that of personal responsibility, which suppresses all vicarious responsibility in the punishment of the guilty.

   c) In constitutional law: the *Qur'an* establishes that "those who answer the call of their Lord and establish worship are those whose affairs are decided by counsel among themselves" (*ash-Shura* 42:38).

   d) In international law: the *Qur'an* declares: "O mankind! We have created you male and female, and have made you nations and tribes that you may know one another (and be good to one another). The noblest of you with God is the best in conduct" (*al-Hujurat* 49:13). This injunction clearly affirms the oneness and moral unity of humankind, from which it follows that international peace will only be achieved when nations come to know one another, treat one another well, rid themselves of all superiority and inferiority complexes, and recall that the best in the eyes of God are those who are best in conduct. These are all principles without which no international law can exist. What is the use of international law if it does not aspire to cultivate harmony among nations?

2. From the very beginning, these precepts were meant to deal directly with actual events. This law was concrete, not hypothetical. That is, presupposition was basically excluded from its philosophy of legislation, in contrast to other codes of law which legislate upon the presumption and calculation of probabilities. This trend in Islamic law is deliberate and not a matter of coincidence. The Prophet Muhammad said: "God has enjoined certain obligations, so do not abandon them. He has imposed certain limits, so do not transgress

them. He has prohibited certain things, so do not fall into them. He has remained silent about many things, out of mercy and deliberateness, as He never forgets, so do not ask me about them."

3. As a rule, everything that is not prohibited is permissible. Islamic law was not meant to paralyse people so that they might only move when explicitly allowed to. On the contrary, humankind is repeatedly called upon by the *Qur'an* to consider the whole universe as a divine grace meant for them and therefore to exhaust all their resources of wisdom and energy to get the best out of it.

4. Even in the area of prohibitions, the *Qur'an* sometimes adopts the method of patience. It does not prohibit an evil immediately and absolutely, but awaits a gradually emerging readiness in society, in the light of reason and its own experience, to implement restraint and prohibition. A good example is the prohibition of intoxicants.

5. All that the *Qur'an* and the *sunna* have prohibited becomes permissible whenever pressing necessity arises. This is reiterated throughout the *Qur'an*. It is generally an accepted rule (known as *dharurat* or "duress") among jurists that "necessity renders the forbidden permissible."

6. The door is wide open to the adoption of anything of benefit or utility, of whatever origin, so long as it does not go against the texts of the *Qur'an* and the *sunna*. The Prophet, in a *hadith* which is universally held to be authentic, stated this most significant principle when he remarked that "it is but for the perfecting of morals that I have been sent to you," thereby not only affirming all the virtues that had been practiced before him but also including them as an inseparable part of his own mission.

K. Haridas, "Islamisation of State and Society," in Othman, ed., *Shari'a Law,* 91–93.

Applying the Shari'a

Shari'a consists of a set of principles on morality, or dogma, as well as practical legal rules which are contained in the *Qur'an* and *sunna*. The clear injunctions, or *nusus,* of the *Qur'an* and *sunna* represent the binding corpus of the *shari'a* and it is the cardinal duty of the state in Islam to enforce them. The state is a necessity in Islam if only for this purpose. Muhammad Asad observed that "the real eternal *shari'a*" consists of commands and prohibitions expressed in self-evident terms in the *Qur'an* and *sunna.* It is concise, clearly conveyed and relatively small in volume, and hence does not provide, nor was it ever intended to, detailed legislations for every contingency of life. We should add to this that the *Qurʾan* and *sunna* also provide a set of broad and general principles which constitute the substance of what is described as the *maqasid al-shariʿa:* that is, the philosophy and objectives of *shariʿa,* which are timeless and comprehensive. The concrete injunctions and the broad principles of the *Qurʾan* and *sunna* embody the real eternal *shariʿa.* The detailed, supplementary and additional legislation is provided through the exercise of *ijtihad:* that is, through independent reasoning which is in consonance with the spirit and principles of Islam and which aims at the realisation of *maslahah* (benefit) of the people.

Protecting the faith and implementing the law of Islam is a *raison d'etre* of the *umma.* The *Qurʾan* declares to this effect:

> You are the best *umma* created for mankind. You command good
> and you forbid evil and you believe in Allah (*al-Imran* 3:110).

"Commanding good and forbidding evil" here means in the first place implementing the *shariʿa,* although the scope of this Qurʾanic concept, also known as *hisbah,* is wider than the *shariʾa.* The latter part of the text explains the earlier, that is, why Allah intends it as the best *umma.*

In response to a question as to the position of Islamic law in Egypt, the Egyptian scholar Muhammad Yusuf Musa writing in the early 1950s affirmed our entitlement to demand that the *shariʿa* be the principal source of legislation. The Egyptian nation and its legal order, he maintained, have suffered intellectual colonialism and domination, especially from the French. But it is now time to reject such influences and return to our own heritage. We ought to encourage, Musa continued, specialised studies of *shariʿa* and *fiqh* in our universities. We also need to adopt the *fiqh* to changing conditions. For it is unrealistic to expect solutions to new issues to be found in the works of the *ulama* of the past, who were not faced with these questions. To support his views Musa refers to Abd al-Razzaq al-Sanhuri, who offered a positive appraisal of the value and resourcefulness of the legal heritage of Islam and its capacity for adaptation.

As the main source of *shariʿa,* the *Qurʾan* does not embody a constitution since it does not address constitutional themes on the devolution and transfer of power or provide direction concerning other matters of state. It is rather a source whose guidance needs to be reflected and given expression in evolving state activity and legislation. In that sense, Yusuf Musa is right to suggest that the *shariʿa* should be designated as a principal source of legislation. The Egyptian constitution of 1973 in fact includes a provision to that effect. Similar provisions are also found in the applied constitutions of many Islamic countries.

Mohammad Hashim Kamali, "The Islamic State and Its Constitution," in Norani Othman, ed., *Shariʿa Law* . . . 49–50, 51.

Holy War

The Koran sanctions war against unbelievers. During the conquests everyone took part and later volunteers joined the regular troops. One of the earliest ascetics was a fighter though he refused to take his share of the booty. There was an attempt to exalt the holy war into one of the pillars of religion as is proved by traditions like, "the monkery of my people is the holy war." On the other side are opinions like, "he who takes part in the holy war does so for his own (temporal) gain," and, "the holy war is only one of the duties." The attempt failed, perhaps as a reaction against the behaviour of the Kharijis. Some of the Muʿtazilis would have declared any land, where their pet doctrines did not rule, the abode of war.

The schools of law (except Ibn Hanbal and following him the Wahhabis) regarded it as an obligation if certain conditions were fulfilled. These were that unbelievers should begin hostilities, it should be sanctioned by a duly constituted imam, there should be a reasonable hope of success, and the determination to win. As the Shiʿa have no visible imam the holy war is not possible for them. . . .

One, who fell in such a war, was a martyr and went straight to paradise where his soul is in a green bird. His corpse was not washed and he was buried in the clothes in which he was killed. Later another meaning was given to this term, "the holy war has ten parts; one is fighting the enemy of Islam, nine are fighting the self." The real war is against sin. There was another extension of meaning, "he who loves, fades away, conceals his love, and dies, is a martyr."

A. S. Tritton, *Islam* (London: Hutchinson, 1954), 29.

Jihad, or Holy War, in Islam

Jihad is the most sensitive word in the Islamic vocabulary. It is always used, heard and understood in a very emotional way, either positive or negative. To non-Muslims, jihad is a holy war against them, a raised sword not easily sheathed. To many Muslims, jihad is a religious duty to guide non-Muslim peoples to the right and true faith. Militants believe jihad is a divine precept to impose Islam, the ultimate faith, on non-Muslims. Only a minority of Muslims live jihad's moral and spiritual meaning.

The literal meaning of the Arabic word *jihad* is striving, contention or struggle. Jihad, then, has many meanings: obstinate opposition or resistance; contending resolutely with a task or a problem; strenuous efforts toward an end; doing something difficult; a strong effort, or series of efforts, against any adverse agencies or conditions, in order to maintain one's existence or manner of life.

In the initial Meccan phase of the Qur'anic revelation (610–622 C.E.) the word *jihad* was used in an ethical, moral and spiritual sense. Initially, jihad meant to maintain one's faith and serenity in the midst of adverse conditions. In the Meccan period the Prophet was told through revelation to be patient with the Meccans, to suffer quietly, and not meet force with force: "Remind them [the people of Mecca], for thou art but a remembrance, Thou art not at all a dominator over them" (Sura 88:22). "But be patient [Muhammad] with a patience fair to see" (Sura 70:5). "Say [it is] truth from the Lord of you [all]. Then whosoever will, let him believe, and whosoever will, let him disbelieve" (Sura 29:18). And to the Muslim community as a whole, the Prophet recited: "Exhort one another to truth and exhort one another to endurance" (Sura 103:3).

Then how did jihad come to mean holy war? In the Medinan phase of the Qur'anic revelation (622–632 C.E.), the word *jihad* came to include the struggle of the individual or the community with the Meccans: "We have enjoined on man kindness to parents, but if they strive to make thee join with me [God] that of which thou hast no knowledge, then obey them not" (Sura 29:8). It is also written: "As for those who strive in us [God], we surely guide them to our paths" (Sura 29:69). "So obey not the unbelievers, but strive against them with a real endeavor" (Sura 25:52).

The Meccans continued to persecute the new Muslim community. The Prophet and the new Muslim community were forced to migrate to Medina, about five hundred kilometers to the north, in the historic flight called the *hijra*. They left their homeland, families, trades and fortunes. . . .

Because of the circumstances of the period, the initial spiritual meaning of jihad, striving and struggle, gave ground to the new material meaning, to struggle together against the evil and harmful aggression of the people of Mecca. Eventually, the material meaning came to dominate the spiritual meaning. Muslims threatened Meccan caravans coming from Syria and occasionally attacked them in order to force the Meccans to recognize the new Muslim community and to allow Muslims to visit Mecca where their families, possessions and memories remained. Mecca to them—and to all

Muslims—has a great significance; it is the axis of Islam. In Mecca is found the *Kaʿba* (a small stone building said to be initially built by Abraham and Ishmael). The pilgrimage is made to the Kaʿba and other prescribed places in Mecca.

Still the Meccans kept up their resistance against the new Muslims. The Meccans prepared an army of a thousand men to fight three hundred Muslims. They went to the north to exterminate the Muslims in 624 C.E. Jihad took on a new meaning in its second manifestation; it came to mean a holy war. . . .

The real first battle between Muslims and Meccans, the battle of Badr (624 C.E.) was won by the Muslims. On their way back to Medina, the Prophet said to them: "We (the Muslims) have turned from the minor jihad to the major one [struggle]." Clearly the Prophet saw the battle of Badr for what it was: minor jihad. The more important and more difficult struggle continued—ethical, moral and spiritual jihad. This jihad is a strenuous effort, or series of efforts, to discipline oneself against greed, avarice, cowardice, fear, tyranny, ignorance, submission to negative elements, yielding to evil desires and giving way to passion. This jihad avoids a meaningless existence and an empty, if not easy and comfortable, life. This is the major jihad. While armed conflict and warfare may be associated with jihad, jihad is much more than physical force or holy war.

Later, in 626 C.E., a segment of the Jewish community (the Bani Qurayza tribe of Medina) renounced their agreed upon allegiance with the Muslims. At this time the Muslims were close to being defeated by the Meccans. A verse was revealed commanding the Muslims to protect Islam by fighting the Jewish covenant breakers: "Fight against such of those who have been given the Scripture [People of the Book] as believe not in God [Allah] nor the last day, and forbid not that which God [Allah] hath forbidden by his Messenger, and follow not the faith of truth, until they pay the tribute readily" (Sura 9:29). Because this Jewish tribe betrayed the Muslims and renounced their allegiance to them, the tribe was considered unfaithful to their own faith, or apostates. It is very clear from this verse that to fight against the People of the Book is conditional and not general or absolute. Moreover, the Qurʾan says nothing of converting the People of the Book to Islam or of eliminating them. In fact, the Qurʾan warns: "Forbid not that which has not been forbidden by the messenger [Muhammad]."

Thus, in its third manifestation, jihad came to mean to fight those who believe not in God or the Last Day and to force them to pay a tribute as a sign of their surrender to the Muslim community. The concept of tribute was applied to the People of the Book—Christians or Jews—living in the

Muslim community. The tribute was a substitute for becoming a soldier, since non-Muslims could not fight in the Muslim army. The tribute was a tax to be collected by the state as a subsidy to the army from those unable or not allowed to fight.

In its fourth manifestation, after the conquest of Mecca (630 C.E.), the meaning of jihad or holy war came to include the coercion of all Meccans to Islam. All Meccans were to confess that God is one God, and that the Prophet Muhammad is his messenger (Sura 2 and Sura 9). Hence, the meaning of jihad was the conversion of non-Muslims to Islam.

To summarize: Jihad is always major, as the Prophet stated, when one fights the negative elements in oneself in order to grow in serenity and strength. Jihad as warfare is just the minor jihad, not to be confused with or compared to the major jihad. The major jihad implies self-improvement and legitimate self-defense. Many scholars who have influenced the thinking of Muslims believe that jihad is always a war against non-Muslims. They believe that this war will continue until Islam becomes the sole faith of all peoples of the world. War, then, becomes a permanent attitude. This understanding of jihad is a grave departure from its original meaning.

Emphasis on armed aggression results from the wrong use of a Qur'anic verse and two prophetic traditions: "O ye who believe: Fight those of the disbelievers who are close to you" (Sura 9:123). On closer examination, this verse is not to fight all unbelievers (non-Muslims who do not believe in the Prophet Muhammad and his message) in every place and at all times; rather it has a strategic meaning—to fight only the unbelievers who are living geographically close to the Muslim community. Its emphasis is on self-defense and on the security of the community. Application of this verse can be seen in the action taken by the Prophet just before his death. In 632 C.E. the Prophet prepared an army to invade his enemies to the north. The Muslim community was surrounded by mighty and powerful enemies, the Roman Empire to the north and the Persian Empire to the east. At that time, attacking these enemies was the best strategy for the defense of the new Muslim community. . . .

In sum, jihad has dual meanings: its religious meaning and its historically determined political meaning. In its authentic religious meaning, jihad is a strong effort or series of efforts against negative behavior or unjust conditions in order to keep one's faith strong and one's existence stable and open to progress; it is to instill justice and mercy in one's conscience and then to establish justice and mercy in the community through the individual and the collective conscience. In its historically determined political meaning, jihad is self-defense and nothing more. It is not aggression, hostility or confrontation. It is unfortunate that the misunderstanding of jihad has become so prevalent. Jihad is mercy, not a sword; and justice, not violence. And Islam is not a state for some people but a path of mercy for all people; not an empire for powerful rulers, but a faith for humankind.

Muhammad Saʿid al-ʿAshmawi, in *Against Islamic Extremism: The Writings of Muhammad Saʿid al-ʿAshmawy*, ed. Carolyn Fluehr-Lobban (Gainesville: University Press of Florida, 1998), 112–113, 114–116, 118–119.

Dissemination of the Message

The minds of many, Muslims and non-Muslims alike, have been firmly impressed with the belief that the Message of Muhammad appeared and spread under the shadow of the sword. They believe that the Arab tribes which bore the Book of Allah in their hearts carried the sword of truth in their hands as they pushed on to the West and to the East and utilized that sword to force people to bow to the Koran. Nothing is farther from the truth or more revealing of superficial and distorted inquiry. It is only proper that we regard this matter with more care in order to distinguish truth from error as we follow the course of the dissemination of the Message during different periods of time.

Perhaps the reason this false notion spread was that the emergence of the Message outside the Arabian peninsula coincided with the rise of the Islamic state; this had led some to confuse the conquests of the polity with religious conversions, and explains why they cannot distinguish between the adherence of peoples to the faith and their acceptance of the message of *tawhid* (belief in the oneness of God) on the one hand and, on the other, their submission to the political authority of the rising Islamic state.

There is a tendency to ignore the fact that Mecca and other places were conquered by an army consisting of thousands of the oppressed who had accepted the guidance of the new faith prior to the period of conquest. These had been persecuted publicly for becoming Muslims and forced to forsake their homeland as they crossed the sea twice, seeking refuge in Abyssinia, and fled subsequently to Yathrib, imploring the protection of every person of ability and means.

ʿAbd al-Rahman ʿAzzam, *The Eternal Message of Muhammad* (New York: New American Library, 1964), 155–156.

Politics and War

The clash between Islam and Christendom began during the lifetime of the Prophet. In the earlier stages of his career, when the main fight was against Arab paganism, his attitude to the Jews and the Christians was friendly and respectful. The leadership of the community brought him into contact and then conflict with both. At first the Jews, strongly represented at Medina, were the immediate enemy, while the Christians remained potential allies and converts. Later, when the expanding influence of the community of Medina brought the Muslims into collision with Christian tribes in Arabia and on the northern borders, relations with Christianity, as with Judaism, culminated in war. . . .

According to Muslim tradition, in the year 7 of the *hijra* (A.D. 628), the Prophet sent letters from Medina to Caesar and Chosroes—the Roman and Persian Emperors—informing them of his mission, and summoning them to accept Islam or suffer the penalties of unbelief. The text of these letters, and even the story of their being sent, are now generally regarded as apocryphal, but, like so much of the Muslim tradition, they reflect an accurate, if subsequent, assessment of realities. Whether Muhammad really contemplated the conquest and conversion of the two great Empires is a matter on which scholars have differed. There can, however, be no doubt that he initiated the processes by which this was in large measure accomplished.

The first Islamic conquest was Khaybar, an oasis some 100 miles north of Medina, on the road to Syria. It was inhabited by Jews, including some who had been evicted from Medina. In 628 Muhammad led an army of about 1,600 men against Khaybar, and in six weeks was able to conquer the whole oasis. The Jews were allowed to retain their families, and practice their religion. Their lands and property were forfeit to the conquerors, but they were allowed to remain in possession of their fields and till them, in return for paying half the harvest to the new owners.

At a later date the Jews of Khaybar were expelled from their oasis by the Caliph ʿUmar, allegedly so that there should be only one religion, Islam, in the holy land of Arabia. The arrangement originally imposed on them by the Prophet, however, became, with minor variations, the pattern followed in later conquests. The expansion to the north, into Christian territory, began during Muhammad's last years; his successors brought under Muslim rule vast regions of Christendom, including the Christian heartlands in the Near East, the whole of North Africa, Spain, parts of France and Italy, and most of the Mediterranean islands.

Bernard Lewis, "Politics and War," in *The Legacy of Islam,* ed. J. Schacht and C. E. Bosworth (London: Oxford University Press, 1974), 180–182.

Religious Law

Islamic law is a particularly instructive example of a "sacred law," but even the two other representatives of a "sacred law" which are historically and geographically nearest to it, Jewish law and canon law, are sensibly different. Islamic law is much less uniform than both. It is the result of a scrutiny, from a religious angle, of legal subject-matter which was far from uniform, comprising as it did the various components of the laws of Arabia and numerous elements taken over from the peoples of the conquered territories. All this was unified by being subjected to the same kind of scrutiny, the impact of which varied greatly. This inner duality of legal subject-matter and religious norm is additional to the outward variety of legal, ethical, and ritual rules which is typical of a "sacred law." Jewish law was buttressed by the cohesion of the community, reinforced by pressure from outside. Canon and Islamic law, on the contrary, are dominated by the dualism of religion and state, where the state is not, in contrast with Judaism, an alien power but the political expression of the same religion. But their antagonism took on different forms; in Christianity it was the struggle for political power on the part of a tightly organized ecclesiastical hierarchy, and canon law was one of its political weapons. Islam, on the other hand, was never a "Church," Islamic law was never supported by an organized power, consequently there never developed a real trial of strength; there merely existed a discordance between the sacred law and the reality of actual practice of which the regulations framed by the state formed part, a gap more or less wide according to pace and time, now and then on the point of being closed but continually reasserting itself. . . .

The central feature which makes Islamic law what it is, which guarantees its unity in all its diversity, is the assessing of all human acts and relationships, including those which we call legal, from the point of view of the following concepts: obligatory, recommended, indifferent, reprehensible, forbidden. Law proper has been thoroughly incorporated in this system of religious duties; these fundamental concepts permeate the juridical subject-matter as well. It might therefore seem as if it were not correct to speak of an Islamic law at all, as if the concept of law did not exist in Islam. The term must indeed be used with the proviso that Islamic law is part of a system of religious duties, blended with non-legal elements. But though it was incorporated into that system, legal subject-matter was not completely assimilated, legal relationships were not completely reduced to and expressed in terms of religious and ethical duties; the sphere of law retained a technical character of its own, and juridical reasoning could develop along its own lines.

Joseph Schacht, "Law and the State: Islamic Religious Law," in Schacht and Bosworth, eds., *The Legacy of Islam,* 392–393, 396.

Jurisprudence

. . . Muslims have defined jurisprudence as "knowledge of the practical rules of religion." The Muslim legists scrutinize human actions and classify them in agreement with Allah's rulings. This procedure makes jurisprudence, in Ibn Khaldun's words, "the knowledge of the rules of God which concern the actions of persons who own themselves bound to obey the Law respecting what is required, forbidden, recommended, disapproved, or merely permitted."

The body of these rules is called *fiqh,* which originally and even as late as the Koran means merely "knowledge" of any kind. Together with *kalam,* scholastic theology, *fiqh* builds the *sharic͏a,* the "straight path," the Sacred Law, where "sacred" relates to the source rather than the subject matter of the regulations.

. . . in its widest sense it (*fiqh*) covers all aspects of religious, political and civil life. In addition to the laws regulating ritual and religious observances, as far as concerns performance and abstinence, it includes the whole field of family law, the law of inheritance, of property and of contract, in a word, provisions for all the legal questions that arise in social life; it also includes criminal law and procedure and finally constitutional law and laws regulating the administration of the state and the conduct of war.

Before the word *fiqh* attained to this comprehensive meaning it had been used together with, or in opposition to, *c͏ilm,* which denoted the accurate knowledge of Koran, tradition and legal precedent, whereas *fiqh* carried the connotation of independent finding of judgment. Thus it could be said, Wisdom consisted of Koran, *c͏ilm* and *fiqh.*

The encyclopedic system of jurisprudence, worked out, to use this old terminology, through *c͏ilm* and *fiqh,* arranges the individual subjects in a manner strikingly different from that suggested by Western legal thinking—even if we overlook the absence in *fiqh* of the fundamental Western division of private and public law and if we acquiesce in having the criminal law distributed over a number of sections.

The Shafi'ite *faqih*, Abu Shuja' al-Isfahani (eleventh century), divides the material into sixteen books which treat of ceremonial purity, prayer, the poor rate, fasting, pilgrimage, barter and other business transactions, inheritance and wills, marriage and related subjects, crimes of violence to the person, restrictive ordinances (e.g., concerning fornication, drinking, apostasy; a chapter of miscellanies), holy war, hunting and the slaughter of animals, racing and shooting with the bow, oaths and vows, judgment and evidence (i.e., legal procedure), and manumission of slaves.

The actual codification of the good life as proposed by *fiqh* would, of course, depend on the source material which the legislator would recognize as authoritative. The assumption seemed obvious that the statute of Allah's commonwealth ought to be promulgated by the Lord himself. But equally obvious was the observation that he had not done so. Only by a dangerous extension of the interpretative abilities could it be maintained that the Koran supplemented by the Prophet's *sunna* contained or implied the answers to every question brought up by the change of events, the change of conditions. But to admit any other source of law was to acknowledge the impossibility of building the life of the individual and the life of society exclusively on the command of Allah; it meant the renunciation of the ideal for whose realization the Muslim community had been called into being. Not to admit any other source was, on the other hand, a dishonest evasion of the facts; at best, a pious fiction bound to result in disastrous inadequacy in meeting the exigencies of everyday life.

Viewed in this light, the acrimonious fight among the law schools concerning additional sources of legislation entirely loses the character of a squabble over words. In the last analysis no legist could escape the necessity of using "opinion" or "analogy" besides Koran and *sunna*, whether he openly acknowledged them as "bases," *usul*, or whether he admitted them covertly through subtle and elaborate interpretation of the Holy Book. The identity of their plight and the essential identity of their solutions lend the disputations of the schools a flavor of futility. However, while a sizable proportion of their debates and of their differences amply warrants this condemnation, the great cause at stake actually resolved itself into the burning question whether or not the Lord had revealed the full statute of a *civitas Dei*, whether or not the concept of divine rulership of man and society could be carried through to its logical conclusion, whether or not through a compromise a human element had to be admitted into the structure.

The Prophet apparently was unaware of the dilemma. He does not seem to have considered the completeness of revelation or custom. We are told that once he was sending a judge to the Yemen and asked him on what he would base his legal decisions.

"On the Koran," he replied.

"But if that contains nothing to the purpose?"

"Then upon your usage."

"But if that also fails you?"

"Then I will follow my own opinion." And the Prophet approved his purpose.

Gustave E. von Grunebaum, *Medieval Islam,* 144–147.

2

The Islamic Establishment in Decline

In his essay "Politics and War," Bernard Lewis describes the uniqueness of Islamic law and the Islamic polity. Muslims, he points out, "like Christians, governed and made war; like them, too, they managed to involve their religion in both activities." But in the manner and nature of the two involvements there were great differences, he adds.

The Founder of Christianity bade his followers "render unto Caesar the things which are Caesar's; and unto God the things which are God's"—and for three centuries Christianity grew as a religion of the oppressed, until Caesar himself became a Christian, and initiated the processes by which the Church became involved in the State, and the State in the Church. The Founder of Islam was his own Constantine. During his lifetime, the Muslims became a political as well as a religious community, with the Prophet as sovereign—governing a place and a people, dispensing justice, collecting taxes, commanding armies, conducting diplomacy, and waging war. For the early generations of Muslims, there was no long testing by persecution, no apprenticeship in resistance to an alien and hostile state power. On the contrary, the state was their own, and the divine favour manifested itself to them in this world in the form of success, victory, and empire.

For Muhammad and his companions, therefore, the choice between God and Caesar, the snare in which not Christ but so many Christians were to be entangled, did not arise. In Islam, there was no Caesar, there was only God, and Muhammad was His Prophet, who both taught and ruled on His behalf. The same authority, from the same source, sustained the Prophet in both tasks; the same revelation provided the content of the one, and the basis of the other. When Muhammad died, his spiritual and prophetic function—the promulgation of God's message—was completed; his religious, and with it his political work remained. This was to spread the law of God among mankind, by extending the membership and authority of the community which recognized and upheld that law. In the leadership of this community, a deputy or successor to the Prophet was needed. The Arabic word *khalifa*, by which that successor was known, combined the two meanings.[1]

Islamic religious motifs featured prominently in the bitter debate that raged in the Arab world in the early 1990s between those who backed Iraq, however conditionally, and those who condemned Saddam Hussein's invasion of Kuwait out of hand and sought to justify the presence of foreign troops on Muslim soil. The arguments used by the two sides were always duly supported by relevant passages from the Qurʾan and from Islam's oral tradition, some of which are shown to prohibit Muslims from seeking help from "the infidels" while others appeared to allow such help if it is sought for purposes of self-defense.

The great frequency with which these religious motifs were evoked in that controversy was by no means untypical. In the Arab world religion seems always to be dragged into such political disputations, not only because Islam is an all-pervasive faith that cannot be separated from the general sociopolitical order but also because Muslim rulers, whether religiously oriented or strictly secular themselves, find it convenient to use their willing clerics for promoting their worldly pursuits and obtain religious edicts (fatwas) in support of practically any measure they might take.

In such recent debates, however, there is one more good reason for turning to Islam and its teachings for help. For the fact is that Saudi Arabia happens to house Islam's two most revered holy places—the Kaʿba and the tomb of the Prophet Muhammad. This apparent coincidence is considered of such significance that the Saudi monarchs proudly and loudly carry the title *Khadim al-Haramain ash-Sharifain*—Servant of the Two Exalted Sanctuaries—since the establishment of the dynasty.

The lead roles in the heated Gulf War squabble were played by the ʿulema of Egypt, Saudi Arabia, and Syria on one side, and of Iraq, Jordan, and the Palestinians on the other. But the most vocal discussions were conducted—as always—in Egypt, where even some of the opposition parties engaged in quasi-theological disputations. (One of these was the Labor Party, Hizb al-ʿAmal, whose chairman and deputy chairman were locked in a fierce controversy between themselves over whether Islam allows the usurper to get away unpunished.)

Inside the religious establishment of Egypt itself, however, there was complete unanimity of views. The two leading luminaries of the establishment were the sheikh of al-Azhar, Jad el-Haq ʿAli Jad el-Haq, and the mufti of the republic, Dr. Muhammad Sayyid Tantawi. The fatwas the two issued, quite early in the proceedings, are as learned as they are lengthy, and the verdicts given therein are backed by ample passages from the Qurʾan and other sources. The fatwas, of course, were subjected to merciless scrutiny and criticism by the muftis of Iraq, Jordan, and the Palestine Liberation Organization, who seemed to have had no difficulty in collating quotations in refutation of the verdicts passed by their Egyptian counterparts.

What emerges from these disputations is, in the main, that the decline in stature and in influence of the Muslim religious establishments in general, and of that of Egypt in particular, continues unabated. The decline is most pronounced in the case of al-Azhar, the oldest and for many centuries the most venerable house of religious learning in the Muslim world. Attempts to reform its methods of teaching, which started with the emergence of a strong reformist movement toward the end of the nineteenth century, bore fruit only in the early 1960s.

Established in 970 in New Cairo by the Fatimid conquerors, the Mosque of al-Azhar (Jamiʿ al-Azhar) over the centuries taught and trained Muslim religious judges, muftis, and preachers from all over the Muslim world. It sent out teachers and issued fatwas in response to questions and queries from all over the world, organized Muslim conferences, published and distributed religious publications, and encouraged Islamic missionary work in Africa and the Far East. The sheikhs and the ʿulema of al-Azhar also often dabbled in politics, occasionally making a show of independence and issuing fatwas opposing the policies of the existing powers of the day.

While it continues to perform most of these functions, however, al-Azhar today is not what it used to be, having lost much of its splendor. (The Arabic word *azhar* means "resplendent.") It was Gamal Abdel Nasser— who, by the way, never tired of invoking Islam to justify his politics and his ideology—who decided that the time was ripe for modernizing and thus taming and restraining the ancient institution.

In June 1961, after integrating all the judiciaries in Egypt and abolishing the religious (shariʿa) courts in 1955–56, Nasser completed the process by reorganizing al-Azhar and turning it into what for all intents and purposes is a state institution and a tool of the republic. In accordance with Law 103 the institution became one of the five state universities of Egypt. The religious character of al-Azhar was preserved, to be sure, and its sheikh kept issuing fatwas against Egypt's enemies and in support of its government's policies—and it is these fatwas that usually lead to controversy, especially when they touch upon points of dispute between Arab and Muslim regimes, as in the case of the Gulf War, resulting in grave accusations and counteraccusations.

It is notable that such sharp exchanges are fairly characteristic of these debates, which rage not only between ʿulema of various nationalities and predilections but also between them and the secular establishment. It often happens, too, that the fatwas pronounced by them are later contradicted by others issued by the selfsame religious savants. In Egypt, especially, the debate between the ʿulema and the secular intellectuals has always been fierce. Some years ago—to give only one example—wondering whether Islam was at all capable of adapting to the modern world and, if so, who among Muslims was to take the initiative in such a reform movement, the Egyptian writer and publicist Ahmad Bahaeddine had very harsh things to say about the ʿulema.

"Throughout history," Bahaeddine said in the course of a symposium, "we meet Muslim theologians and religious savants twice, and consistently. We meet them once prior to change, when they rule that it is forbidden, and once after the change has taken place, when they protest that Allah had already envisaged such change long ago and permitted it. . . ." In recent decades, in fact, after the rise of modern nation-states in the Arab-Muslim world, the basically secular regimes there managed to reduce their respective religious establishments to a position where they became little more than willing tools and mouthpieces, ready to explain and justify every measure and policy taken by their governments. Again, suitable fatwas were readily issued, invariably backed by ample quotations from the Qurʾan and the Hadith.

Al-Azhar and its successive sheikhs were no exception. In 1961, when Gamal Abdel Nasser had cause to be displeased with the institution and its leaders, he pronounced what may prove to be the last word. "Of course," he wrote in al-Azhar's own publication, "the sheikh does not think of anything except his turkey and the food with which he fills his belly. He is no more than a stooge of reaction, feudalism and capitalism."[2] Upon which the sheikh duly turned into a stooge of progress, socialism, and Arab nationalism—Nasser style.

Hasan Turabi's Vision

"Even the Muslims themselves sometimes don't know how to go about their Islam. They have no recent precedent of an Islamic government." Thus

Hasan Turabi, the veteran Muslim revivalist now widely considered the uncrowned head of the Islamic government of Sudan. Turabi, a trained lawyer with degrees from the Sorbonne and the University of London, made this instructive remark when confronted by an interviewer with examples of arbitrary measures taken by the authorities in Khartoum—such as after-dark arrests, morality police, and restrictions on women, some of whom having complained that in offices and schools where they work they had been threatened with the loss of their jobs if they went on wearing Western dress.

That present-day Muslims do not quite know how to go about Islam—how, that is, to interpret it or reinterpret it as the comprehensive, all-inclusive code of life and government it is said to be—is apparent to anyone who follows the endless intra-Islamic controversies raging these days in the Arab world. So-called Muslim fundamentalists, for one, all advocating a return to pristine Islam, appear to be hopelessly divided on the question as to what such a revival actually means. There are, for example, certain leading ʿulema and dignitaries whose views are considered anathema in Saudi Arabia, a famously Islamic state.

Again, to take an example from Egypt, the two highest religious authorities there—the grand mufti, Sheikh Jad el-Haq, and the grand imam of al-Azhar, Dr. Tantawi—speak in two entirely different voices on many a theological and juridical subject touching upon the everyday life of Muslim men and women in that largest of Arab-Muslim countries. An article printed in the Cairo weekly *Rose el-Yusuf* not long ago contains a number of instructive examples. Carrying the heading, "Who Are We to Believe—the Grand Mufti or the Grand Imam?" the article opens with short remarks about the almost identical backgrounds of the two men. Both, it appears, had attended the same university, studied the same theological treatises, the same Qurʾan commentaries, and the selfsame compilations of Hadith.

"However," adds the author of the article, "the distance between the two is very long indeed if you happen to read their fatwas. A Muslim can cross oceans and negotiate mountains, and yet he wouldn't know which of the two to believe—the mufti or the imam." Differences between these two seem to cut across the spectrum of the pressing issues of the day—birth control, transplantation of organs, savings and interest, among others. On each of these subjects, the imam and the mufti have issued diametrically opposing fatwas.

At the root of the confusion here is the multitude of individuals and committees authorized to issue fatwas—or just believed by popular consensus to be fit to do so. The phenomenon can reach absurd dimensions. The author of the article in *Rose el-Yusuf* quotes a popular Egyptian saying:

Leave it all to the ʾalim
All else is vain.
And thus secure and safe
You will remain.

The meaning is clear: You can get any fatwa you want— so do your own thing and leave the rest to the ʿalim or the imam.

"In Egypt," adds the writer in *Rose el-Yusuf,* "you can stop at any news stand and have your pick of whatever ʿalim on whose neck you choose to hang your misconduct. You will find a whole variety of leading sheikhs to choose between—Shaʿrawi, Ghazzali, Yusuf el-Qardhawi, Yassin Rushdi. Each has a different opinion and each the right quotes from the Qurʾan and the Tradition."[3]

Needless to say, such wide differences of opinion and interpretation extend all the way from everyday matters like family planning and banking to the criminal code and to affairs of state. On this latter subject especially—that is, the precise nature of an Islamic government—the views are often diametrically opposed. As these differences all have some basis in the Scripture, moreover, Muslims have always felt free to choose whatever version seems suitable—to their temperament, to their immediate circumstances, or both.

Take the case of Islamic law itself. There have always been two fairly different approaches to that law, corresponding to the two portions of the Qurʾan revealed to the Prophet in Mecca and Medina. In the former, where Muhammad's mission was threatened, the precepts of the law were far stricter than those revealed in Medina, by which time Islam ruled uncontested.

Thus, for the contemporary Islamist to lean on the Meccan precepts is to be the more militant, the more literalist, and accordingly the less tolerant of minority opinion and of the followers of other faiths. Those who choose to base their programs on the Medinic version, on the other hand, are the more "liberal," and politically the more pluralistic.

Or that is what they profess anyway. As Hasan Turabi has put it on more than one occasion and in a variety of ways, the Islamist movement is one of intellectual renewal and of active social reform, representing a revolt against "the dormancy and dogmatism of traditional societies." With regard to the impracticability of the rules of the shariʿa, he points out that although that law has been in force in the Sudan for over a year, there has not been a single amputation of a burglar's hand yet—which for him is proof that the law has proved to be a very effective deterrent.

In an exhaustive interview with Hassan el-Tal, editor of the Jordanian daily *Al-Ra'y*, Turabi said the Islamist tide spread considerably after the Kuwait crisis and the Gulf War. This, he added, helped expose the fallacies of those "who clamoured for democracy, but who, when their Islamist adversaries won the elections in Algeria early this year, turned their backs on democracy . . . and called openly for suspending the elections and closing this option for a return to Islam." "The only difference between the democratic state and the Islamic state," Turabi said in conclusion, "is that in the latter one code of laws guides all government institutions—i.e., the *shari'a.*"[4]

The shape of things in the Arab-Muslim world after the guns fell silent in the Gulf War of the early 1990s is a topic of much discussion both in and outside the Middle East. One of the subjects on which speculation has been rife is that of change—social, political, economic, and cultural change, change that had already been considered overdue but that the war is deemed to have made inevitable or at least to have hastened considerably.

Although so far they have largely failed to respond, monarchs and rulers of traditional Arab-Muslim nations are no doubt aware of the existence in their midst of increasingly vocal minorities calling for more personal freedoms, an equitable distribution of wealth, a free press, and democratically elected governments. With the exception of the Hashemite Kingdom of Jordan, however, where an earnest and so far successful leap has been taken in the direction of representative government, responses to such calls have been far from encouraging.

Saudi Arabia is a case in point. On November 8, 1990, three months into the Gulf crisis, King Fahd suddenly announced that a shura council would be set up, and that other laws—including "a constitutional law"— would soon be promulgated. Spokesmen of the regime went on record that these measures constituted "a new policy based on choice and the wishes shared by the leadership and the citizen."

Grand enough talk—and equally reassuring. What it all amounts to, however, is far less clear. Plainly, the operative term here is the Arabic word *shura*. When they refer to a shura council, Saudi and Arab commentators equate the term automatically with parliament. The sole point of similarity between a Western-style parliament and a Muslim shura council, however, is that both are places in which people "speak" and tend to discuss and consult about things, in this case affairs of state.

And indeed the word *shura* means "consultation," and a shura council (*majlis shura*) is an assembly of representatives of a people, and can also be the supreme legislative authority for that people. But the shura council the Saudi monarch promised his people differs in one cardinal point from a parliament as the term is understood in a democracy: Rather than being elected on the popular level, the promised majlis is to be rooted firmly in the rules of the Islamic shariᶜa, which the Saudi monarchy is said to be "absolutely and permanently committed to follow equally as a faith, a program, and a basis for government, and from which there can be no deviation whatsoever."[5]

"Islamic Democracy" Defined

The exact nature of the shura way of government—which some Muslim writers have called Islamic democracy—has never been properly defined as a working system with clearly articulated rules for its being put into practice. Like almost every other Islamic practice, however, the shura system is based on the teachings of the Qurʾan and on Islam's oral tradition, Hadith. In this particular case the practice originates in a brief Qurʾanic ordinance which states, "The Believers' communal business is to be transacted in consultation among them." Muslim thinkers consider this injunction to be the fundamental, operative clause of all Islamic thought relating to statecraft. In the words of one prominent Muslim theologian, the ordinance "makes the transaction of all political business not only consequent upon, but synonymous with, consultation—which means that the legislative power of the state must be vested in an assembly chosen by the community specifically for this purpose."[6]

The question, however, is how to put together such an assembly. In more plain language: Who is to choose those who are to consult among themselves on state business? Answers to these questions were advanced by the Saudi monarchy since the early 1930s, when Abdul Aziz Al Saud assumed the title of king of Saudi Arabia. His "consultative council" comprised heads of tribes and prominent urban families—a simple and effective enough practice, considering the tribal character of the country more than six decades ago.

This system worked fairly efficiently until the early 1960s, when the traditional Saudi monarchy found itself threatened by revolutionary regimes in Cairo, Baghdad, and Damascus, and when the civil war in neighboring Yemen became a struggle between the old regime and anti-monarchist elements actively supported by Nasser's regime. Then, as now, a promise was made by the monarchs to the effect that, Allah willing, a consultative council would be set up.

This promise was duly forgotten after the threats were lifted, with Nasser's 1967 fiasco and the withdrawal of his divisions from Yemen. In 1979, and again in 1980, similar promises were made by King Khalid, but again nothing came out of them, despite the fact that Khalid named an eight-man commission to draw up the relevant legislation and prepare the assembly, for which even a building was planned. Though the building, in marble and glass, was duly finished, it stood empty on a hill above Riyadh. More recent promises made by the king may, conceivably, have meant that the imposing construction would be occupied once the Gulf War was over.

Whatever happens to Fahd's promise of a majlis shura, and even if one is duly put together, one thing is certain: The Saudi monarchy is going to continue to insist that Islam is the source of all its laws and ordinances. The Saudi stand on the subject of elections and representative government is propounded in great detail in a Ph.D. dissertation prepared by none other than a Saudi prince. To get his degree from the University of California, Prince Faisal ibn Mashʿal ibn Saud ibn Abdul Aziz chose the subject "Democratic Practice through the Open Councils in Saudi Arabia," in which, among many other things, he set out to explain the reasons why the practice of democracy as it is known in the West is not suitable for that country.

In the West, writes Prince Faisal, there is a tradition of respect for and observance of laws—"such as traffic and tax laws"—which are observed as if they were religious edicts, whereas in Saudi Arabia "law and order are, and will continue to be, based on religious ordinances." According to him, political consciousness and the literacy rate in any country are extremely important factors when it comes to choosing the kind of political system most suited to that country. Popular elections, he adds, are not practicable in a country like Saudi Arabia, where 60 percent of the population were, until thirty years ago, divided into tribes used to a life of nomads and living in a state of permanent warfare between themselves. This is why, he concludes, popular elections in the Saudi monarchy today would result in the same state of rivalry and struggle between various sections of the population.[7]

This, roughly, is the Saudi monarchy's basic approach to the subject of representative government. To do him justice, however, it must be added that King Fahd in his November 1990 promise did not refer to anything like popular elections. The terms in which he spoke were vague enough for him to come out with some kind of consultative council, which eventually he did.

By way of conclusion to this preliminary survey, in which an attempt has been made to explain why Islam, both as religion and as polity, is unique among the three monotheistic religions, I quote here from a relatively recent work by an American student of the subject. In his book *The Islamic Threat*, Georgetown University professor John L. Esposito writes under the heading "Diversity and Change":

> The experience of the past decade alerts us to the need to be more attentive to the diversity behind the seeming unity of Islam, to appreciate and more effectively analyze both the unity and diversity in Islam and in Muslim affairs. In the past, the oneness of Islam (of God, the Prophet, and the Book) gave rise to many movements and interpretations: Sunni, Shii, Kharaji, Wahhabi, and different schools of law, theology, and mysticism. So too today, different contexts have spawned a variety of Islamically oriented nations, leaders, and organizations. The diversity of governments—the Saudi monarchy; Qaddafi's populist state; Khomeini's clerical republic in Iran; and the military regimes of Zia ul-Haq in Pakistan, and Gaafar Muhammad Nimeiri and now Omar al-Bashir in the Sudan—their differing relations with the West, and the variety of Islamic movements are undercut and distorted by the univocal connotation of the term *Islamic fundamentalism*.

Beyond the common reference to an Islamic alternative and to general ideological principles, and as one looks across the wide array of governments, societies, and Islamic organizations, one discovers multiple levels of discourse. "There are," Esposito writes, "often as many differences as similarities in Muslim interpretations of the nature of the state, Islamic law, and the status of women and minorities as there are sharp differences regarding the methods (the ballot box, social service centers, violent confrontation) to be employed for the realization of an Islamic system of government." He concludes:

> Ironically, non-Muslim scholars sometimes sound more like mullahs. When faced with new interpretations or applications of Islam, they often critique them from the vantage point of traditional belief and practice. On the one hand, Islam is regarded as fixed, and Muslims are seen as too reluctant to accept change. On the other hand, when change occurs, it is dismissed as unorthodox, sheer opportunism, an excuse for adopting that which is outside Islam. Yet all we are witnessing is a natural process of reinterpretation by individuals and communities, another stage in the interpretation and development of the

Islamic tradition. The reinterpretation of traditional Islamic concepts such as *shura* (consultation) and *ijmaᶜ* (community consensus) are excellent examples of this progress. Change is a reality in contemporary Islam and in Muslim societies. It may be found at every level, in every quarter, and across social classes. The issue is not change but the amount, pace, and direction of change. The flexibility of the Islamic tradition is demonstrated not only by those whom some regard as modern reformers, such as Ali Shariati or Sadiq al-Mahdi, but also by the Ayatollah Khomeini's interpretation of the doctrine of governance by the jurist (*vilayat-i-faqih*), as well as by the constitution of the Islamic Republic of Iran's acceptance of a constitutional parliamentary form of government.[8]

Readings

The Nature of Islamic Modernism

The problem Muslim reformists have had to grapple with during the past century or so can be formulated in a variety of ways. . . .

. . . Broadly speaking, attempts on the part of modern Islam to meet the West's assault in the cultural, political, and military spheres have been of two kinds—the one showing an instinct to absorb and find compatibles, the other displaying a tendency to reject and affirm distinctions. It must be pointed out, however, that these two modes of reaction—which denote the two extreme tendencies in the struggle of the assaulted culture against the dominant one—do not exhaust all possibilities of dealing with the problem. If these two sharply contrasted reactions of absorption and rejection can be likened—as has been done by Toynbee—respectively to those of the Herodians and the Zealots in Hellenic times, there then must be a third way, namely, that of the Pharisees. This original, positive mode of reaction to alien cultural pressure has been called one of "withdrawal and return." It is perhaps to this third tendency that we have to refer the main body of the great reform movement in Arabic Islam in modern times.

. . . It is not easy to formulate a satisfactory definition of the term "modernism" in its Islamic context—or in any other context for that matter. Roughly speaking, the modernist movement in Arabic Islam can be described as an expression of the necessity of an intellectual response, within the religious faith, to the pressure of new circumstances and ideas as they bear upon traditional dogma and behavior. The movement's driving force, insofar as it had one such distinguishable force, was the desire to demonstrate, in practical terms and in response to particular concrete issues, that Islam was equal to the needs and demands of the modern world. Its protagonists and leading exponents were informed by a desire to rid Islam of a backward-looking mentality that they thought disqualified its followers from participation in a progressive, forward-looking mode of life. They sought to destroy the spirit of obscurantism, which encouraged authoritarian loyalties to old schools of law and custom and barred the introduction of reasonable change.

Yet, contrary to what might seem both logical and desirable, Islamic modernism did not seek any far-reaching theological reconstruction. The basic theological and orthodox doctrines of Islam have not, except in very rare cases, been involved in the debates of the modernists. Their main emphases have fallen on institutional adaptation and adjustment to new situations and on the liberation of the minds and ways of men from the paralyzing restrictions imposed by *taqlid,* the slavish imitation of traditional interpretations. Though it is true that some of the positive achievements of the movement have had important doctrinal implications, these have tended to be only indirect and sometimes unconscious. One can conclude with fairness that the modern reform movement in Islam, especially where the Arabic-speaking world is concerned, has not attempted any radical intellectual reexamination of Islam or sought a revision of its basic precepts.

As a matter of fact, the directions in which the exponents of the movement have expressed themselves were for the most part practical rather than speculative, adaptive rather than creative—with the notable exception of the Indian school of Islamic modernism led by Muhammad Iqbal. The modernist Muslim strives, in fact, to evoke an Islam that takes cognizance of all its duties in the present without inhibition from the past—an Islam which does not, as a religion, resist the pressure of social morality but rather encourages and adopts it to itself.

This reluctance on the part of the modernists to deal with issues of basic doctrine was no accident. By concentrating on practical rather than speculative aspects of the subject, the exponents of Islamic reform managed, at least for a time, to avoid the main issue, which was simply how to modernize Islam itself and not merely its followers. But only for a time. This is why their work was left uncompleted and is likely to remain so for a long time.

Nissim Rejwan, *Arabs Face the Modern World: Religious, Cultural, and Political Responses to the West* (Gainesville: University Press of Florida, 1998), 2–3.

The ʾUlama and Legal Reform

For the *ulama,* the modern period has brought a serious erosion of their traditional power and authority. Educational and legal reforms have greatly curtailed the dominant roles of the *ulama* in education and law, restricted their sources of revenue, and raised serious questions about their competence and relevance. In most Muslim countries, modern secular educational systems have been set up alongside the traditional religious (*madrasa*) schools. Countries have tended to favor national schools, as have students who wish to be trained for and compete for jobs as modern professionals. More often than not, the *madrasa*s have attracted less state support and fewer of the talented students. They are regarded as seminaries rather than as universities; their diplomas have a more limited value and usefulness. Similarly, the introduction of modern law has seen the rise of a new class of civil lawyers and judges emerge, as the expertise of the *ulama* was restricted to family law courts. Whereas Islamic law was determined by religious scholars, modern legal reform has been accomplished through the action of rulers or parliamentary bodies, most of whose members were laymen, and enforced by civil courts.

The *ulama*'s sense of disenfranchisement has been heightened by the abolition of religious endowments (*waqf*) or their administration by government agencies, further reducing the economic independence and social role of the *ulama.* The state, by controlling revenues and paying salaries, has increased its control of religious institutions and social-welfare programs. Moreover, the greater value placed on modern education has also resulted in the general tendency to hold the *ulama* responsible for the ills of Muslim societies. Among Sunni Muslims in particular, secularists, Islamic modernists, and many neotraditionalists alike, the *ulama* have been regarded throughout much of the twentieth century as ignorant and obscurantist religious leaders incapable of providing necessary leadership. Like Sufism, the *ulama* are often regarded as a major cause of Muslim weakness and decline. . . .

However, increasingly one finds Muslim voices who, while not directly challenging the existence of the *ulama* as an institution, do attempt to redefine their role and areas of competence. In order to limit the scope of *ulama* authority and justify lay input, they remind their followers that Islam knows no clergy and that all Muslims are equal and responsible before God. They argue that the title *alim* (pl. *ulama*) simply means "learned," one who has knowledge or is an expert. Thus, the title belongs properly not to a specific clerical group or class but to any Muslim who is qualified. This point is made subtly by Dr. Hassan al-Turabi, leader of the Sudan's

Muslim Brotherhood and a former attorney general, in discussing the role of the *ulama* in parliamentary deliberations regarding legislation in an Islamic state. . . .

However, for the majority of the *ulama*, any attempt to limit the area of their competence is to be resisted. Thus, the authority of the *ulama*, along with the nature of Islamic law and the question of legal reform remain pivotal issues facing the Muslim community.

John L. Esposito, *Islam: The Straight Path* (New York: Oxford University Press, 1988), 183–185.

"Translating" Traditional Texts

The hallmark of Islamist modernism is its admission of the possibility, even the necessity, of the translatability of traditional texts; thus *shura* becomes democracy, even parliamentary democracy; Islam becomes a charter for socialism; and the cosmic calamities indicated in the early apocalyptic chapters of the Koran become premonitions of modern scientific discoveries. For the radicals, however, Islam is *sui generis,* and is utterly distinctive; it is therefore totally unrelated to democracy, especially parliamentary democracy, and any talk of relating it to socialism is polluting by implication, for the term "socialism" is contiguous with communism, and communism is atheistic, and neither socialism nor democracy occurs in the Koran or the salutary tradition. In radical Islamism, translation is precluded, and the utopia which is sought is a literalist one whose institutes have already been fully established. Fundamentalism here becomes, fully, *integrisme,* not even precluding (for some radical groups) the reclamation of slavery. The present thus being no more than a shadow of unreality in comparison with the full ontological weight of the salutary example, it will be seen that such radical discourse rarely even adulterates itself with specifying matters arising in the present. Wahhabite discourse, for instance, rarely refers to its present, regarding it in some way as a register running parallel to itself, while it takes the form of a metonymic representation of present realities when it discourses on matters that occurred in the days of the Prophet.

It has long been realized that Islamist revivalism is heavily impregnated with Western notions. This is perhaps most clearly so in the foundational texts of this revivalism: these are by ʿAbduh (d. 1905), Afghani (d. 1897) and (to a lesser extent) Rida (d. 1935), who produced a repertoire of ideas which have infused Islamist discourse until the present. This is entirely unsurprising, given the circumstances of its emergence in the late nineteenth century in a milieu which was neither beholden to the religious hierarchy

of the Azhar and similar institutions, nor particularly fond of it—
Muhammad ʿAbduh spoke of decades spent in sweeping out of his head
the filth deposited in it by Al-Azhar, then the major seat of Muslim learning in Egypt and beyond. ʿAbduh, Rida and their spiritual descendants spent
considerable effort trying to translate koranic and other traditional pronouncements into terms current in the political and scientific life of their
days. . . .

In political and social matters, translation took the form of pairing various notions from tradition with matters of contemporary relevance. One
of the major such notions is *shura,* consultation among Arab tribal grandees
at the time of the Prophet, which was reclaimed as the fount and origin of
popular presentation. As the political polemic of the early Islamic revival-
ists such as ʿAbduh, Afghani, Kawakibi and Rida has essentially been directed against despotism, this is hardly unsurprising; and in the course of
its long career, the notion of *shura* has taken on many shades spanning the
entire spectrum of the possibilities in Rousseau between direct democracy
and a sort of sectoral senate containing representatives of various corporate and other groups. Other notions of the same order include the appro-
priation of socialism, especially under the Baathist and Nasserite regimes.

Aziz al-Azmeh, *Islams and Modernities* (London: Verso, 1993), 79–80.

Al-Afghani's Legacy

The only substantial work [al-Afghani] left behind was *The Refutation of
the Materialists,* which he wrote while in semi- exile in India. Charles Adams
summarizes the final section of the book, entitled "The Means by Which
the Happiness of Nations May Be Attained," which gives an example of
the more constructive side of his teachings and contains many of his fundamental ideas. In order that the happiness of nations may be attained, Afghani
maintains the following:

1. The minds of the people should be purified of belief in superstitions
   and foolish notions. Islam requires this, especially because the
   doctrine of the unity of God requires the clarifying of the mind and
   forbids such foolish and extravagant notions as idolatry, or incarna-
   tions and suffering of the Deity.
2. The people should feel themselves capable of attaining the highest
   levels of nobility of character and should be desirous of being so. The
   only thing that cannot be reached by him who desires it is prophecy,
   which God confers on whomsoever he will. If all the people were
   persuaded of the possibility of attaining perfection of character they

would vie with one another in endeavors to attain it. Islam made possible perfection for all. . . .

3. The articles of belief of the religion of the nation should be the first subject taught to the people, and this should be done by teaching also the proper reasons and arguments in support of these beliefs; the religious beliefs of the people should not rest upon mere acceptance of authoritative teaching. . . . Islam is almost alone among the religions of the world in addressing itself to man's reason and demanding that he accept religious belief only upon the grounds of convincing argument and not of mere claim and supposition. Contrasted with Islam are other religions, such as those requiring the belief that one can be more than one and the many can be one, a belief which its professors justify on the ground that it is above reason and cannot be grasped by reason.

4. In every nation there should be a special class whose function is to educate the rest of the people and another class whose function is to train the people in morals. One class would combat natural ignorance and the lack of instruction, the other would combat natural passions and the lack of discipline. . . . Islam is the only religion by which the happiness of nations can be attained. If it be objected, "Why then are the Muslims in the evil state in which you find them?" The answer may be given in the words of the Koran: "Verily God will not change the state of a people until they change their own state" (XIII:12).

The student will probably be struck by the remarkable similarity between Afghani's contention in point three above and the teachings of the Protestant movement in Europe. His reference, for instance, to "a religious party that claimed the right of investigating religious beliefs for themselves" is an obvious reference to that movement. Indeed, [one of his biographers] quotes Afghani as having told Abd al-Qader al-Maghribi that there should emerge in Islam a reform movement "akin to that of Martin Luther's Protestantism . . . to eradicate mistaken notions which have taken roots in the minds of the populace and of some of the theologians alike."

However, despite the fact that Afghani's ideas about religious reform were clear, well argued, and systematic, his chief appeal to the young Muslims of his time was political. This can be readily understood, since the field of political agitation offered these patriots not only a seemingly quick and easy way to national independence but also an opportunity for the expression of vociferous nationalistic sentiments. This appeal was wide. Afghani-inspired political revolutionaries and venerable scholars, in equal measure, advocated both local nationalism and Pan-Islam and agitated for liberation from both internal despotism and foreign domination.

Nissim Rejwan, *Arabs Face the Modern World*, 11–12.

Two Views of Islamic Law

The attempt to reintroduce what Islam's early generations understood as Islamic law has been characteristic of one response to the modern Muslim predicament.

After the glories of its early history, Islam was in early modern times eclipsed by the West. Many Muslims wondered how this humiliating and demoralising setback was to be addressed.

For some, the way forward was to do what the West itself had done, but better and in one's own way: that is, to embrace modernity, but to find an authentically Muslim way of doing so, consistent with the progressive, rational, morally egalitarian, emancipatory, and democratic spirit of the *Qurʾan* itself.

But for others, a different path seemed indicated. If Islam had been eclipsed, then the way to its restoration was by a return to the sociopolitical institutions, laws and practices of the triumphant early *umma,* especially those of the first generation of Muslims who lived under the Prophet Muhammad's leadership in Medina.

The first tendency is that of Islamic modernism, both religious and social. It is the tradition which, in common with their predecessors, Malaysia's current political leaders notably exemplify. This is an approach which sees every generation as not merely entitled but also obliged to rethink Islam anew, in an effort to find new and ever more inclusive ways of giving effect to its enduring social and moral imperatives.

For this approach, history as it unfolds holds out new and ever greater possibilities for the actualisation of the Qurʾanic ethical and social vision— and of giving constantly evolving sociolegal form to those new possibilities and understandings—that were not available to previous Muslim generations, including even the wisest thinkers and noblest spirits among them.

To the adherents of the second approach, who seek to move Islam forward by taking the *umma* back to the supposed security of its past practices, the early generations of Islam—being closer to the life and example of the Prophet himself—were giants, or at least exemplars, who necessarily knew better from their involvement in early Islamic history than do we, or any of their successors ever could.

For the supporters of this second approach, as for all Muslims, the *Qurʾan* itself is divine, sacred and authoritative. But they also treat as virtually no less authoritative and binding the interpretations of that sacred text that were made—under the often limiting sociolegal conditions then prevailing—by the early Muslim legal scholars who codified Islamic law in its traditional or classic formulations.

For the adherents of this approach, history offers not new possibilities but imposes a troubling remoteness, even alienation. As history advances, it takes the *umma* even further away from the paradigmatic ideal of its founding generations, from the secure example and guidance of those who enjoyed a direct understanding of Islam in its authentic and formative phase.

For them, accordingly, the way to close that gap—to heal the wounding distance imposed upon modern Muslims by relentlessly advancing history— is to reaffirm and to reimpose in the present the understandings of Qurʾanic ethical imperatives of those early times: that is, as they were first codified in their not simply premodern but actually most archaic legal forms.

Seen in this way, the desire to implement what its proponents regard as the essence of Islamic law—including the *hudud* punishments—becomes understandable. But it can also be recognised for what it really is: an anachronistic attempt to impose in modern times and upon modern Muslims of good faith what is not the essence or culmination of Islamic law but only Islamic law in its most archaic, provisional and historically unevolved form.

Norani Othman, "Hudud Law or Islamic Modernity?" in *Shariʿa Law and the Modern Nation-State,* ed. Norani Othman (Kuala Lumpur: Sisters in Islam Forum [Malaysia] Berhad, 1994), 148–149.

Applying the Shariʿa

. . . The call for the application of the shariʿa rests upon a simplistic view of thought and history. . . . It starts from the assumption that there is a single, stable, and immutable conception and content of what is conventionally called the *shariʿa,* and that just because we are disobedient servants (in the best and most merciful of assumptions) we refuse to take hold of that clear conception and content and apply it to our crisis-ridden reality. [But] the matter is not that simple. The principles and rules of the *shariʿa* are not instruments in themselves ready for governing any society at any time. They become so once the instruments of our reason come into play. . . . The *shariʿa* consists of goals: the preservation of religion, of the mind, of honor, of property, and of the person. It consists of indubitable texts in the Qurʾan and *sunna.* It consists of an *ijtihad* that treats these texts in detail. And finally the *shariʿa* consists of the practical application of all this.

While the *shariʿa* was officially the law of the land, the matter was not so clear on the practical level. Public order was solely governed by the law of oppression, tyranny, might, and force. Private law—that is, the relations of lesser importance between the common people—was governed by principles of Islamic jurisprudence administered by Islamic judges, and even here the application of the *shariʿa* was not quite generalized, and the competence of the Islamic judge to cover them was not comprehensive. . . .

Consequently—and this is the important thing—the era that preceded the introduction of national laws with French roots was not a golden era of Egyptian society ruled by the *shariʿa*. Not only was the era not golden, but the *shariʿa* was not reigning either.

Muhammad Nur Farahat, in Alexander Flores, "Secularism, Integralism, and Political Islam: The Egyptian Debate," in *Political Islam: Essays from* Middle East Report, ed. Joel Beinin and Joe Stork (Berkeley: University of California Press, 1997), 87.

Facing Western Influences

Today, in nearly every Muslim land one can discern a struggle between Islam and Western ideas and institutions, both within the borders of each country and also within the souls of men. Nationalism has placed boundaries between Muslim peoples who, before, lived in a single world. A generation educated in the West or influenced by modern ideologies of different colours rules over most Muslim lands and upholds many ideas which are often in contradiction to the beliefs of the majority. In fact for the most part the vast majority of Muslims remains completely faithful to the teachings of Islam while the small but influential minority which holds power has ceased to belong completely and totally to the tradition because of the influence of the West. The pattern is not identical in every Muslim country but the general trend is similar. Faced with different kinds of economic and military pressures of the non-Muslim world, both Communist and Western, the leaders of the various Muslim countries concentrate all their energies on economic and material development, mostly along Western lines, and sometimes adopt measures that are not conformable with the Islamic view. This cleavage naturally creates a tension within society which characterises much of the Islamic world today.

Yet, even among the modernised classes many Islamic elements continue to survive, manifesting themselves at often unexpected moments. Islam continues as a living force which moulds the life of the vast majority of the Muslim peoples and still determines many of the values of the modernised classes. It is the most essential element in the life of that segment of the world which Westerners call the Middle East, and which for over a millennium has been the locus of a civilisation which had the closest contact and exchange with the West, particularly during the Middle Ages, before the West began to deviate from the common path followed by the two civilizations for many centuries.

Sayyed Hossein Nasr, "Islam," in Michael Adams, *The Middle East: A Handbook* (London: Anthony Blond, 1971), 183.

The West's Inroads

In the independent Islamic countries the demand for European education usually arose out of a realization by the rulers of their military inferiority. In order to have an army on the European model they had to have a measure of European education for their officers. From such beginnings there grew a complete system of Western education, stretching from primary schools to universities. While this was happening in the "secular" sphere, the religious leaders showed no interest whatsoever in the new education. The old educational system continued alongside the new, with its Qur'an schools in the villages and its traditional-type universities like al-Azhar in Cairo. The result of having two educational systems functioning side by side has been to create two distinct classes of intellectuals—the ulema or old-fashioned religious intellectuals, and the new Western-educated intellectuals. Both of these, moreover, are largely cut off from the common people, the ulema because of their excessive philosophizing and because of the rigidity which prevented adaptation to changing conditions, and the moderns because they had become almost completely Western in their outlook.

It is in the practical sphere first of all that the ulema have become alive to the need for reform, and they have devised various methods or stratagems for bringing the legal practice of Islamic countries more into line with the general world outlook. On the intellectual side they have been much slower. Until after the Second World War hardly any of the ulema in Egypt, for example, could read books in a European language. Thus their ideas of the modern world were derived at best from a limited number of translations or from the secular writings of Arabs who stood in the European tradition. This was all their equipment for dealing with the intellectual problems of young Muslims who had been studying science in Europe and reading the works of scientific humanists. To make matters worse the traditional suspicion of Christianity among Muslims has led these young students to prefer the humanistic and anti-religious European writers. In this predicament we find some of the ulema turning to "heretical" Arabic philosophers like Avicenna and Averroes; but it is a gesture of despair.

Where is the Muslim of today, inescapably bound to this situation, to look for intellectual renewal? What is needed is a set of ideas which is both a development of traditional theological conceptions and also relevant to contemporary problems; and this relevance really implies that intellectual renewal and social reform must go hand in hand. Where is this set of ideas to be found? Who is to produce it? The ulema are unlikely to do so, because they are insufficiently familiar with European ideas and therefore unable to communicate easily with the modern-minded politicians who have the actual power. The modern intellectuals are likewise incapable of producing a suitable set of ideas; they tend to think in European conceptions (including Marxist) and, though they are able to speak to the politicians, they are unable to link up with the traditional categories of Islamic thinking, and thus cannot carry the religious leaders and masses with them.

The situation varies, of course, in the different countries. Turkey is at one extreme, in that it has turned away from Islamic ideas and officially accepted a Western outlook. If the present attempts to revive Islamic theology in Turkey are successful, the results should be most important. Pakistan is also interesting, since it has had a longer effective contact with Europe than a Middle Eastern country like Egypt, and its reactions therefore tend to be more mature. There are also features of interest in Tunisia, Egypt, Syria and Iraq. It is from these countries that intellectual renewal is most likely to come, and not from the peripheral ones and the less advanced. The situation in Persia is similar to that elsewhere, but it is difficult for it to help the other countries much since it is officially Shiꞌite, and therefore in many ways cut off from them. . . .

W. Montgomery Watt, *Islamic Philosophy and Theology* (Edinburgh: Edinburgh University Press, 1962), 174–178.

The Travails of Modern Islam

Many reasons have been offered for the difficulties Muslims face in modernizing. . . . The great majority of the problems took form before the rise of Western Europe in the eighteenth century; the context in which Muslims acted already existed well in advance of their encounter with the modern West. . . .

It would be wrong, however, to conclude . . . that nothing Islamicate fitted Western patterns, for some did, such as a resistance to inherited rights and an acceptance of social mobility. Also, political concepts such as justice and freedom were not incompatible. Overall, however, compared with other non-Western civilizations, the Islamicate background is the least propitious for modern life; Muslims faced greater obstacles than did the Indians, Chinese, or Japanese. This can be illustrated by a comparison with non-Muslims with regard to two key matters: conquest by Europe and nationalism.

Falling under the control of Europe affected Muslims more severely than other peoples. In the first place, Islamicate civilization places an especially heavy emphasis on the control of land, so that loss of control to Europe had an alarming effect. India and China had for centuries been under foreign control before the Franks came, ruled by Turks and Manchus, respectively; both had accommodated to this fact and maintained their cultural integrity while subjugated. British conquest did relatively little damage to Hindu civilization, either in India itself or in its outposts abroad. China had an extremely powerful political tradition which had many times overwhelmed and absorbed foreign conquerors; if a Briton had ruled in Peking, even he may have eventually fit its structures and ways. As it turned out, the predicament of Confucian lands was eased by the fact that most of them escaped direct European control. Muslims lacked such versatility; conquest by Europe meant passing from Dar al-Islam to Dar al-Harb, with all the trauma that implied.

Second, Islamic autonomism provided Muslims with a unique drive to defy foreign domination. Other colonized peoples resisted the Europeans initially; then they accepted colonial rule without much protest. It was not until they learned about Western ideologies such as nationalism, liberalism, and democracy that they were aroused to action again. In contrast, the autonomist impulse made Muslims resist foreign control more consistently and it caused them more suffering. Because Islam requires its adherents to wield political power, the colonial experience especially bruised Muslims.

As for nationalism, it was incorporated by non-Western peoples other than the Muslims without great tribulation. The political units of East Asia—China, Japan, Korea, Mongolia, Vietnam, Cambodia, and Laos—fit the framework of the nation-state far more easily than do those of East Europe. In India, sub-Saharan Africa, Southeast Asia, and the Americas, indigenous political traditions were usually too weak to resist nationalism, which reigned supreme and almost unchallenged after World War II. Even in Africa, where the state boundaries have an especially arbitrary quality, they have acquired a sacrosanct character and are rarely questioned. The

Organization of African Unity (O.A.U.) established as its cardinal rule the preservation of existing borders, a decision that has given the continent a certain stability. Africans accept the status quo, regardless of its inadequacies, because they have no alternate vision to it, because no other political order rivals the national ideal left behind by the Europeans. What were once arbitrary lines on the map drawn by European diplomats lost the colonial associations and became almost universally accepted.

Daniel Pipes, *In the Path of God: Islam and Political Power* (New York: Basic Books, 1983), 186–188.

Islamisation

The term "Islamisation" is increasingly gaining in popularity, connoting for some a process of "converting" (in Malay, one might perhaps literally use the term *memuallafkan*) all un-Islamic things—including an aspect of life or a system—into a form acceptable to or within Islam. The underlying assumption of this approach is clear: that, as a result of the penetration of Islamic societies by and the imposition within them of exogenous ethnocentric values, existing aspects of life and the social systems through which it is organised are in fact un-Islamic. They must therefore be realigned and transformed in accordance with Qurʾanic doctrine and the teachings of the Prophet Muhammad s.a.w.

What Is Islamisation?

To me Islamisation means basically reviving an awareness that each human being is a creation of the higher divine power. As such every individual is accountable in all matters to his or her Creator who, as the creator of all that exists, knows what is best for the whole of creation. This awareness that we are subjects of an awesome and divine power does not reduce us to passive and helpless servants of the Creator, nor does it mean that our human mental and intellectual capacities are limited. That awareness does not make us inert or static. Rather it is a dynamic force that provides impetus to daily human life in all things.

Yet the methods of Islamisation differ from one group to another. Some insist upon Islamising the outer form of social relations and human existence but leave their inner substance untouched. What they accomplish may therefore appear Islamic, yet in content and in its core elements it still remains un-Islamic. Others, on the other hand, enthusiastically urge Islamisation of the substance, but without transforming the existing secular framework of our existence. This approach accommodates Islamic elements, but only partially, and then justifies this containment of their full meaning and impact by invoking Qurʾanic verses and *hadith*. But all that it accomplishes is accomplished within and limited by the existing and dominant secular structure of social life.

If the substance is to be changed yet the form remains unchanged, does one really have control of the process of changing the substance anyway, and can one determine what part of the substance will be changed? But if the impetus for change remains focused on questions of form, what happens to substance?

Both approaches are partial and limited, and neither can really achieve what it hopes to. In either case, those who pursue Islamic change remain dependent upon and limited by inappropriate methods that are not their own. Muslim intellectuals are still unable to escape from the entanglement of knowledge in structures of power and domination outside the *umma*. They are unable to dissociate their approach and actions from the dominant Western methodologies and paradigms. Although labelled "Islamic," their analyses are conducted not simply by using the prevailing or dominant tools of analysis but within the dominant secular perspective where those borrowed tools and methods originate.

In economics, for example, such scholars still advocate ideas, objectives and assumptions and pursue approaches that emerged from within Western economics: either neo-classical theory or the radical derivatively Marxist alternative. What makes their work different is the addition of justifications based upon reference to the *Qurʾan* and *sunna*. Providing justifications of this kind—for work of an entirely conventional nature that is simply dressed in apparently Islamic clothes—is an important ingredient or feature of so-called "Islamic" economics. There are parallel instances in other fields as well.

Their work tells a familiar story, and offers familiar remedies. The main objectives that we still find in them are the need to maximise productivity, to increase income and purchasing power and to maximise consumption. They offer no redefinition of any basic philosophy, concepts and assumptions.

Muhammad Syukri Salleh, "Islamisation of State and Society: A Critical Comment," in Othman, ed., *Shariʿa Law*, 106–107.

Political Islam in Egypt

The administrative and police treatment of political Islam—by arrests, torture, blockade, and defamation—has transformed that tendency from a wide to a narrow horizon. . . . The removal of the artificial factors standing in the way of a real intellectual, social, and political struggle in Egyptian society will give each tendency its real scope. The majority vote for the ruling party is no less artificial than the influence of the Islamist groups—rather, they are two sides of the same coin. The factors guaranteeing this majority—arresting the real political struggle, obscuring the opinions of the other parties and tendencies, especially those on the left, limiting their influence, defaming their positions, and outlawing them—also benefit the groups of political Islam. They also benefit from the chaotic economy protected by the ruling party. The fight for real democracy will create a strong public opinion able to distinguish between the tendencies and to choose from among them according to its interest. . . .

Confronting this [Islamist] tendency from a non-Islamic standpoint gives [the Islamists] a wonderful opportunity to win any battle over the correctness of its interpretation of Islam and its social slogans. . . . The ideological struggle against [the Islamists] must essentially be left to that nonexisting tendency that was originally stipulated by the conception of the Tagammuᵓ as one of its constituent parts, namely the enlightened religious tendency. The continued ideological and organizational absence of that tendency is the most serious mistake of the left, and it is high time to correct it.

Salah ᶜIsa, in Flores, ed., "Secularism, Integralism, and Political Islam," 92.

3

Islam and the Orientalists

In the late 1980s, ʿAli Akbar Rafsanjani, then president of the Islamic Republic of Iran, paid a four-day visit to the Sudanese capital, Khartoum, accompanied by an entourage two hundred strong. The much-publicized visit, which Tehran called "historic," caused tremors in neighboring Egypt, whose regime views with trepidation the prospects of having an Iranian-style fundamentalist regime in what many Egyptians consider almost an inseparable part of a unified Nile Valley. The aim of the visit was to encourage Sudan's fundamentalists in their drive to establish a Khomeini-type Islamist regime. Did such efforts have any chance of success or were they bound to fail along with those made by previous Sudanese regimes?

An adequate answer to this question involves an examination not only of the subject of church and state in Islam, but also, ultimately, of the place of Islam in the modern world. Like many fellow monotheists—only perhaps more so—Muslims are emotionally strongly attached to their religious traditions. At the same time, contemporary Muslims are keen on living in the modern world and on being part thereof. This naturally calls for building modern, largely Western-type states and societies. And there, as the phrase goes, is the rub.

The difficulty arises, in the main, from the need to reconcile two essentially opposing trends—the one pulling back to traditional ways, the other pushing toward the modern state. Islam as a religion stands in the way because, rather than being mainly a personal matter of piety and observance, it is both a system of beliefs and practices and a law for the community of the believers. To put it briefly, in Islam religion and state are inseparable. This particular point has been the subject of much study and reflection, by Western students of Islam and of Muslim societies as well as by Muslims themselves.

Another aspect of this subject is how a genuinely Islamic polity is to conduct its affairs in a largely secularized, non-Muslim community of nations. In the early 1990s, after barely surviving a ruinous eight-year armed struggle with neighboring Iraq, Tehran sent forth calls for an all-out jihad (holy war) against Israel. The calls, coming at a time of excitement and jubilation that accompanied the start of the Middle East peace negotiations in October 1991, got scant attention from the media, despite the long days of high rhetoric and fierce war cries spent in the Iranian capital by Muslims from all over, not excluding the Palestine Liberation Organization and a number of Arab countries whose governments had named delegations to attend peace talks with Israel in Madrid.

The calls from Tehran and the resolutions adopted by the delegates were calls for an all-out jihad against the Zionist entity, with at least one Iranian spokesman boasting that his government could easily mobilize five million believers for such a war and finally wipe Israel off the face of the earth.

It was not the first time the Islamic regime in Tehran had issued such threats—and not only against Israel. Nevertheless, the tone and the absurd dimensions of the claims sounded like something of an anomaly. Just finished with the war with Iraq—and seeing that, high talk of jihad against the "infidels" notwithstanding, their Islamic republic had to continue to deal with the non-Muslim world—even the most radical among Iran's fundamentalists could reasonably have been expected to have second thoughts. For the truth is that a political entity or a sovereign state based strictly on the teachings of Islam is no longer possible or practicable—if indeed such an entity had ever existed at any time in the past.

This, however, is something that few Muslim believers, let alone the fundamentalists among them, would admit or resign themselves to. The problem is not new. Even before the dismemberment of the Ottoman Empire earlier in this century, but especially after the establishment of the modern Muslim nation-states that were to succeed it, Muslims realized that they had to come to grips with the problems of building modern, Western-type state apparatus without formally breaking with their religious traditions.

From the point of view of the believing Muslim this poses a real and rather ponderous dilemma. Put briefly, the problem lies in the fact that, as stated above, in Islam state and church are inseparable, ruler and religious potentate are one. This subject has been treated in some detail by a number of Western Orientalists and not a few Muslim ʿulema. They all agree that the distinction between the "governing institution" and the "religious institution" in Islam, relevant as it may be to the later Islamic empires, has no relevance to early Islam. Such pairs of words as religious and secular, spiritual and temporal, clergy and laity, even sacred and profane, had no real equivalents in Islamic usage until much later times, when new terms were devised for new concepts; in classical Islam the dichotomy which these terms denote was unknown and therefore unexpressed.

Von Grunebaum's Appraisal

Gustave E. von Grunebaum, a renowned Orientalist and late professor of Islamic studies at the University of Chicago, deals with this and many other related points in his book *Medieval Islam: A Study in Cultural Orientation,* which many consider a classic in the field. Von Grunebaum's general appraisals of Islam, its character, and its attainments are far from flattering. "Mastery of nature, public morality, and the condition of the common man," he writes, "have been suggested as measures of backwardness or achievement of a civilization." It does not require elaborate demonstration, he adds, that by these standards the Islamic world "has but a small contribution to make." In Islam, he explains,

> there has never been a concerted effort to put natural resources to such use as would insure progressive control of the physical conditions of life. Inventions, discoveries, and improvements might be accepted but hardly ever were searched for. Despotism, foreign rule, a certain lack of organizational stamina, and otherworldliness prevented the perpetual verbal attacks on corruption from taking effect and never allowed the concept of the opposition as a constructive political force to take root. The misery of the lowly is made permanent by the contempt of the squalid masses that has animated the leading castes throughout Islam, individual charity and religious equality notwithstanding. The finest accomplishments of Muslim civilization remained confined to a relatively small circle. Social consciousness never grew sufficiently strong to raise the value of human life not protected by any claim to special consideration, such as power, wealth, or education.

"Islam does not reach to the stars," von Grunebaum explains. It is realistic, which is only a euphemism for being timid. "And this timidity comes from the realization that the combination of the many disparate elements which make up Muslim civilization might split under the impact of the unknown. . . . There is no authoritative guide to progress, and human wisdom is not to be trusted. The awareness of man's frailty and the futility of his works stunts that undaunted self-confidence which is the basis of the will to progress."[1]

From the viewpoint of what it set out to do, von Grunebaum concludes,

Islam failed to make good its universalist claim, but it succeeded in providing the believer with a civilized and dignified form of life. "Islam has not conquered the world," he adds, "Muslim civilization grew through its tolerance of alien elements, but their variety defied complete integration and the intellectual basis of its Arab roots proved too slim to carry and unify the legacies of the many pasts which Islam found itself called upon to administer." The Muslim's world is at rest, and he is at rest within it, von Grunebaum adds.

> His immediacy to God and his acceptance of the divine order were never, during the Middle Ages, seriously disturbed. Resignation and submission to the inevitable and abdication of searching reason before the inscrutable were rewarded by the consciousness of fitting perfectly and naturally into the great preordained scheme of things that embraces mankind as it embraces the genii, the angels, and the stars. The Muslim knows and accepts man's limitations. In fact, he is inclined to underrate man's capabilities. He finds happiness in attuning himself to the will of the Lord as it is revealed in the wondrous world around him. God has vouchsafed him enough of the truth to understand what needs understanding and to trust divine wisdom where understanding ends.[2]

One of the more astute critics of von Grunebaum's assessments is Bryan S. Turner, the social scientist. In a paper entitled "Gustave E. von Grunebaum and the Nemesis of Islam," he takes on the whole subject of what he calls the Orientalist version of Islam, which he says "is defined by a limited, but highly persistent, bundle of interpretative themes which have the effect of bringing into question the authenticity of Islamic religion and culture." "There is firstly," he writes, "the dominant theme of historical decay, retreat and decadence because of which the explosive rise of Islamic society was followed by an equally rapid and total decline." The consequence is that Islam is a religion "which either fails to fulfill some latent promise or which represents some retardation of the prophetic monotheism of the Abrahamic faith."

Secondly, the "failure" of Islam "is located within a broadly teleological conception of history in which the unfolding of Islam and its interruption are explained by reference to certain innate and ineradicable features of the 'Muslim mentality,' the favored characteristic being Leibnitz's 'Mahommedan Fate.'" In its sociological version, this conception of an inherent flaw in Islamic social structure concentrates on alleged gaps in the "civil society" of Islam.

Thirdly, there is the Orientalist notion that Islam, if not exactly a defective form of Pauline Christianity, is then at least a parasitic and arid religion. "The expansion and appeal of Islam can thus be partly explained by its alleged simplicity, both in theological formulation and ritual practice. While Islam is typically held to be merely dependent on the Judaeo-Christian tradition in spiritual terms, Islamic philosophy and natural theology are themselves highly dependent on decadent forms of Hellenism, namely the Neo-Platonic compilations of Plotinus."

Finally, while the Orientalist is professionally immersed in his subject, "there is characteristically an emotional gap and cultural hostility which alienates the Orientalist from Islam, producing a covert antipathy towards the Orient. The personal distance between Orientalist and Orient serves to reinforce the notion of the uniqueness of the unbridgeable gulf between Orient and Occident."[3]

Von Grunebaum, says Turner, adopted a view of Islam as lacking some of the most significant features of great civilizations, and that, like anthropologist A. L. Kroeber, he also held that "there is nothing new, nothing specific to [Islam]" and that, "ideologically, the peculiarities of Islam are restrictions."

For von Grunebaum, Turner adds, "Islam suffered from conservatism and lack of cultural integration"—and that, "arrested in its growth during the eleventh century, it has remained an unfulfilled promise. . . . It stagnated in self-inflicted sterility."

According to Turner, there are two "very general" objections to von Grunebaum's analysis.

Firstly, he examines Islam from the outside and indeed regards it as an academic duty to sit in judgment over Islam. It is not simply that he brings external criteria to Islam, but that he considers Islam in terms of elitist, normative and exacting Western criteria. The standards which signify the "failure" of Islam would in fact also signify the failure of Christianity. . . . Put simply, von Grunebaum's perspective is colored by prejudice and ultimately by an almost virulent dislike of Islam.

Secondly, there is a striking relationship between von Grunebaum's style and the repetitious, mimetic character which he ascribes to Islam. His discourse is peppered by erudite references, by quotations from a variety of philosophical and linguistic sources and by a curious mixture of social anthropology and philology. Despite his apparent commitment to social science, there is curiously little significant intellectual development in his work, little change in his account of classical Islam and little modernization of his views on Islamic literature. [He] not only repeats himself, but reproduces all the mimetic themes of Orientalism.[4]

Orientalists under Attack

Bernard Lewis, author of *The Arabs in History, The Middle East and the West, Islam in History, The Middle East: Two Thousand Years of History,* and several other weighty volumes on Islam and the Arabs, is universally acknowledged as one of the leading Orientalists working in the West today and perhaps the best in the English-speaking world. However, according to one Arab-American scholar and university lecturer, Dr. Khalil Samʿan, Lewis is a "Zionist apostle," anti-Arab, anti-Muslim, ill-willed, and with no sound knowledge of Arabic.

Samʿan is not the first Arab to savage Western Orientalists nor is Lewis the only non-Arab Islamic scholar to be subjected to such assaults. Orientalists have in fact always been an easily accessible target for Arab-Muslim critics and denigrators, even though many of the best Arab scholars and historians of this century have always made good and rather profitable use of the findings of these Western students of Islam and Arabic culture and literature.[5]

While a few of the charges and criticisms leveled at Western Orientalism in general seem appropriate enough, the bulk of them are patently unfounded, motivated as they were by political considerations and religious bigotry rather than by objective scholarly concerns. A few examples will illustrate my point.

Karam Khalla, who wrote a book, in German, on the history of the Arabs, claims in an interview in the Cyprus-based Arabic weekly *Al-Ufuq* that the Orientalists' approach to the Arabs and to Islam was "racist," since "imperialism cannot survive without a racialist ideology." Abdennabi Astif, a Syrian professor of comparative literature and the author of works on Anglo-American Orientalism, told a reporter in the U.K.-based Muslim weekly *Al- ʿAalam* that the reason why Western Orientalists depict such "a miserable picture of the Arabs, the Muslims and of Orientals in general," presenting them "as the enemy and the negation of all that the West represents," is that in order to defeat an enemy "you have first to denigrate him, then try to justify the wrongs that you do him, and finally to furnish an ideological cover for your actions by defending them on moral, cultural and political grounds." Astif conceded, however, that contemporary Oriental studies in the West differ from the old ones in that they tend to give "a human face to Arabs, Muslims and Orientals, and ultimately a more authentic picture than the distorted one drawn by their predecessors."[6]

Another attack on Orientalism is written by one of the editors of the fundamentalist-oriented *Al-'Aalam*, Abdul Rahim Hasan. While merely reiterating the usual complaints against Orientalists and their work, Hasan directed his fire mainly against Arab-Muslim scholars and historians suspected of borrowing from or following in the footsteps of these Orientalists, such as the Egyptians 'Ali 'Abdel Raziq and Taha Husain, who both wrote in the 1920s. Hasan's main victims, however, are those contemporary Arab scholars who he claims are now trying to rectify the damage done to the Orientalists, partly by praising the works of those Arab scholars like Husain and 'Abdel Raziq who drew their knowledge and inspiration from those Western sources. These transparent efforts at defending Orientalism, Hasan concludes, "represent desperate attempts to stop the continuing depletion in the ranks of the secularists and to prevent cutting them off from their roots." (The reference here, of course, is to Muslim secularists, whose roots are claimed to extend to the older generation of Arab-Muslim scholars who had studied Arab and Islamic history and culture in European universities, where the most eminent Orientalists of the century taught.)[7]

The most venomous, unbridled and totally unwarranted personal assault on any Orientalist in recent years is the one launched by Sam'an and directed specifically against Lewis. Sam'an himself, who had left his native Syria in the 1940s to study Western European languages and cultures at Georgetown University in Washington, stayed in the United States ever since, teaching Arabic and Arab civilization in a number of colleges and universities. However, now retired after nearly four decades in academe, Sam'an still has no substantial book to his name, having spent his time and energy—as he claims in a long interview in the Beirut weekly *Al-Hawadith*—in defending Arabs and Muslims against their many denigrators in the West.

According to Sam'an, all would have gone well with Western Orientalism's attitude to Islam and to Muslims, which had its origins in a miscomprehension dating back to the Crusades, "were it not for the Palestine war." Zionism, Sam'an explains, "made its entrance here and spoiled . . . our relations with the West." Colonizing Palestine was not Zionism's sole objective, Sam'an says; another aim was presenting itself "as the only ideology that is in harmony with that of the West." Ill will prevails especially among "small-fry Zionist Orientalists, who write against Arabs and Muslims in a manner that often makes one want to throw up; they say for instance that the Arabs have no poetry and no literature, and that they are primitive people with no theater, no music and no songs to their name."

Sam⁽an then proceeds to classify today's Orientalists. Some American Orientalists, he asserts, are "extremely good"; but many of the minor ones are "of the worst possible." Not all Zionist Orientalists belong to the latter group, however. "There are Zionists of the kind of General [Mattityahu] Peled who, though an Israeli, when he lectures on Arabic literature he does this with fairness, good taste, and objectivity." Other Zionists, however, "lack the first elements of objectivity." Of these latter Sam⁽an gives only one example. "Menahem Milson," he says, "who used to be military governor of the West Bank, is a professor of Arabic literature but knows nothing worth mentioning about that subject. He does read Arabic though, and his professorship grants him entry into Western universities, where he spreads his racist venom through his lectures."

Sam⁽an's own venom, however, is directed against Bernard Lewis. In answer to an obviously planted question about Lewis and his "Crusader assault on our heritage and our history," he calls Lewis "a Zionist Orientalist." "Bernard Lewis," he goes on to say, "came to the United States when Zionism failed to find an apostle to spread its word in the community of Oriental studies. They brought him from England following the death of Gustave von Grunebaum." Toward the end of his outburst, Sam⁽an breaks the news that Lewis's influence has of late been on the wane, "especially when his counsels to the State Department" ceased to be listened to or sought, as in the past. "Lewis," Sam⁽an decides, "has gone bankrupt both ideologically and politically; but he continues to be a Zionist plenipotentiary, and he is greatly valued in Zionist circles in America. . . . He is a Jew and a Zionist." Not to mention that his knowledge of Arabic is highly inadequate.[8]

Two Western Critics

Criticism of Western Orientalists and their works comes not only from Arabs and Orientals but also from Western and Western-educated scholars, some of them experts in the field in their own right. One of these is John L. Esposito of Georgetown University. In his book *The Islamic Threat: Myth or Reality?* he discusses, among many other things, the subject of Muslim responses to a triumphant West. "The image of Islam as both a potential threat to the Christian West and a retrogressive force and thus a source of Muslim backwardness and decline," Esposito writes, "dominated the worldview of European colonialism." It also "provided a ready-made rationale for 'crown and cross.'"

Esposito accuses the first colonial officials and Christian missionaries of becoming "the footsoldiers of Europe's expansion and imperial hegemony in the Muslim world." The British spoke of the "white man's burden" and the French of their "mission to civilize." As the balance of power and leadership shifted from the Muslim world to Europe, he adds, "modernity was seen as the result not simply of conditions that produced the Enlightenment and the industrial revolution, but also of Christianity's inherent superiority as a religion and culture."[9]

European colonialism posed both a political and a religious challenge, according to Esposito.

> It abruptly reversed a pattern of self-rule in the Muslim world which had existed from the time of the Prophet. By and large, the vast majority of the Muslim community had possessed a sense of history in which Islam had remained triumphant. Despite past divisions, civil wars, and revolts as well as invasion and occupation, Islam had prevailed—Muslims had ruled Muslims. To be a Muslim was to live in a state which at least nominally was a Muslim community guided by the laws and institutions of Islam. . . . However, this sense of Muslim history and belief now seemed to be unraveling, owing to internal as well as external threats to the identity and fabric of Islamic society. Muslim communities had already been struggling with internal problems. . . . The political challenge of European colonialism was intensified by the threat posed by the wave of Christian missionary activity which sought to win souls for Christ and openly questioned the viability of Islam in the modern world.[10]

Another student of Islam who finds some of the views of Orientalism and Western images of Islam objectionable is Akbar Ahmed, whose work was quoted briefly earlier in this discussion. "The blind spot of Muslims," he writes, "the incapacity to see how others see them, has historically created a false sense of self-sufficiency in Muslim society."

However, he adds, the pictures on television and in the newspapers of Muslims, death in their eyes, burning books in Bradford, were not a figment of the imagination. "Others reinforce the Bradford ones: Libyans killing a policewoman in London; Palestinians hijacking passenger planes; Iranians seizing foreign embassies; and Indonesians blowing up the Borodubar temple in Java." However, the images invoked by such incidents "stem partly from a lack of understanding of Islam among non-Muslims and partly from the failure of Muslims to explain themselves. Many of the negative images of Islam are not based on fact or reason. But as Johnson said: 'Prejudice not being founded on reason cannot be removed by argument.'"[11]

The burning of books in Bradford, writes Ahmed, brought into the open the present encounter between Islam and Western civilization. "The encounter involves not only questions of religious belief and practice but also those of power and politics. An entire civilization is involved. On the surface, both civilizations appear vigorous and confident. Take Islam: about forty-four nations (around fifty with the Soviet Central Asian Republics) and about a billion people . . . (Muslims tend to inflate their numbers). The present rash of political eruptions . . . points to the vitality in their societies."

The encounter, he adds,

is coloured by the two earlier encounters, the first lasting centuries. It began with the rise of Islam, the arrival of its armies in Sicily and France, the duration of the Crusades, and ended in the seventeenth century when the Ottomans were stopped at Vienna. . . . The brevity of the second encounter was matched by its ferocity. Lasting perhaps a century, the consequences of this encounter were devastating and in many ways are still with us. Social, cultural and intellectual life was affected and in parts damaged. . . . At the end of the second encounter, after the Second World War, when Muslim nations began to emerge as independent powers, the difference between a triumphant Western civilization surging forward and a Muslim civilization racked with loss of intellectual confidence and direction was apparent. What the European imperialists did still matters in the Muslim world; it matters most in the creation by European fiat of the present political boundaries. Arabs in the Middle East, for instance, have good cause to blame outsiders for their political problems. Indeed, even the very term "the Middle East" is Eurocentric; for Indians the region is "the Middle West" or "West Asia." [12]

Ahmed concludes with a quotation from the Aga Khan, who feels that Islam as a threat to order, as darkness, is never far from the Western mind:

With Islam encompassing such a large area of the world with significant populations, western society can no longer survive in its own interest by being ill informed or misinformed about the Islamic world. They have to get away from the concept that every time that there is a bush fire or worse than that, it is representative of the Islamic world.

So long as they make it representative of the Islamic world, they damage both themselves and their relations with the Islamic world itself because they are sending erroneous messages back. There is what I would call a "knowledge vacuum." It is hurting everyone.[13]

Readings

"Instrument of Patience"

Among European writers who traveled to the Middle East in the middle and latter part of the nineteenth century, one very frequently finds the experience of its strangeness expressed in terms of the problem of forming a picture. It was as though to make sense of it meant to stand back and make a drawing or take a photograph of it; which for many of them actually it did. "Every year that passes," an Egyptian wrote, "you see thousands of Europeans traveling all over the world, and everything they come across they make a picture of." Writers from Europe wanted to make pictures in the same way. They wanted to portray what they saw in words with the same chemically-etched accuracy, and the same optical detachment, as the daguerreotype or the photographic apparatus, that "instrument of patience" as Gerard de Nerval described it, ". . . which, destroying illusions, opposes to each figure the mirror of truth." Flaubert traveled in Egypt on a photographic mission with Maxime du Camp, the results of which were expected to be "quite special in character," it was remarked at the Institut de France, "thanks to the aid of this modern traveling companion, efficient, rapid, and always scrupulously exact. "The exact correspondence of the image to reality would provide a new, almost mechanical kind of certainty. The publication in 1858 of the first general collection of photographs of the Middle East . . . would be "an experiment in Photography . . . of surpassing value," it was announced in the *Art Journal*, "for we will *know* that we see things exactly as they are. . . ."

Since the Middle East had not yet been organised representationally, Europeans found the task of representing it almost impossible and the results disappointing. "Think of it no more!" wrote Nerval to Theophile Gautier, of the Cairo they dreamed of describing. "That Cairo lies beneath the ashes and dirt, . . . dust-laden and dumb." Nothing encountered in those Oriental streets quite matched up to the reality they had seen represented in Paris. Not even the cafes looked genuine. "I really wanted to set the scene for you here," Nerval explained, in an attempt to describe the typical Cairene street, "but it is only in Paris that one finds cafes so Oriental." His disappointment resulted from the failure to construct representations of the city that were to serve, as so often, very practical purposes. . . . Nerval finally despaired completely of finding "real Egypt," the Cairo that could be represented. "I will find at the Opera the real Cairo, . . . the Orient that escapes me." In the end only the Orient one finds in Paris, the simulation of what is itself a series of representations to begin with, can offer a satisfying spectacle. As he moved on towards the towns of Palestine, Nerval remembered Cairo as something no more solid or real than the painted scenery of a theatre set. "Just as well that the six months I spent there are over; it is already nothing, I have seen so many places collapse behind my steps, like stage sets; what do I have left from them? An image as confused as that of a dream; the best of what one finds there, I already knew by heart."

Timothy Mitchell, *Colonizing Egypt* (Cambridge: Cambridge University Press, 1991), 22–23, 29–30.

Western Orientalism Scrutinized

Orientalism is Western when it takes the West not as an event, but as an idea preordained in all eternity, complete and final from the beginning. And if it starts from this point, it has to construct its subject-matter as an explicitly, totally different item, reduced to the form it had at its birth. The two assumptions are clearly related; if the West is a fulfilled promise, the non-West has to be unfulfilled since unannounced. If the first is predetermined the second is necessarily accidental. In both cases no evolutionary process is ever conceived. Positive changes, when detected in the West, are predicated on preexistent seeds, and so are defects, flaws, wants in the non-West. One is a welcome miracle, which can change and remain the same, while the other, particularly Islam, is an unwelcome accident, not permitted to change without betraying itself.

It is clear that these assumptions are common to the Western Orientalist and the Muslim fundamentalist. The latter, ancient or modern, also refuses to take history seriously into account; he apprehends the West as a concept given once for all, and compares it in every respect with what he calls true or pure Islam.

The direct consequence of such an anachronism is that the arguments on both sides are usually opportunistic. Eclectic subjectivism is more apparent in Islamic writings about the West, but it can be detected easily in Orientalist works as well, even when they are not openly polemical. Having, I hope, made myself clear about what I mean by Western Orientalism, I go on now to state the main theme of this talk. Whoever affirms categorically that

such and such Western value-system, be it liberalism, rationalism, humanism, etc., is incompatible with Islam is talking theology and therefore, while
he may well be right in his domain—I mean theology—he is in no way
entitled to translate his idiom into sociology or political science. His assertion means no more than that the West, as he defines it, is never to be
found in the non-West. I see the same tautology behind the so-called uniqueness of Islam, and during the last two decades my main concern was to
unveil it to Muslim audiences. I continue then the same battle, in different
circumstances, using the same language, the same logic.

Abdallah Laroui, "Western Orientalism and Liberal Islam: Mutual
Distrust?" *MESA Bulletin* 31 (1997): 4–5.

The Critics Criticized

. . . [One] area of difficulty with the critique of Orientalism [is] its analysis,
or rather absence thereof, of the ideas and ideologies of the Middle East
itself. Edward Said himself has, in his other writings, been a trenchant critic
of the myths of the Middle East and of its politicians, and nowhere more
so than in his critique of the poverty of the intellectual life of the Arab
world: while the rulers have constructed numerous international airports,
he once pointed out, they have failed to construct one good library. But the
absence of such a critique in his *Orientalism* does allow for a more incau-
tious silence, since it prevents us from addressing how the issues discussed
by the Orientalists and the relations between East and West are presented
in the region itself. Here it is not a question of making any moral equiva-
lence between the myths of the dominators and of the dominated, but of
recognizing two other things: first, that when it comes to hypostasis, stereotyping, the projection of timeless and antagonistic myths, this is in no
sense a prerogative of the dominator, but also of the dominated; and, second, that if we analyse the state of the discourse on the contemporary Middle
East, then the contribution of these ideologies of the dominated has been,
and remains, enormous, not least because those outside the region who try
to overcome the myths of the Orient rather too quickly end up colluding
with, or accepting, the myths of the dominated within the region. One of
the most cogent critiques of Said, made with this in mind, was that of
Sadeq al-Azm, published a decade ago in *Khamsin*. If there is a condition
such as *gharbzadegi*, there is also one which I would call *sharqzadegi*, the
uncritical reproduction of myths about the region in the name of anti-im-
perialism, solidarity, understanding, and so on. Here, of course, the myth-
makers of the region see their chance, since they can impose their own

stereotypes by taking advantage of confusion within their own countries and without.

No-one familiar with the political rhetoric of the region will need much convincing of this tendency to hypostatisation from below: a few hours in the library with the Middle Eastern section of the *Summary of World Broadcasts* will do wonders for anyone who thinks reification and discursive interpellation are the prerogative of Western writers on the region. The uses made of the term "the West," to denote one single, rational, antagonistic force; the rantings of Islamists about *jahiliyya;* the invalidation of ideas and culture because they are, or are supposed to be, from the West; the uncritical but often arbitrary imposition of controls and customs that are supposed to be genuinely from the region, an expression of some *turath* (heritage) or other; the railings against Zionists, Persians, kafirs, traitors and so on with which Middle East political leaders happily puncture their speeches, without apparent qualm or contradiction, or awareness that they themselves are promoting prejudice, all confirm this point. Of course, the hypostatisation is most evident in the discussion of the idea of "Islam" itself, for no-one is more insistent on the unitary, determinant, timeless, and, in his version, orthodox interpretation of Islam than the fundamentalist. Equally, while brave and critical souls in the West have tried to break the usage of the term "Muslim" as a denotation of an ethnic or cultural identity, whether in its British or French colonial usages, the reifiers of the region are keen to re-establish this link. In this they are joined by communal politicians in western Europe, who purport to treat all "Muslims" as one social, cultural or even ethnic group.

Fred Halliday, "Orientalism and Its Critics," *British Journal of Middle Eastern Studies,* 1993, 160–161.

The Middle East Is Not Unique

. . . in approaching the analysis of the Middle East the element of particularism, uniqueness, or impenetrability has been greatly overrated. Let me mention four issues on the analyses of the contemporary Middle East familiar to us all: the structure of states, the prevalence of conspiracy theory in political culture, the role of the Islamic religion, and the difficulties in establishing and sustaining democracy. It is easy to construct analyses of each of these that locate themselves in the influence of Islam, in the workings of the "Arab" or "Persian" mind, or in the particular havoc wrought in the region by imperialism. But other, less particularistic, explanations are also possible, starting from the obvious enough point that many of the phenomena analysed in this way are seen elsewhere in the world: the Middle East is not unique in the incidence of dictatorships, or of states created by colonialism, or of conspiracy theories. Every nation thinks its own conspiracy theories are greater and more inventive than those of others, but a comparative survey would suggest this may not be so. While I would certainly, if pushed, give the gold medal to the Persians, one can find some fine examples in Latin America, in China, in Greece, not to mention the USA. It would, moreover, be possible to provide explanations of conspiracy theory in terms of historical and material, as well as purely cultural, features of the countries in question.

. . . If we turn to the question of the dictatorial state, and its impact not just on opposition political activity, but on economic activity independent of the state, there is no doubt that this has been an enduring feature of many Middle East states, and that, for dictators and for analysts alike, the cause has been found in those aspects of Islamic tradition that allow the state to exert such power. But this is to beg the question, since, as is equally well known, other interpretations of Islam are possible and in some countries—Turkey being an obvious example—a flourishing private sector and a degree of opposition politics exist. Any analysis of the contemporary Middle East has to confront the enduring power of dictatorship, in many cases enhanced by the flow of oil revenues to the state; there are clear, and in some cases specific, obstacles there. But it is doubtful how far a hypostatized Islam can explain this.

The Middle East is not unique, except possibly in the content of the myths that are propagated about it, from within and without. The political, economic, social, and cultural activities of the peoples of this region have their peculiarities and differences, as much between each other, as in terms of one Middle East contrasted with the outside world. Material concerns, jokes, the pleasures of good food, and the horrors of political oppression, are theirs as much as of any other peoples in the world. The development of social science in general will never be completed, and each specific issue, or country, or incident, poses questions for it. But we are no more precluded by our concepts from understanding the Middle East, and no more limited in our ideas, whatever their origins, than in addressing any other area of the world. In normative terms, we have, perhaps, allowed the discussion to be too inflected by relativism and doubt as to the validity of universal standards, in the face of a mistaken, and often self-interested, critique of imperialism and Western norms. Perhaps I could sum this up by adapting a slogan: *na gharbzadegi, na sharqzadegi,* neither westoxification nor eastoxification. Let us therefore go beyond this unnecessarily polarized and in some ways methodologically impoverished debate and continue with the job of studying these societies. . . .

Fred Halliday, "Orientalism and Its Critics," 162–163.

Strong States, Weak Societies

The classical Orientalists argued that orthodox Islam promoted political quietism. Supposedly the great medieval Islamic thinkers, horrified by the periodic rebellions and civil wars that wracked their community, decreed that obedience to any ruler—even an unworthy or despotic one—was a religious duty. "As the great divine Ghazali (d. 1111) declared: "The tyranny of a sultan for a hundred years causes less damage than one year's tyranny exerted by the subjects against each other." As a result of this blanket prohibition of all dissent, there could be no question of representative bodies being set up to carry on a dialogue between ruler and subject; neither could there be institutions of local self-government in town or countryside; nor could craft or professional associations flourish unhindered, since they would always be suspected of limiting the sway of the government over its subjects. The upshot of the suppression of such groups was a despotic regime in which the state is stronger than society.

Among Western experts, the idea that in the Middle East the weakness of society assured the dominion of the state persisted until quite recently, although there had always been a handful of unorthodox scholars who argued that the prevailing consensus underestimated the real strength of society. They insisted that groups, solidarities, and classes had been historically influential and that their collective action remained a critical force. The size of this minority grew as political scientists found studies of clientage networks increasingly unsatisfying and began to identify authentic interest groups in Islamic societies. Historians began to question the idea that the state had always been dominant. Ervand Abrahamian noted, for example, that although a late eighteenth-century Qajar Shah could execute anyone who attended his court, he probably enjoyed less real control over the countryside surrounding his capital than did a contemporary French monarch.

The popularity of these dissident ideas exploded after the Iranian revolution of 1979. Until then, most students of Iran shared the Orientalist assumption that Islam had the effect of promoting despotic authority and claimed that Twelver Shiᶜism was, if anything, an even more quietistic faith than Sunni Islam. After the revolution Western experts quickly reversed their views, and now portrayed Iran as a country where society had traditionally been strong and the state weak. The Iranian clergy and its supporters among the traditional bourgeoisie of the bazaar and the new urban middle classes formed a genuine civil society capable not only of challenging the state but of toppling it. Shiʿism, with its cult of martyrs and delegitimation of secular authority, was now an ideal revolutionary ideology that had a long history of encouraging insurrections.

This revisionism was not confined to Iranian studies. During the 1980s, three new trends were discernible in Middle Eastern studies. First, as Islamic or Islamist movements grew more potent and challenged the ruling authorities, a host of studies of "radical Islam" appeared to reveal how Islamic doctrine disposed believers to form militant groups and contest the authority of the state. Second, as oil prices declined and government revenues dried up, scholars came to appreciate that states in the region were less powerful than they had once appeared. Finally, as the intellectual foundations for the idea of "weak" Middle Eastern societies collapsed, there was a slow growth of interest in studies of mafias, mobs, interest groups, solidarities, and classes that *might* act as the equivalents of "civil society" in the region.

In 1987, the Social Science Research Council launched a major program to fund research on the now-trendy theme of "Retreating States and Expanding Societies" in the Middle East. There was already a sense that the growing weakness of states would create opportunities for civil society to assert its independence in the region. Today most scholars confidently affirm that both intermediate powers and autonomous social groups exist in the Middle East. Both Harvard and New York University have sponsored large-scale research projects on these questions. An articulate minority of scholars are even prepared to argue that civil society is sufficiently well grounded to serve as a platform for the development of democracy in the Middle East.

Yahya Sadowski, "The New Orientalism and the Democracy Debate," in *Political Islam: Essays from* Middle East Report, ed. Joel Beinin and Joe Stork (Berkeley: University of California Press, 1997), 38–39.

Orientalists Old and New

It is clear that the neo-Orientalist argument is seriously flawed. Patricia Crone, Daniel Pipes, and Ernest Gellner have retained exactly those ideas that vitiated classical Orientalism. They too portray Islam as a social entity whose "essential" core is immune to change by historical influences. Crone describes how the *ʿulamaʾ* wrote their tribal biases into the structure of

Islamic doctrine—and claims that this bias continued long after the Arabs settled down; the *ʿulamaʾ* grew sedentary, and Muslim society became largely detribalized. Like the classical Orientalists before them, the neo-Orientalists portray Islam (the religion) as a kind of family curse that lives on, crippling the lives of innocent generations after the original sin that created it. They claim that Muslim efforts to build durable states—from Ibn Khaldun's radical insights in the fourteenth century to Ottoman tax reformers in the seventeenth century or Islamist revolutionaries today—have not, and never can, bring about a change in the essential antistate and therefore antimodern core of Islamic dogma.

As a corollary to this essentialism, the neo-Orientalists also (like the classical Orientalists) downplay the importance of imperialism. A fairly consistent refrain in Orientalist analyses is that in the Middle East the impact of European imperialism was late, brief, and for the most part indirect. For Orientalists of all varieties, there is no point in dwelling on the fact that half the populations of Libya and Algeria died during the course of their colonial occupation. The fact that the Ottoman and Qajar empires were effectively deindustrialized when European imports wiped out their proto-industrial manufactures during the nineteenth-century era of "free trade" is irrelevant to issues of economic development. According any weight to these events would tend to undermine the claim that the obstacles to development are overwhelmingly internal and have not changed during the fourteen hundred years of Islamic history. Essentialism and the dismissal of Western colonialism and imperialism are commonly paired together, since each make the other more plausible.

Neo-Orientalist analyses do not prove that states in the Middle East must be weak, any more than classical Orientalism proved that states had to be strong. But does this mean that the alternative proposition—that the strong societies of the Middle East provide a groundwork for democratization—is correct? The fact is that both traditional and neo-Orientalist analyses of civil society are deeply flawed. Both claim that the key to building effective states and successful democracies lies in the proper balance of power between state and society. They disagree only over what the proper balance is, over how strong society should be. The traditionalists claim that society must not be too weak; the neo-Orientalists claim it must not be too strong. Perhaps there is a narrow range where society is neither too strong nor too weak but just right.

Yahya Sadowski, "The New Orientalism and the Democracy Debate," in Beinin and Stork, *Political Islam* . . . 42–43.

Who Decides Modernity?

Three attitudes have emerged among Middle Easterners faced with the alien civilization from the West. One is expressed in [V. S.] Naipaul's image of the supermarket: we take what we can adapt and use, without allowing ourselves to be infected by a superseded religion and an inferior civilization. This view comes in an extreme form nowadays in the writings and utterances of the so-called Islamic fundamentalists, who see Western civilization, and particularly American popular culture, as immoral and dangerously corrupting. In this strain is the Ayatollah Khomeini's denunciation, taken up by his successors in Iran, of the United States as the Great Satan. (No intelligence service is needed to interpret this epithet—just a copy of the Koran. The last verses, the best known along with the first, talk about Satan, describing him as "the insidious tempter who whispers in the hearts of men." Satan is not a conqueror, not an imperialist, not a capitalist, not an exploiter. He is a seducer. He comes with Barbie dolls and cocktails and provocative TV programs and movies and, worst of all, emancipated women.)

Others have talked hopefully of a marriage of the best elements of both civilizations. When civilizations meet and clash, however, what all too often results is not a marriage of the best but a promiscuous cohabitation of the worst.

The third attitude could be summed up in this way: The world has seen many civilizations. Each has grown and flourished in its day, then passed away. At this moment in history only one is still alive. We must join it or be uncivilized. This was the line that Kemal Ataturk and his ideological predecessors in the Young Turk Movement pursued.

The modern process of change was undoubtedly initiated by the West, but is it Western in its origins? The West was not born like Aphrodite from the seafoam, and much of it is of non-Western origin, distinct from the Greco-Roman and Judaeo-Christian roots of Western civilization.

Bernard Lewis, "The West and the Middle East," *Foreign Affairs* 76, 1 (January-February 1997): 126–127.

Orientals Orientals Orientals

. . . Where, then, does Arabic influence the Arab mind? Exclusively within the mythological world created for the Arab by Orientalism. The Arab is a sign for dumbness combined with hopeless overarticulateness, poverty combined with excess. That such a result can be attained by philological means testifies to the sad end of a formerly complex philological tradition, exemplified today only in very rare individuals. The reliance of today's Orientalist on "philology" is the last infirmity of a scholarly discipline completely transformed into social-science ideological expertise.

In everything I have been discussing, the language of Orientalism plays the dominant role. It brings opposites together as "natural," it presents human types in scholarly idioms and methodologies, it ascribes reality and reference to objects (other words) of its own making. Mythic language is discourse, that is, it cannot be anything but systematic; one does not really make discourse at will, or statements in it, without first belonging—in some cases unconsciously, but at any rate involuntarily—to the ideology and the institutions that guarantee its existence. These latter are always the institutions of an advanced society dealing with a less advanced society, a strong culture encountering a weak one. The principal feature of mythic discourse is that it conceals its own origins as well as those of what it describes. "Arabs" are presented in the imagery of static, almost ideal types, and neither as creatures with a potential in the process of being realized nor as history being made. The exaggerated value heaped upon Arabic as a language permits the Orientalist to make the language equivalent to mind, society, history, and nature. For the Orientalist the language *speaks* the Arab Oriental, not vice versa.

The system of ideological fictions I have been calling Orientalism has serious implications not only because it is intellectually discreditable. For the United States today is heavily invested in the Middle East, more heavily than anywhere else on earth: the Middle East experts who advise policymakers are imbued with Orientalism almost to a person. Most of this investment, appropriately enough, is built on foundations of sand, since the experts instruct policy on the basis of such marketable abstractions as political elites, modernization, and stability, most of which are simply the old Orientalist stereotypes dressed up in policy jargon, and most of which have been completely inadequate to describe what took place recently in Lebanon or earlier in Palestinian popular resistance to Israel. The Orientalist now tries to see the Orient as an imitation West which, according to Bernard Lewis, can only improve itself when its nationalism "is prepared to come to terms with the West." If in the meantime the Arabs, the Muslims, or the Third and Fourth Worlds go unexpected ways after all, we will not be surprised to have an Orientalist tell us that this testifies to the incorrigibility of Orientals and therefore proves that they are not to be trusted.

Edward W. Said, *Orientalism* (New York: Pantheon, 1978), 320–321.

The Matter of Arabic

"For the Orientalist (to quote Edward Said), the language *speaks* the Arab Oriental, not vice versa". . . . [Bernard Lewis], after he has "carefully" examined such concepts as *dawla, fitna,* and *bughat,* also examines and describes the meaning of *thawra* at the very end of his essay. "In the Arabic-speaking countries," he writes, "a different word was used for *thawra* [revolution]. The root *th-w-r* in classical Arabic meant to rise up (e.g. of a camel), to be stirred or excited, and hence, especially in Maghribi usage, to rebel. . . . The noun *thawra* at first means excitement, as in the phrase, cited in the Sihah, a standard medieval Arabic dictionary, *intazir hatta taskun hadhihi al- thawra,* wait till this excitement dies down—a very apt recommendation. The verb is used by al-Iji, in the form of *thawaran* or *itharat fitna,* stirring up sedition, as one of the dangers which should discourage a man from practising the duty of resistance to bad government."

Lewis's intention is to associate the concept of "revolution" with nothing more noticeable than a camel raising itself from the ground! He then gives a goodly number of possible associations such as excitement, sedition, and resistance. Lewis's surprisingly abrupt remark "wait till the excitement dies down" is not without cynicism, and his comment that this is "a very apt recommendation" is even more frustrating. Whatever the word means, Lewis's "sarcastic scholarship" cannot go unnoticed. The association of the word, on Lewis's part, with camels and with excitement (not with political, *human* struggle) hints much more broadly than is usual for him that the Arab is scarcely more than a neurotic, sexual being. Each of the words or phrases he uses to describe revolution is tinged with sexuality: *stirred, excited, rising-up.* A prolific scholar like Bernard Lewis, who distinguishes himself as an established historian of what he calls the Middle East, must be aware that his choice of words is slippery, and it has much more belittling and devastating nuances than one may imagine at first.

It must, in conclusion, be emphasized that Western understanding of Arabic has always suffered from much the same stereotyping and exoticism as that of Chinese, aggravated perhaps by historical, political, and religious factors. In a review of Jonathan Raban's *Arabia: A Journey through the Labyrinth* (1979), one encounters generalizations like the following: "The very language of Arabia, according to the author, is a labyrinth of ambiguities in which there are hardly any literal meanings, only symbolic gestures. It is a language in which the same work, with a slightly different inflection, means both 'sexual intercourse' and 'socialism.' Is it any wonder that Arabs are difficult to understand?" As we see, it has not been unnatural for Western "specialists" who are concerned with Arabic to go on to adopt the centuries-old view that the language the Arabs speak, write, understand, use, and in which they communicate, is merely "a labyrinth of [exotic and fabulous] ambiguities." This kind of description is clearly intellectually discreditable—it turns Arabic into a "mythic" language, that is to say, expressive of a "myth" created by Orientalism and the Orientalists.

Morwan M. Obeidat, "Arabic and the West," *Muslim World* 88, 2 (1998): 195–196.

4

The Anthropologist's Approach

It can well be argued that the study of Islam is too important a business to be left solely to the Orientalists, and that a share in that effort ought to be borne by the social scientists. It was von Grunebaum who was the first to attempt such a joint effort, in a book published some fifty years ago under the auspices of the American Anthropological Association—*Islam: Essays in the Nature and Growth of a Cultural Tradition.*

The editors of the series of which von Grunebaum's book is a part make a very persuasive case for a joining of efforts between humanist and social scientist in the study of cultures and civilizations; they argue that as things stand now these studies are incomplete, for while the humanist looks to the past of a civilization, the social scientist looks to its present.

This departmentalization has resulted in a loss of continuities between past and present, text and context, philosopher and peasant. What is needed, the editors add, is an overall view of the subject whereby the anthropologist receives heavy reinforcement from the humanities, while the historian and the Orientalist draw similarly on the findings of the social sciences.

Von Grunebaum managed to do this fairly admirably, and the result is salutary. Papers on "Islam and Hellenism," "Westernization in Islam and the Theory of Cultural Borrowing," and similar subjects read like a superior synthesis between the work of a good cultural anthropologist and that of an Orientalist. They also have the virtue of being readable and quite free from technical jargon.

Tracing the origin and growth in Islam of an identification between itself and Arabism—"an identification which is analyzable into political, religious and cultural constituents"—von Grunebaum shows how Islam and Arabism came to be almost identified through a variety of factors such as that Islam was founded by an Arab prophet, codified in an Arabic sacred book, developed by an Arab state, and promotes Arab supremacy.[1]

It is interesting to note here, however, that von Grunebaum nevertheless questions the validity of the theory that Islam, in combination with language, can be cited as a decisive factor in accounting for the cohesion of an "Arab culture." To do this, he maintains, would be to disregard the fact, among others, that Christian Arabs have everywhere been prominent in awakening Arab consciousness. He does not find it surprising, however, that in its fight for a new unity Arab nationalism should avail itself of the traditional feeling of religious unity permeating the majority of its actual or prospective converts. In other words, Arab nationalists are prone to using religious faith merely as a means to enroll supporters—and when aspiring young politicians and officers make a show of going to a mosque to pray, or fulfilling the Muslim precept (*faridha*) of pilgrimage, they are not to be suspected of religious fervor!

Another aspect of the Arab nationalist movement which the nationalists would like to see reconciled with Islam is the fundamental difference between the traditional Islamic concept of government and the Western brand of representative government that the nationalists favor, verbally at least.

These and other difficulties and contradictions lead von Grunebaum to draw a striking portrait of today's modernized Muslim. This individual, he writes, is a man "leading two types of life, in the family circle and outside, each with its own set of conventions. . . . He will at the same breath hate and love, admire and despise, the West. He is enthusiastic and headstrong, but at the same time torn between two ideals that have as yet not been reconciled and neither of which he is ready to abandon."[2]

"I have not yet seen," Hamilton Gibb, another Western Orientalist, once complained, "a single book written by an Arab of any branch in any Western language that has made it possible for the Western student to understand the roots of Arab culture . . . [nor] any book written in Arabic of Arabs themselves which has clearly analyzed what Arab culture means to the Arabs."[3]

This somewhat sweeping verdict is partially belied by a major contribution to the subject made by von Grunebaum in a chapter entitled "Attempts at Self-Interpretation in Contemporary Islam." In this summary-analysis he presents comprehensive summaries of the opinions of ten outstanding Arab and other Muslim thinkers, literary figures, and spokesmen of contemporary Islam on the position of their religion in a changing world. They range from al-Afghani, who started agitating for a return to pristine Islam in the 1880s, to Taha Husain, the prominent Egyptian scholar and thinker who until his death in the mid-1970s was called the doyen of Arabic letters.

The conclusion drawn by von Grunebaum in connection with these self-interpretations is that the present state of the Muslim East "stimulates such discussion of religion and civilization as falls easily in any one or more of the following categories":

a) Apologetics of one sort of another.
b) Reformist or "reactionary" theology.
c) Appeals for Westernization.
d) Political discussion and political propaganda.

"Whatever the modern Near Easterner has to say about his own background and about the West," von Grunebaum concludes, "is primarily a political judgement." On the tricky subject of Westernization in Islam, he observes that throughout the thirty to forty years ending in the mid-1950s the political advancement of the Muslim countries "outran the cultural." Here he presents a theory of cultural borrowing and culture diffusion which differs from the one held by most students of the Orient—an outlook that is full of new vistas and insights on a subject which continues to be of great relevance and topicality.[4]

Approaching the subject from a slightly different angle, Raphael Patai, an anthropology professor and Orientalist in his own right, chooses to focus on what he calls the Islamic component of the Arab personality and the role of religion among Muslim Arabs. Pointing out that the normative function of religion is manifested in the extent to which it regulates everyday behavior through positive and negative commandments, Patai asserts that in the West, at least since the onset of the Industrial Revolution, this function of religion has shrunk considerably. "Religious doctrine and ritual, even for those who follow religious precepts meticulously, cover but one area of life, separate from most of the everyday pursuits. Religion has thus become divorced from the essentially secular goals and values which constitute the bulk of modern Western culture." Moreover, "most people, especially in the large metropolitan centers, do not feel religious or, at the utmost, are quite lukewarm in their attitude to religion. Religion does not regulate our lives. Indeed, in the West religion has largely lost its normative function."

In the Arab world, in contrast, before the impact of Westernization, "Islam permeated life, all of which came under its aegis. Religion was not one aspect of life, but the hub from which all else radiated. All custom and tradition was religious, and religious do's and don'ts extended throughout all activity, thought, and feeling." Most important, "all the people in the Arab world were religious in the double sense of unquestioningly believing what tradition commanded them to believe, and obeying the ritual rules with which religion circumscribed their lives. Religion was—and for the traditional majority in all Arab countries has remained—the central normative force in life."

Beneath the thin veneer of official doctrine, however, "are old popular beliefs, held by the masses who know little of the theological tenets of their religion." In the West, little of this popular religiosity has survived, Patai asserts.

A belief in the existence of the Devil, which, incidentally, is also part of the official doctrines of both Islam and Christianity, does survive on the popular level; but in order to find a living belief in demons, spirits, the evil eye, and other supernatural forces, and an actual worship of local saints, one has to go to the Mediterranean, a region transitional between the West and the Arab world. In the Arab world itself, popular religion places even more emphasis on demons. There is belief in innumerable demons and spirits, jinn, ghouls, ʿifrits, the evil eye, and the like, as well as belief in, and ritual worship of, numerous saints who, especially at their tomb-sanctuaries, wield great supernatural power.[5]

On what he calls "the issue of sex" in the Arab world, to which he devotes a substantial chapter, Patai asserts that, "in the final analysis," this issue "comes down to the question of whether or not women should enjoy the same sexual freedom as men—or to put it differently, whether or not the double standard of sexual morality should be maintained." He again singles out "Arab culture," in which, he says, "traditional sexual mores are focal concerns." This being the case, Patai concludes, "protracted struggles" around the issue will ensue, in which "the innovators will be accused . . . of trying to introduce into the Arab world fallacious notions and vices from the Western lands of moral darkness," and the West "will be accused of an entirely new type of 'sexual' imperialism, which will devote to opponents of innovation perhaps the most vicious, because most insidious, attempt of the West to impose itself upon the Arab East."

From this excursion on the issue of sex in Islam, which concludes a chapter entitled "The Realm of Sex," Patai turns to an analysis of "the Islamic component of the Arab personality." Following a short introductory section, "Religion East and West," the author of *The Arab Mind* writes in detail about two main such components—predestination and improvidence. He again uses the doubtful device of contrasting Islam to the "modern West." In the modern West, he writes, "the spiritual vacuum" left behind by the "progressive decay of religious belief" which Toynbee bemoaned "has, at least partly, been filled by an attitude of self-reliance and a drive to know and understand the world." It is no coincidence that the great urge to explore the universe methodically arose as religion began to wane, he adds. "Whatever the shortcomings of the scientific approach, it implies a firm belief in man's ability to understand and improve things around and within him, and expresses the conviction that it is his moral duty to make every effort to do so. This, ultimately, is the intellectual, moral, and, if you will, spiritual foundation of modern Western culture."

In contrast to the West, Patai adds, the Arab world still sees the universe running its predestined course, determined by the will of Allah, who not only guides the world at large, but also predestines the fate of each and every man individually. "The very name *Islam* indicates that the one overriding duty it imposes on man is to obey God; it is derived from the verb *aslama,* which means to submit, to surrender oneself wholly, to give oneself in total commitment." Hence, *Islam* means primarily "submission [to the will of God]."[6]

"A Reduction of Judaism and Christianity"

Patai here writes as an Arabic scholar and as an expert on Islam. The anthropologist A. L. Kroeber had no pretensions to such expertise. Nevertheless, in *The Nature of Culture,* one of his standard works, he ventures upon a brief but far-reaching appraisal of Islam as a religion, a culture, and a civilization. As a civilization, he writes, Islam "manifests unusual cohesiveness and uniformity in spite of its vast spread; and it possesses not only a 'universal' idea system or church . . . but a universal language and writing in Arabic."

Yet Islam lacks some of the most significant features of other great civilizations, Kroeber asserts.

> It had no infancy and no real growth, but sprang up Minerva-like full-blown with the life of one man, something as German world dominance would have sprung with the will of Hitler if it had become realized. The formally basic law of Islamic civilization is still colored by the idiosyncrasies of the person Muhammad—his greeds, his astuteness, his amorousness, his practical wisdom and fervor, his intellectual illiteracy. The religion which is the patent spring and reason of Islamic civilization is not an enlargement of monotheistic Judaism and Christianity, but a reduction of them. There is nothing new, nothing specific to it, other than the accidents of the man Muhammad and

his home town and the meteorite that once fell there. Ideologically, the peculiarities of Islam are restrictions.

Continuing in the same vein, Kroeber writes:

> There are to be no idols, no other gods, no room for any Holy Ghost, Virgin, or future Messiah; no wine, no gambling, no usury, no industry but by hand and core caches of coins or consumable luxury goods. Now, how could a church whose only distinctive features were negations give rise to a civilization which has for a millennium and a third competed with the intrinsically so much richer ones of the West, of India, and of China—often successfully, as shown by its having gained territory from all three; and which is still maintaining itself? There is no parallel in history.[7]

Part of the explanation for this, says Kroeber, is that Islam arose at a time when constructive cultural impulses had long since moved out from the Near Eastern area. "There was apparently no longer any hope, in our seventh century, for a really creative new great civilization—creative by the standard of total human culture—to spring up in this Nearer East, among the palimpsested, tired, worn societies of Egypt, Syria, or Mesopotamia." There was, though, a chance for "a reduced, retractile civilization, an anti-Hellenic, anti-Sassanian, anti-Christian civilization, to throw off the foreign cultural yoke and to establish its own free society—without art, without much intellectual curiosity or profundity, without many of the aspirations customary in civilizations—but fervid over its new autonomy and well satisfied at being at last able to impose its culture on others once more—no matter at what level—instead of having their culture and influence imposed upon it."[8]

Muhammad was of the Arab nation—that people which had then for three or four thousand years lived in a back alley around the corner from civilization. "They were in touch with higher cultures, but not partaking of them; until at last they had come to prefer to avoid the responsibilities of being civilized. With that they had remained ignorant, renegade, illiterate, poverty-stricken in possessions as in ideas; but proud and covetous and untamed and tumultuous. They were a proletariat—not, indeed, dulled with oppressive toil in metropolises, but of the waste places, and passionate of an empty freedom and spiritual beggary."

Muhammad appeared and gave them a society and civilization of novel cast. "The civilization was new precisely in . . . its appeal to the common denominators and therefore to the commonnesses of men; its discarding of much of the heritage of the past; its simplification of ideas; its leveling and denunciations; its long list of prohibitions. The new society asked little else of its members than adherence; but for that it offered unity, success, power, and wealth. . . ." Kroeber concludes:

> The argument, in fine, is that Islamic society was effective and successful because it reduced and simplified culture, and that this contraction was necessary for any civilization which was to succeed, without the long-worked and worn "heart area" of higher civilization, at a time when the crucial front, the firing line, of innovating and progressing civilization had long since moved out beyond the Near East. This inference in turn validates the concept of a historically interconnected totality of culture throughout the main mass of the Eastern Hemisphere—the old range of the Oikoumene: not only as a fancy in which we may indulge if inclination so leads us, but as a tool which should be included in intellectual operations if our aim is the completest possible understanding of the highly complex history of civilization.[9]

Kroeber, an eminent anthropologist of the older school, here leans heavily on the conclusions and generalizations Arnold Toynbee makes in his *Study of History*. Isma'il al-Faruqi, an acknowledged authority on Islam and a Muslim himself, approaches the subject from an entirely different vantage point. In a paper entitled "Islam as Culture and Civilization," he analyzes a wide range of the aspects of his subject—Islam and Arabism, and Islam's view of the ultimate reality, of truth, of man, of nature, and of beauty. In the section on Islam's view of society and history, he writes that in Islam, "society is neither an evil nor a happenstance, nor an inevitable growth of nature in satisfaction of basic material needs." These, he adds, "are respectively the views of Christianity, Indian religions and utilitarianism."

The Islamic view of society differs from those of the first two, "which deprecate the social aspect of life by assigning all ethical value to the subjective-personal aspect exclusively." It also differs from the third, "where society is said to have evolved out of the need for exchange of economic goods, for collective services such as defence, transportation, etc." Islam, he explains, "affirms society as the realm for actualization of the highest ethical values; and it regards societal action as such, as embodiment of a higher order of moral existence." The Islamic view is also different from those theories "which regard the social order as the creation of heroes, kings and princes, an outgrowth of their courts and entourage, or as an accidental outgrowth of the family, clan, tribe or village, which came to exist naturally and without preplanning; but once it developed, it provided such advantages as made it worthy and/or necessary in the eyes of its beneficiaries."[10]

Islam views society as a divinely ordained institution, a pattern of God, as necessary for man's fulfillment of the purpose of his creation as nature, al-Faruqi writes.

> Society is necessary for knowledge. Without consultation, criticism and validation by other humans, all claims to the truth are suspect. All knowledge must be tested against evidence, and would be more trustworthy the larger and more varied the evidence, the other views, against which it is rubbed. The principle of *shura* (consultation, dialogue and argument) is declared by the Qur'an the method of felicity and is buttressed by the prescription of collective pursuit of knowledge. Jurisprudence added the principle of consensus (*ijma*) as a practical check upon the creative flight of the individual, as well as a confirmation of the creative breakthrough achieved by the individual. Every person is entitled to reinterpret, re-understand, re-crystallize the truth; but it is his duty to convince his peers of the validity of his findings. The right to creativity (*ijtihad* in its general sense) belongs to all; the duty to follow it up with *shura* until consensus is reached makes exercise of that right responsible and beneficial.

Society is necessary for morality, al-Faruqi adds. "Ethical values require the existence of others, interaction with them, and conditions under which there are needs to which the moral subject responds if ethical action is to take place. It is impossible for love, charity, justice and sacrifice, for example, to be realized unless there are other humans to be loved, to be charitable and just to, to assist and rescue through sacrifice. . . ."

Society is also necessary for history. "Judaism and Christianity grew and developed in history in situations of weakness and persecution, over protracted durations of centuries," al-Faruqi adds. "This weakness in their formative period so impressed itself upon the minds of Jews and Christians that it determined the very nature of their faiths. It is primarily responsible for making Judaism and Christianity essentially religions of messianism and redemption; i.e., religions offering a hope for better things—whether eschatological or realized in internalist subjectivity, or both at once—in face of the desperate hopelessness of the real present." Al-Faruqi explains:

The state of exile, of homes and country shattered, of men and women a-whoring after other gods and tyrannizing over one another, of a decaying Roman imperium bent on the pursuit of power, and a corrupt society caring for little more than *panem et circences*—all these facts repulsed the conscience and turned men away from the world. It was a violent reaction to an extreme situation. World-denial, mistrust of the human self, condemnation of nature within as flesh, of nature without as sin and mammon, of the process of history as doomed never to realize the absolute, were the result of this pessimism. The "Kingdom of God" was understood as an alternative to this kingdom, the former as absolutely good and the latter as absolutely evil. Man looked forward to it as bringing cessation to the misery of the present. The Day of Judgement was interpreted as the cataclysmic passage from one to the other. Life and history under this scheme could have little value besides that of bridge, or transient passage, to the other side.

Islam Is Different

Not so Islam, which conceives of God's purpose of creation as the realization of His will, the highest part of which is the moral, al-Faruqi adds. "It conceives of the morally imperative as fulfillment of all the potentialities of creation—the natural and the ethical—by human free choice, decision and action. The morally imperative is indeed possible of realization; otherwise human existence would be the tragic game of a trickster-god, not the purposive creation of the benevolent, beneficent God Islam recognizes. Therefore, history and its processes are the theatre for the morally imperative. Involvement in them is the meaning of normativeness; actualization in history of the ought-to-be of value is the objective of human existence on earth."[11]

That is why Islam does not countenance any separation of religion and state, al-Farugi continues.

> The state is society's political arm which, like society itself, is meant to bring about the realization of the absolute in history. Between the state proper, society with its other organs and institutions, and man as person, there is only a division of labour, a distinction as to function. All are subject to the same purpose and goal. The transitiveness of man's actions demands a public law to regulate it. It cannot be satisfied with the verdict of conscience. That is why Islam had to

develop the *shariʿa*, a public law governing the personal as well as the societal fields of action. That is why Islam must be relevant to the economic, social, political and international realms, as surely as it is relevant to the subjective realm where conscience alone rules supreme. . . . To live as a member of the society Islam seeks to create is to do so in an open brotherhood where every member is equal—except in righteous achievement. In this field, Islam invites all humans to compete and prove their moral worth.

The arena is open to all mankind. "Within it, all of them are equal until they have distinguished themselves from one another in deeds. Their lives are subject to no arbitrary authority, the ultimate and supreme criterion being the law of God." The nature of political authority is executive, al-Faruqi concludes. The caliph or chief of state, his ministers and all their employees are workers hired to implement the divine law. "Both the executives (as subjects) and the citizens (as objects of law-implementation) shared under the authority of the jurists in interpretation of the law. It is the jurists who spend their lives in its study, analysis and elaboration that know it best. . . ."[12]

Another aspect of Islam which is generally only occasionally taken into consideration are its universalistic and abstract principles and how these have been realized in various social and historical contexts "without representing Islam as a seamless essence on the one hand or as a plastic congeries of beliefs and practices on the other," in the words of Dale F. Eickelman in his essay "Changing Interpretations of Islamic Movements." To this end—which Eickelman considers a challenge for the student of Islam—"the earlier conceptual dichotomy of 'great' and 'little' traditions can retrospectively be viewed as a significant first step." As initially employed in the late 1940s, he adds, "this conceptualization contained an historical component and was used to explore the possible relationships between religious traditions, as known through the texts and exegeses of a cultural elite on the one hand, and the religious expressions and interpretations prevalent in . . . 'folk' contexts, on the other." Unlike the earlier doctrine of "survivals," which Eickelman says presumed that folk traditions were vestiges of earlier civilizations and less permeable to change than "high culture," the notion of great/little tradition made no gratuitous assumptions concerning the historical precedence of some civilizational elements over others. Yet as ordinarily reported, great and little traditions were more often juxtaposed than used as the basis for analysing their complex interrelationships. Literate traditions were taken to be closer to orthodoxy, and 'local' ones were variously assumed to be misinterpretations of the 'vulgar' or even 'pre-Islamic' vestiges, rather than indications of the key points at which the Islamic tradition is continuously undergoing an internal dialectic of adaptation and self-renewal."[13]

Of equal importance were anthropological efforts in the 1950s to represent the full complexity of religious tradition in specific localities, Eickelman adds.

> An antithetical but productive reaction to the essentialist tradition, inspired by the heyday of structuralist studies in the 1960s, was the suggestion that the term *Islam* be replaced by *islams*. This approach emphasizes the multiplicity of Islamic expression and asserts that in all historical and social contexts the islams of elite and non-elite, literate and illiterate, theologians and artisans, tribesmen and peasants, are equally valid expressions of a fundamental, unconscious (in the structuralist sense) set of principles. The islams approach can thus be seen as a reaction against both the orientalist search for an ahistorical Islamic "essence" and the somewhat parallel venture of Muslim fundamentalists who declare their own beliefs and practices to be "Islamic" in opposition to the jahili [pagan] practices of other Muslims.
> . . .
> Ironically, by considering all expressions of Islam as transformations based upon a single set of principles, the conceptual end-product of the islams approach likewise reduces Islamic tradition to an essentialist, ahistorical core. The islams approach also disregards the fact that most Muslims quite consciously hold that their religion possesses central, normative tenets and that these tenets are critical to an understanding of Islamic belief and practice. Further, ideas and practices take on radically different meanings depending upon who introduces, advocates and supports them. Some understandings of Islam are more highly valued than others because of their identification with certain carriers and groups. The islams approach neglects this important social dimension of the transmission and reproduction of ideas and organizations. The islams approach, like that of cultural "orientations," falls short of accounting for the historical conditions which favor the emergence of particular institutional arrangements or cultural notions over alternative, coexisting ones.[14]

On the nature of Islamic government and the ways in which it differs from Western systems of governing, Akbar Ahmed draws an interesting analogy. He finds it "very striking" that, where Western polities speak of the city, crown, state, or people, classical Islam named God as the ultimate repository of authority. "The community was God's community, *ummat Allah*," he writes, "its property was God's property, *mal Allah*; its officials, army, even booty, were similarly ascribed. Its enemies, naturally, were God's enemies, *ʿaduww Allah*."

The subject of the caliphate received a good deal of attention from Muslim scholars and thinkers. In Islam, as elsewhere, men sought to define the nature of political authority and to regulate its exercise. "In the West," Ahmed explains, "these tasks have been variously discharged by theologians, philosophers, politicians, constitutional lawyers, and social scientists. In the Islamic world, a somewhat different classification is required. By far the most important body of Muslim writers on the State is that of the Sunni jurists whose approach . . . is theological and legal at one and the same time." The starting point in their work is God's concern for man and intervention in human affairs.

> Though man is a political animal, he is by nature warlike and destructive, and is incapable by himself of attaining to a knowledge of the good or achieving an orderly social existence. These deficiencies are remedied by revelation and divine law. To uphold and apply the law, a supreme ruler is required, whose office is thus part of the divine plan for mankind. This is the Caliph, or, to use the term favoured in juristic and theological writings, the Imam. The appointment of such a ruler, and obedience to him once appointed, are an obligation of the Muslim community—a religious obligation, failure in which is a sin as well as a crime. As there is only one God and only one divine law, so there must be only one supreme ruler on earth, to represent God and enforce the law.[15]

Readings

The Nature of Muslim Civilization

. . . Is it legitimate to speak about "Muslim civilization"? To what degree can this notion be justified and defined? The faithful of the Islamic religion have from early times constituted a goodly sized body of human beings, which has not stopped growing even in our day, occupying a more and more extensive, almost continuous, territory, roughly oriented in a direction parallel to the equator but noticeably overflowing any fixed geographical zone. Does this population belong, from the very fact of the religious distinctiveness of its members, to some specific "civilization," crossing the barriers of place and time? This is far from a matter of course. In any general classification of historical civilizations—there is no completely satisfactory one today—it seems likely that the large-scale criteria cannot uniformly be of the same nature. The fundamental cultural characteristic can very well have been at one time a material technique, at another a belief. The religious criterion is admissible, at this high taxonomic level and for large populations, if it stands out as a predominant characteristic which differentiates the multitude of believers from the rest of humanity in an extensive area and in all sorts of cultural fields; and that is true only if the religion in the case can be regarded as a determining factor, not only for feelings and for thoughts, but also for the many public and private branches of human activity. Is this true for Islam?

It is, naturally, not the tentacle-like normative attempts of classical Islam, that of the severe theoreticians, that should suggest our answer to us but an objective consideration of reality, which everyone knows is often far from a close fit to what the doctors teach. In examining this reality, it is also proper to avoid confusing the truly "Islamic" character of the civilization studied with the depth or sincerity of religious feelings or with a sufficient respect for ritual directives. In spite of the fact that the one is frequently bound up with the other, there is not any necessary concomitance; and if we want to treat cultural history, properly speaking, and not religious history in the narrow sense, when we speak of Muslim civilization, we ought to base our studies essentially not on the quality of belief or the degree of religious observations, as some have a tendency to do, but on the effects this belief exerts in many cultural sectors, from humble material usages all the way to the most complex or most exalted psychocultural manifestations.

At first glance, this condition seems to be satisfied at certain times, in certain countries; for example, in the Middle Ages, in the Arab or Arabized countries. It is true that even in so favorable an instance, which it is tempting a priori to consider as optimum, some closer observations, which may seem to be reservations, must be stated: some non-Muslims, in compact nuclei, participated then in more than one aspect of this "Muslim civilization" and contributed to it; on the other side of the relationship, the Islamized Arab Bedouins were undergoing Islam's imprint on their mode of existence in only the most limited way. Among the urban population as among the rural, the new religion seems to have had no noticeable effect on the

general level of techniques (for their diffusion in detail the case was otherwise), so that the material substructure, which in other cases often has a
predominant taxonomic validity, does not bear out our principle of discrimination at all. And yet the Muslim religion's impact is so manifestly
powerful, in the case we have just mentioned, on so many elements of human culture—language, arts, literature, ethics, politics, social structure and
activities, law—that it would be impossible, taking the situation as a whole,
to refuse to recognize an autonomous civilization there which was marked
not just by the Islamic *element* but by the Islamic *factor.*

There is good ground for distrusting simplistic theses here. The linguistic
argument, for example, which, it is true, is based on an important and
easily observed phenomenon, runs a good chance of turning out, upon examination, not to be the major criterion. An illustrious Arabist, whom I
deeply respect, writes: "It would only be exaggerating the expression of a
correct observation, were one to say that a Muslim people has Muslim
institutions just to the extent that the idiom it speaks is close to the language of the Koran." Is this so certain? To mention only a single objection
that seems to me to invalidate the proposition, did not the Persians and
Turks embody "Muslim civilization" in the course of their history better
than did the Arabic-speaking nomads of the desert? Would not giving pre-
eminence to the spoken language—which is also to be distinguished carefully from the cultured language, the vocabulary of which is separately
diffused—be only a snare and a delusion? . . .

Is it more legitimate to envisage, as a working and hence provisional
hypothesis, that the degree of a group's "Muslim civilization" varies above
all with the degree of application of Muslim law in all the various domains
of life, as that law was fixed by the doctors? To take a more precise formula: with the degree of application of the *fiqh* [jurisprudence]? Perhaps
there would be room for initial criticism, from a sociological standpoint, in
the reference to an ideal, sometimes artificial construct rather than to concrete, impartially analyzed facts. The *fiqh*, from another standpoint, however totalitarian it may seem, is far from covering the whole field of human
activities, at least in a decisive and methodical way. It admits its own limits
and shares generously with secular regimentation, with local customs, or
with discretionary judgment, being limited, in many legal matters, to loose
directives (portions on public law and penal law) or to elementary ethical
precepts (portions on business law). In all these fields of life, too, many
usages exist which, while traditionally linked with Islam for centuries in
the minds of many Muslims, would find only a doubtful or uneasy support

in the *fiqh:* in matters of art, clothing, and eating habits, notably, and including some ritual practices endorsed by the most scrupulous orthodoxy. Lastly, the *fiqh,* which in one sense is so characteristic of classical Islam, has notwithstanding this no monopoly on transmitting the imperatives of Muslim spirituality into the real world: this spirituality antedates the *fiqh* by at least a century; and during the course of the Middle Ages, before a sort of lasting compromise was worked out, the mystic movement, for example, tended to orient its adepts' behavior into paths very different from the ways of the *fiqh.*

Robert Brunschvig, "Perspectives," in *Unity and Variety in Muslim Civilization,* ed. Gustave E. von Grunebaum (Chicago: University of Chicago Press, 1955), 48–49, 52–53.

Unity in Diversity

The civilization which the conquering Arabs brought out of the Peninsula was . . . the result of a first integration of local cultural elements with elements derived from the Jewish, the Christian, and, through their mediation, the Hellenistic traditions, with the message of Islam serving at the same time as an additional constituent and as the crystallizing catalyst. This first Islamic integration imposed itself on a sizable proportion of the subject populations while it was undergoing a keen struggle with the autochthonous cultures. As a result of this *Auseinandersetzung* the philosophical and scientific potential of Islam was actualized and restated in terms acceptable to the representatives of the older traditions with which the new religious civilization had to deal. Persian administrative and political thinking, Hellenistic techniques of philosophizing and of secular science, Indian mathematics and medicine were mastered effortlessly. The linguistic Arabization of the borrowings contributed to their assimilation—the foreign viewpoint when expounded in an Islamized setting and in an Islamized terminology would be experienced as genuinely Islamic; on the other hand, the progressive expliciting of the primitive data of the faith and of their cultural implications would enlarge the basis of intercivilization receptivity. The flowering of the Abbasid Empire between A.D. 760 and 840 thus came to represent a second integration of Islamic civilization, in which room had been made for "local" traditions which were in part admitted in a bookish fashion but which mostly forced themselves into the new synthesis through the realities of an actual symbiosis.

This second integration was that classical Islamic civilization which com-

peted with Byzantine civilization, which had to withstand the rise of Iranian nationalism in the ninth and tenth centuries, and which, most important of all, found itself exposed to the criticism of a competing attempt at
integrating Islamic and local elements undertaken by the radical Shi'a and
at times propagated by the political power of the Fatimids. With the help
of the Seljuq Turks and the unwitting assistance of the Christian Crusaders, the threat of the Batinite integration was eliminated, and the emergent
Sunnite orthodoxy consolidated Islam in a third ecumenical integration
which was, by and large, completed by the middle of the twelfth century,
and has so far remained the universally accepted self-definition of the Islamic world.

In this third integration, which is only now slowly yielding under region-
ally disparate reactions to the West, the piety of the popular strata was
more securely anchored than it had been before the equipollence of local
traditions was assured by an elastic application of the *consensus doctorum*
as the verifying authority; a keener sense was shown of what elements of
Hellenism are compatible with the Muslim aspiration, and an inclusive
feeling about membership in the community which, notwithstanding the
awareness of local variations, came to be experienced as increasingly unified in doctrine and lore, made possible the rise of a body spiritual whose
hold over the faithful was well-nigh independent of the political realities of
the day.

The stability which, in the consciousness of the believers, Islam as constituted in this third integration had reached in providing a balance between
the claims of the universal and of the local tradition neutralized the disrup-
tive effects of the supplanting of the multinational empire of the early
Abbasid caliphs by an increasing number of rival local, and in certain cases
clearly national, states. It also counteracted the disintegration potential of
the local renaissances to which in the later Middle Ages Islam owed most
of its significant cultural acquisitions. A limited cultural pluralism within,
and under the protection of, the ideal unity of Islam—such was the solution provided by the third integration to the inescapable conflict of cultural traditions. Theology and the law, on the one hand, and the forms of
conceptualization, argument, and presentation, on the other, provided the
most potent means of communicating a sense of cohesion to the overex-
tended and disorganized domain. . . .

The universal culture of Islam disposes of several means to further the
adjustment to the local cultures. Of those, the most characteristically Islamic is the *ijma'*. The *consensus omnium*, narrowed down to a *consensus*

prudentium, is authorized to rule on the legitimacy of any individual belief or practice which the community may have adopted. Its verifying verdict includes its object among the normative elements of the Muslim tradition. There is no appeal against the *ijma*ᶜ except to a later *ijma*ᶜ. It has often been shown how significant elements of local and popular piety were allowed to enter the orthodox norm. A typical progress leads from appraisal of a phenomenon as *bidᶜa* [innovation] *sayyi*ʾ*a* (bad) to that as *bidᶜa hasana* (good) and thence to fissureless integration in the teachings of the doctors of the faith. The existence of a merely local *ijma*ᶜ is recognized. But while the *ijma*ᶜ of the *Haramain* (Mecca and Medina) may count for more than that of an outlying area, and while attempts may be made to bring the local *ijma*ᶜ in line with that of more holy or more advanced places, yet even the local *ijma*ᶜ will serve to ward off from the native Muslims the suspicion of heresy; it will serve also to prevent the cleavage between universal norm and traditional practice from rendering an "Islamic" life impossible.

Gustave E. von Grunebaum, "The Problem: Unity in Diversity," in von Grunebaum, ed., *Unity and Variety in Muslim Civilization*, 23–24, 31.

Government and Constitution

Neither the *shariᶜa* nor the juristic doctrine of Muslim scholars provides a specific pattern for the constitution of an Islamic state. Since there is no consensus on the essential features of such a state, the matter has remained open to initiative and *ijtihad*. In recent decades statesmen and scholars have produced a body of opinion from which a certain pattern seems to be emerging. But whether the emerging model of Islamic political organisation that they offer will prove persuasive throughout the *umma* remains to be seen.

The lack of any definitive paradigm of political organisation is also attributable to the absence in formative Islam of any clear source or precedent for the idea of a written constitution as the supreme law of the state. The Charter of Medina, also known as the Constitution of Medina, that was enacted after the Prophet's *hijra* to Medina may be considered as providing Muslims of later times with validating authority for the introduction of written constitutions. The question of the harmony or otherwise of any such document with the principles of Islam is of course another matter.

But despite the enactment by the Prophet of the Charter of Medina, in their own time his successors among the companions did not promulgate a written constitution, perhaps because they saw no need for one. This pattern prevailed and Muslim rulers did not introduce written constitutions or a bill of rights. Apart from the ordinances of the *ulu al-amr,* which addressed issues of constitutional law, constitutional matters were often regulated by reference to custom. Customary rules are naturally slow to materialise and, as one would expect, a certain degree of resistance to anomalous practices is often detectable. The founder of the Umayyad dynasty, Muawiyah was, for example, the first to appoint an heir apparent (*wali al-ahd*) and thereby validate hereditary succession. Notwithstanding the initial protest and the resistance with which it was met, a precedent was nevertheless set which was to become, by the end of the Umayyad period, a generally accepted custom. Custom thus operated as a substitute for a written constitution.

To a question whether constitution-making is acceptable in Islam, Rashid Rida issued a *fatwa* answering the question in the affirmative. Since the cardinal duty of government in Islam is to implement the laws of *shariʿa,* he maintained, the idea of a limited government whose powers are defined by the constitution, and of a consultative government which is committed to the ideals of justice and equality, is acceptable to Islam. If, however, the constitution contains rules which may be repugnant to the teachings of Islam, he continued, then it may be said to be misguided only with regard to its controversial elements. To substantiate this position, Rida observed that in the history of Islamic jurisprudence numerous instances are to be found where jurists have made errors in their *ijtihad* and in the books they have authored. But in such cases, we should only reject the views that are erroneous, not their endeavour in its entirety. What is not defective remains acceptable, so long as the error is corrected at an early opportunity to protect the community from deviation.

Islam advocates only a limited government whose power is restricted in a variety of ways. With reference to sovereignty, we note that the Islamic state is not a sovereign state in the strict sense of the word; its powers regarding legislation are limited by the terms of the *shariʿa.* Politically, this rules out all forms of absolutism; legally, it paves the way for development of constitutional norms and standards by which to limit state powers. The Islamic state is a consultative state. It is bound, as already noted, by the requirement of consultation and must have due regard for the wishes of the community. The powers of the head of state are also limited by reference to *khilafah,* which means that he acts in the capacity of a trustee: of both Allah s.w.t. and of the community of which he is an employee and representative. The community is entitled to depose the head of state in the event of a serious breach of trust, flagrant deviation from *shariʿa,* or loss of capacity to discharge his duties. Furthermore, the individual in an Islamic state enjoys considerable autonomy, since many aspects of his life in the community remain outside the domain of law and government.

The jurists have thus drawn a distinction between religious and juridical obligations. Only the latter are enforceable through formal objective sanctions, but most of the religious aspects of the individual's life in society are private and non-justiciable. Even some of the religious duties such as prayer (*salah*), fasting (*sawm*), the pilgrimage (*haj*) and much of what is classified as recommendable (*mandub*) and reprehensible (*makruh*) are not legally enforceable.

Government, moreover, has no authority to waive or to grant discretionary changes in the private rights of the individual, which are generally known as *haqq al-ʿabd*. The head of state and judges do, on the other hand, enjoy limited powers to grant a pardon or require repentance in certain cases, as well as to order discretionary punishments for violations of public rights (*haqq Allah*).

Government officials, we may further note, including the head of state, are subject to the rule of law in precisely the same way as are other members of the community. They are accountable for their conduct and enjoy no special immunity or privilege before any court of justice. The *shariʿa* provides for no special tribunals or jurisdictions for government officials, nor indeed for any group or class of individuals.

Finally in this regard, the *shariʿa* limits the authority of government regarding taxation in at least five ways: (1) tax must be just and proportionate to the ability of the taxpayer; (2) it must apply to all without discrimination or favour; (3) taxation must aim at the minimum of what is deemed necessary; (4) the well-being of the taxpayer must be observed in determining the quantity and method of collection; and (5) taxation must observe the time limit of one calendar year for the yield upon which tax may be levied to materialise. Abu Yusuf and al-Mawardi both emphasised fiscal moderation by insisting that taxation must in no case deprive the taxpayer of the necessities of life.

Mohammad Hashim Kamali, "The Islamic State and Its Constitution," in *Shariʿa Law and the Modern Nation-State,* ed. Norani Othman (Kuala Lumpur: Sisters in Islam Forum (Malaysia) Berhad, 1994), 52–53, 57–58.

The Social Order

Islam is concerned with salvation or damnation of the individual believer. The believers are equal before God, except for such distinction as is established by their greater or lesser piety. It is explained that "through piety are souls brought to perfection and persons may compete for excellence in it; and let him who desires honor seek it in piety." But the Muslim's personal equality with his fellows in the faith which is guaranteed, so to speak, by his right to a direct relationship with his Lord does in no way preclude elaborate social stratification within the community of Islam.

The Muslim shares, to a very high degree, in the sensitivity about rank which is so characteristic of the Middle Ages. Not only is he rank-conscious but he is keenly concerned with expressing social distinctions through a delicate system of etiquette. Questions of precedence are of considerable importance. Politeness is carefully graded to manifest the relative position of the interlocutors. Conversation as well as correspondence begins with public recognition of the social relationship of the participants. Rank is stressed, not glossed over for the sake of tact or politeness. But this emphasis on social inequality, however offensive it may appear to the modern Occidental, does not touch the core of the personalities involved. The ceremonial registers the accident of their relative position at any given moment. It implies recognition of a social fact that may be short-lived, but it does in no way suggest inequality of substance. Nevertheless, Islam itself has given rise to a new set of criteria to grade and stratify society.

Abu Bakr had divided the spoils of war evenly among the Muslims, no matter whether the recipient was "young or old, slave or free, male or female." 'Umar, although preserving the fundamental assumption of Islam leveling all distinctions of birth, insisted that the Muslims were not equal in the matter of faith. As it would hardly have been practicable to rank the faithful for the depth of their devotion, the caliph adopted two principles of a very different character to determine the share of the individual in the distribution of the booty. Kinship with the Prophet and the date of conversion decided the standing of the believer, inasmuch as this standing expressed itself in the yearly emoluments paid out to him from the public treasury.

Alongside of the idea of a religious aristocracy, other concepts of the structure of society compelled acceptance. The Barmakid vizier al-Fadl b. Yahya (disgraced in 803) is reported to have divided mankind into four classes.

"(1) The ruler, whom merit has placed in the foremost rank; (2) the vizier, distinguished by wisdom and discrimination; (3) the high-placed ones, whom wealth has placed aloft; (4) the middle class, who were attached to the other three classes by their culture (ta'addub). The rest of mankind is mere scum who know but food and sleep."

And long before al-Fadl, al-Ahnaf b. Qais (d. after 687) is supposed to have expressed a similar opinion. The value of culture for social advancement is stressed and the advice is voiced to study history, literature, and astronomy, as the kings are interested in these kinds of information. A litterateur tells how he maintained himself in favor with successive monarchs by achieving proficiency in their respective fields of interest: as-Saffah's (750–54) predilection for sermons was followed by al-Mansur's (754–75) for history; al-Hadi (785–86) preferred poetry—but when Harun was taken with asceticism, our courtier forgot all the information he had amassed in previous reigns.

Gustave E. von Grunebaum, *Medieval Islam* (Chicago: University of Chicago Press, 1961), 170–171.

Law and the State

Islam is the community of Allah. He is the living truth to which it owes its life. He is the center and the goal of its spiritual experience. But he is also the mundane head of his community, which he not only rules but governs. He is the reason for the state's existence, he is the principle of unity, the *Staatsgedanke,* which both upholds and justifies the continuance of the commonwealth. This makes the Muslim army the "Army of Allah," the Muslim treasury, "the Treasury of Allah." What is more, it places the life of the community in its entirety as well as the private lives of the individual members under his direct legislative and supervisory power.

The burden of lawmaking rests on Allah's shoulders. His ordinances may vary in scope but not in stringency. Every order issuing from him carries the same compulsion. It is not for man to grade his rulings as more or less important. Nor is there any differential to separate the sphere of his direct interference from a neutral or purely human zone. The only indifferent areas are those where lack of information bars man from the knowledge of Allah's detailed regulations, and by various methods the community labors to supply the missing instructions.

By its very nature Allah's word must be considered final. He is known to have changed his mind a certain number of times, abrogating specific injunctions given his Prophet and replacing them by "equally good or better ones." The death of the Prophet ended this means of organic, or opportunistic, change.

Conflicts between the inspired precedent of the Prophet's *sunna* and the inspired stipulation of the Koran were but apparent and could be resolved through well-directed ingenuity. It fell thus to the lot of the legist to arrange the relatively restricted number of explicit regulations and the much more numerous records of the usage in the earliest times of the faith in such a fashion as would clearly describe the precedent of the golden prime of the Muslim community.

The ten years of the Prophet's rule in Medina and perhaps the thirty years following his death constituted the age in which human society had come as near perfection as could be hoped for. So the institutional, legal, financial, and, of course, religious precedent of that period was to yield the terms, concepts, and prescriptions of that perfect order which was Allah's.

The political situation of the subsequent times discouraged the majority of the legists from active participation in the government. But even the most harmonious co-operation of jurisprudents and executive officialdom could not have prevented the gap between the ideal and the actual, the normative and the practical, the precedent of sacred law and the makeshift decision of the executive order, from widening until it became unbridgeable. The pious condemned the ruler's deviations from the established norm of the Prophet's days, and in fear for their souls they evaded his call when he summoned them to take office. However ready the state may be to accept the legist's pronouncements, too many emergencies of change would call for arbitrary rulings, and the faithful would risk his salvation by lending his authority to the ephemeral iniquities of power.

Thus the government of Allah and the government of the sultan grew apart. Social and political life was lived on two planes, on one of which happenings would be spiritually valid but actually unreal, while on the other no validity could ever be aspired to. The law of God failed because it neglected the factor of change to which Allah had subjected his creatures. When legal theory stooped to take this element into account, it succeeded in reaching a workable compromise. But it had, unwittingly perhaps, relinquished that grandiose dream of a social body operating perpetually under the immutable law which God had revealed in the fullness of time.

To be sure, God's will was manifest in the transformation of his community. Still there was deterioration and failure in falling away from the standards set in the Prophet's age. To this very day that failure continues, and the Muslim lives under two laws: one, eternal, applicable to him because of his membership in his faith; the other, revocable and subject to modification, a device to cope with the complications and to bridle the sinfulness of this our irremediably backsliding existence.

Gustave E. von Grunebaum, *Medieval Islam*, 142–144.

Adjustment

It is hard to say when Muslim society began to assimilate to European society, if an arbitrary judgment is to be avoided—in Egypt, perhaps under the khedive Isma'il (1863–79), and in the Ottoman Empire under the sultan 'Abd al-'Aziz (1861–76). If Muslim civilization in the French Maghrib and in India resisted assimilation longer than in the free countries, this is because . . . any existing inferiority was felt to be only external, that is, in terms of physical power, and not spiritual. Also assimilation in the other countries, too, ran a slow course. Even in Turkey, where assimilation was enforced by law, many survivals of the old societal forms are alive underneath the European cover. The greater speed of assimilation in the last decades can be attributed to contacts with things Western established by wider strata through films and through the radio.

A few words on the position of women. Its background seems more important to me than the truly accidental rules laid down by the Koran. On one hand, there is the naivete of classical antiquity with which Islam treats sexual matters; on the other, the taboo which is spread over women and which is symbolized by the veil.

This taboo has shown itself to be quite tenacious. The section "The Status of Women in Islam" in Sayyid Amir 'Ali's *The Spirit of Islam* may perhaps be considered a first attempt at weakening this taboo, although the author, in accordance with his apologetic purpose, exalts rather than criticizes the position of women in Islam. Generally speaking, I believe the influence of reformist pamphlets on the process of assimilation to be quite inconsiderable. Assimilation comes to pass through the upper classes imitating European customs and through the lower classes later imitating the upper classes; as to the entering of women into economic life, that is the consequence of economic difficulties. The same process in reverse could be observed in 1939 in the effect which the countermovement, originating in Wahhabi Arabia, had upon the tribes of the Syrian desert: the womenfolk of the great shaikhs were not to be seen, while there was no restriction about talking to the wives and daughters of the other Bedouins.

Werner Caskel, "Western Impact and Muslim Civilization," in von Grunebaum, ed., *Unity and Variety in Muslim Civilization,* 340–341.

Political Organization

It is well known that political organization and behavior are not based on the same principles in the Muslim world as in the Christian world. These

principles, for that matter, are simply the transcription of different historical circumstances. Christianity was born in the framework of the Roman
state. Little by little it built itself a church. Whatever disputes the boundary
line between church and state gave rise to, each acknowledged that the
other had an autonomous domain and so conceived society as governed by
a duality of powers, the temporal and the spiritual. Mohammed, on the
contrary, arising in a society without a state, was, in a manner in which
only modern minds introduce any distinction, the preacher of a faith and
the organizer of a temporal community. Consequently the social law was
an integral part of the religious law, and respect for the social law an integral part of submission to Allah. Revelation was the joint basis of belief
and of temporal organization. The community was in itself its state and its
church, and neither the one nor the other existed as an autonomous system. Naturally Islam is not alone in having set out from this point of view,
which had been that of the Hebrews of Moses under partially comparable
social conditions. Naturally, also, this theoretical unity is a limit which was
never reached, or which at least could not be reached concretely without
naturalizing, as Muslim, usages which were in fact pre-Islamic. The orientation, however, was categorical, and it was not to disappear very soon
from men's minds. It was to have the consequence that the Muslim would
require of his political organization a certain perfection; if this was lost,
the principle of obedience which he owed to it was also lost. In contrast,
the Christian renounced this perfection in advance and yet did not cease to
be bound in his capacity as citizen of a state. It can be easily seen how a
similar turn of mind among Muslims could cover much more concrete attitudes of withdrawal with respect to the state, whether we think of the traditional Bedouin anarchism or of the other forms of externalization which
we meet in the later Muslim world.

In practice, what had been possible in the way of identifying the temporal and the spiritual in the person of Mohammed ceased to be so by his
very death. His successors in the guidance of the community could indeed
direct the fulfillment of the duties of the believers; but it was not for them
to change anything or even to complete anything in a revelation defini-
tively given, unless they accepted, as some were to venture to do later, the
possibility of certain continuation of revelation, which no one then claimed.
In the Roman conception law is constantly capable of reformation, development; in the Islamic conception there could be no theoretical foundation
other than reference to precedent, to tradition—single and unalterable. This
is a state of mind which, for that matter, is not far from that of all peoples

who lack the concept of the state, except for the religious aspect in certain cases; the Christian Occident lived for centuries in a theoretical respect for custom, and for a conception of this custom as being derived from precedents. *Mutatis mutandis,* Arabs and Teutons were of the same human age. Only, in practical reality, things did not happen this way. Mohammed could not have legislated for all the problems of the future. . . .

In reality there was no Islamic political doctrine. There was a fervent but vague aspiration, more and more external to the actual states. To the extent that jurists had formulated a few concrete rules, these did not reveal this general aspiration except in form, and, far from having had some sort of influence on the evolution of the actual institutions, they adapted to them somehow or other—and these institutions resulted from the combination of all the historical, social, national, and other circumstances of the Muslim world, which owed nothing to the intervention of Islam as a doctrine.

Claude Cahen, "The Body Politic," in von Grunebaum, ed., *Unity and Variety in Muslim Civilization,* 133–134, 157.

The Body Politic

[Islam's] lightning conquests, resulting from undertakings integral to the religious doctrine, even though the social reasons for them are in fact clear, had the effect of making it suddenly impossible to maintain the primitive politico-religious organization. The vastness of the territory, the entirely new institutions of the subjugated populations, of which a blank slate could not be made, forced the heirs of Mohammed to undertake or to tolerate things which went far outside the field of simple modalities of application in the Muslim Law. There were then in fact two domains: that of the Muslim Law, applicable only to the Arabs and more and more inadequate even for them, and that of the non-Islamic laws, preserved almost unchanged for the conquered peoples and, in fact, governing the empire. This division could be felt by the members of the primitive community who had stayed in Medina and had been discarded as "rejects" by the new regime, with a bitterness expressed religiously; unlike the warriors scattered across the world, they did not experience the burden and the temptations of the new ways of proceeding. There is no reason to think that for these latter the transformations in their way of life, which they accepted very readily, were to be understood as a betrayal of their faith or that they found any scandal in the non-Arab and non-Muslim peoples' being governed by non-Muslim laws, if only they worked submissively to the benefit of the Muslim Arabs.

The state which takes rough shape under these conditions comprises, in short, two sectors: on the one hand, a rudimentary central organization around the caliph which governs the Muslims—for war, for the obligations of the cult, for distributing the pensions; on the other hand, an administration the revenues of which go to the new masters, but the norms and the personnel of which, by the force of circumstances, continue to be largely those of the previous regimes. The Arabs, at the start, would have been entirely lacking in the experience required for any other policy, which, besides, would have made the establishment of the empire as difficult as this nonintervention made it easy. For populations which had had to complain of the vexatious interference of an invading state or an official church the policy was a partial liberation. In fiscal matters, for example, the Byzantine taxes and the Sassanid taxes continued. How could it have been otherwise? They were set by the nature of the economy and the social structure and not by abstract doctrines. The gradual clothing of these institutions in Arabic terms like *kharaj* and *jizya,* to which the jurists subsequently tried to give a precise Muslim definition, must not deceive us. The researches of [D. C.] Dennett, among others, have demonstrated very clearly how the facts behind these same names differ in Khurasan, in Iraq, in Egypt. Once we have left behind the still narrow framework of the central government, it is therefore not, in the life of the population, *one* regime, but *regimes* with which we must deal. The conquerors themselves had implicitly acknowledged the fact. Precisely because they had no conception of a unitary administration, they had made their conquests empirically and had organized them, not according to a general plan, but by a juxtaposition of local measures. Contrary to what has been believed, it was not at all a construct a posteriori when the later jurists distinguished between territories taken by force and by treaties, and within this second category among as many treaties as territories. Such had very naturally been the actual fact. Certainly there was subsequently a labor of regularization, of assimilation, but one must not be deceived: the later fragmentation of the Muslim world would never have been so easy if this labor had been thoroughly accomplished, and we must get rid of the idea that the centralized, bureaucratized state of the following centuries itself ever did anything but bring together local regimes without casting them in the same crucible. There too the Muslim state seems to us to be of the same age as the Western monarchies.

Claude Cahen, "The Body Politic," 134–135.

5

Coping with Modernity

The predicament of the man of faith in the contemporary world is a subject that has been discussed and analyzed in innumerable books and treatises, with the emphasis generally placed on conditions in the Christian West. Few scholars have turned their attention to the difficulties faced by believing Muslims when they choose to follow the tenets and commands of their religion closely and advocate such fidelity to the faith. Not that the phenomenon had passed unnoticed. Lord Cromer, who was British resident-general and consul general in Egypt from 1883 to 1907, used to quote with approval a saying of Stanley Lane-Poole, the distinguished writer on Egyptian history, to the effect that an upper-class Muslim must be "either a fanatic or a concealed infidel." Of his friend Sheikh Muhammad ʿAbduh, leader of the modernist movement in Egyptian Islam and grand mufti of Egypt, Cromer once wrote that he suspected him of being "in reality an agnostic."

A century has passed since Cromer made his perspicacious observation. Yet the difficulty for a believing Muslim of adjusting to living in the modern world remains as acute as before—and equally far from resolution. To take one example from recent Saudi history: When Prince Faisal ibn Musaʿid assassinated his uncle, King Faisal, in March 1975, it was revealed that the assassin's brother, Prince Khalid, had been killed by the Riyadh police some nine years previously while leading a group of Muslim zealots in a demonstration against the decision to set up a television station, on the ground that the shariʿa (religious law) forbids the representation of the human form in any way.

Again, throughout the past twenty-five years or so, details coming out of Egypt concerning certain disturbances, some of them violent, suggest that the same kind of zeal provided the motive force for several daring plots to overthrow the regime and set up in its place one that would adhere to the teachings and rules of the shariʿa. The plotters—who eventually succeeded in assassinating President Anwar Sadat—represent a new breed of Muslim fundamentalist, one whose zeal and determination surpass anything Arabic Islam had known in recent times.[1]

On the background of these revivalist movements, both historical and theological, John Esposito devotes a few pages of his *Islamic Threat*. Islam, he writes, possesses a rich, long tradition of revival (*tajdid*) and reform (*islah*). "Down through the ages," he explains, "individuals (theologians, legal scholars, Sufi masters, and charismatic preachers) and organizations undertook the renewal of the community at times of weakness and decline, responding to the apparent gap between the Islamic ideal and the realities of Muslim life. As with all things, a return to Islam—that is, to the fundamentals: the Quran, the life of the Prophet, and the early Islamic community— offered the model for Islamic reform."

During the eighteenth and nineteenth centuries, revivalist movements sprang up across the Islamic world. Despite differences, all were movements whose goal was the moral reconstruction of society. "They diagnosed their societies as being internally weak and in decline politically, economically, and religiously. The cause was identified as Muslim departure from true Islamic values brought about by the infiltration and assimilation of local, indigenous, un-Islamic beliefs and practices. The prescribed cure was purification through a return to true Islam. . . . The process of Islamic renewal and reform was based upon a return to the fundamental sources of Islam."

Emulating the example of the Prophet Muhammad, these movements transformed their societies through a religiously legitimated and inspired sociopolitical movement, Esposito adds.

> The ideological worldview of revivalist movements had an impact not only on their societies but also on Islamic politics in the twentieth century. The key ideological components of their program were: (1) Islam was the solution; (2) a return to the Quran and the Sunnah (model, example) of the Prophet was the method; (3) a community governed by God's revealed law, the Sharia, was the goal; and (4) all who resisted, Muslim or non-Muslim, were enemies of God. Members of the community, like the early Muslims of the seventh century, were trained in piety and military skills as these movements spread God's rule through preaching and jihad.[2]

The French Orientalist Maxime Rodinson writes in the same vein. According to him, the phenomenon that had most to do with the conditioning of the European view of the East, particularly after the middle of the nineteenth century, was imperialism. "The economic, technical, military, political, and cultural superiority of Europe was becoming overwhelming," he explains, "while the East was sinking into under-development. . . . The unconscious 18th-century view of things from a European standpoint, guided by the universalist ideology of the age, respected non-European peoples and cultures and rightly found in their historical evolution or their contemporary structures of society universal human characteristics, with pre-critical *naivete* crediting them with the same underlying bases as European civilization, with only very superficial specific differences." The conscious, theoretical European self-centredness of the nineteenth century, on the other hand, made the opposite mistake. "Irreducible specificity was assumed at all levels and universal traits or motives were ignored or denied."

"The humiliating situation in which the Muslim world found itself encouraged Christian missionaries and opened new ways for them. . . . Christianity was made out to be by its very nature favourable to progress, and Islam to mean cultural stagnation and backwardness. . . . The Islamic religious orders, in particular, were presented as a network of dangerous organizations animated by a barbarous hatred of civilization."[3]

Edward Said's Critique

These are only two samples of reservations some Western students of Islam have expressed about the general run of Western Orientalists' work. It was Edward Said, however, who was to produce a fairly comprehensive critique of Orientalism. His book *Orientalism,* published in 1978, will be referred to later in this book. Akbar S. Ahmed, some of whose ideas on the religion of Islam was cited earlier, refers to Said's work in passing while launching his own attack on the Orientalists.

The heat and fury Edward Said generated by arguing that the West can know Islam only in a demeaning and exploitative manner, Ahmed remarks, has obscured a central question raised by him: "Can the West ever hope to understand, objectively and sympathetically, the other, that is, foreign cultures, alien peoples?" Clearly, he adds, these scholars indicate that this is possible, *pace* Said. "Here is scholarship in the highest tradition, and in its humanity it reflects the understanding which academics at their best are capable of achieving."

It is time, then, to move beyond Said's arguments. In an important sense he has led us into an intellectual cul-de-sac. In attempting to transcend the idea of the orientalist system we end up by replacing one system with another. There remains the real danger of simplifying the complex problem of studying the other or the foreign. Said has left us at the end of the trail with what he set out to denounce: stereotypes, images devoid of substance. Orientalism is now an empty cliché, the orient a geographical location only in our imagination.[4]

Joining what Ahmed calls the media persons were numerous academics, including many Islamic experts, who "have abandoned their role as neutral observers and become active participants in the political drama portraying Islam in an unfriendly light," advising governments, preparing reports and appearing on television. "The voices of scholars explaining the gentle aspects of Islamic civilization . . . were drowned by those arguing about geo-political strategy and imperatives. Indeed, some experts argued for the outright invasion of Muslim countries in order to capture their wealth, their oil wells and ports, so as to make them 'safe' for the West."

To prove his point, Ahmed cites a number of would-be specialists. One of these is Conor Cruise O'Brien, who wrote in the *Times* of London on May 11, 1989:

> Muslim society looks profoundly repulsive. It looks repulsive because it is repulsive. . . . A Westerner who claims to admire Muslim society, while still adhering to Western values, is either a hypocrite or an ignoramus, or a bit of both. At the heart of the matter is the Muslim family, an abominable institution. . . . Arab and Muslim society is sick, and has been sick for a long time. In the last century the Arab thinker Jamal al-Afghani wrote: 'Every Muslim is sick and his only remedy is in the Koran'. Unfortunately the sickness gets worse the more the remedy is taken.

"This," Ahmed comments, "from a man once Professor of Humanities at New York University, former Chief Editor of the *Observer* and a member of the Irish Senate; and he was not alone. . . . The intensity of the prejudice against Islam was surprising if only because of the quarters from which it sprang: diplomats, editors, writers, members of Parliament."[5]

What direction will politico-religious developments in Muslim lands take? Will the approach now in force in countries like Egypt, Tunisia, Syria, and Iraq, an approach marked by various degrees of modernity, prevail, or will the opposing approach of Islamic fundamentalism take its place? Erwin Rosenthal's investigations in Muslim countries as disparate as Malaysia, Turkey, Morocco, and Tunisia have produced no conclusive answers to such questions. Yet one has the feeling that he has little faith in the power of Western-educated and Western-oriented Muslim intellectuals to prove equal to the task. An Islamic revival, if and when it comes, is more likely to come from the fundamentalists, who according to Rosenthal are more representative of the true spirit of Islam.

However, while the very complexity of the problem tends to favor the adoption of radical positions, these can only lead to more confusion and contradictions. In order to create a public opinion that is at once "well-informed, rooted in the Islamic past, and determined to support a combined national effort to establish a modern society on the pattern of the Good Society," Rosenthal concludes somewhat inconsequentially, good will and mutual understanding are needed.

Is there a way out? Have any serious attempts been made at what Muhammad Iqbal termed "rethinking the whole system of Islam" and to set Islam again on its old solid foundations—"free from alloy of any kind"? Hamilton Gibb, who held Iqbal in the highest esteem, was extremely skeptical. "Before a beginning could, in fact, be made with the reformulation of Islamic doctrine," he writes in *Modern Trends in Islam*, "it was necessary to isolate the religious element in the reform movement from the emotional influences of the revolutionary or nationalist program."

This was the task taken up and to some extent accomplished by al-Afghani's most influential pupil, Sheikh Muhammad ʿAbduh, in the later period of his active career, says Gibb. He has this to say about ʿAbduh's accomplishment:

> The effect of his teaching was to separate the religious issues from the political conflict, so that (even though they might continue to be associated) they were no longer interdependent and each was set free to develop along its own appropriate lines. If he had been able to win more general support for this doctrine, he might indeed have created a revolution in the thought and outlook of the Muslim world. But among the main body of Muslims, whether conservatives or reformers, it has never been fully accepted. The conservatives rejected it—as they rejected almost all Muhammad Abduh's ideas—a priori and on principle; the modernists, who claim to be his followers, did not understand it and, for external reasons, fell back upon Jamal ad-Din's activism. Although Muhammad Abduh's influence remains alive and is continuing to bear fruit in present-day Islam, the immediate outward consequence of his activities was the emergence of a new funda-

mentalist school calling themselves the "Salafiya," the upholders of the tradition of the fathers of the Islamic church. . . .

Gibb sums up the program which ʿAbduh bequeathed to the reform movement under four main heads:

(1) the purification of Islam from corrupting influences and practices;
(2) the reformation of Muslim higher education;
(3) the re-formulation of Islamic doctrine in the light of modern thought; and
(4) the defense of Islam against European influences and Christian attacks. . . .[6]

The Ottomans' Experience

One highly instructive example of how Muslim theologians and men of religion tried to cope with the challenges of modernity is that of the Ottomans during the last several decades of the empire. In a paper entitled "The Ottoman ʿUlema and Westernization in the Time of Selim III and Mahmud II," the late Uriel Heyd remarks on the phenomenon of Muslim ʿulema supporting policies of modernization and Westernization. The support these theologians lent to the Westernizing reforms of Selim III and Mahmud II, he writes, is understandable "in view of their integration in the ruling class and their active participation in the Government of the Ottoman Empire, which still retained its strongly Islamic character." In their hostility to the reactionary Janissaries and Bektashis they found themselves to be natural allies of the reforming sultans, he adds. "They feared Mahmud II and realized that the internal weakening of their corps had made open resistance to his policy no longer possible. The consistent efforts of both Sultans to prove their religious orthodoxy and appease the ʿulema also made it difficult for the latter to oppose innovations and helped them set their conscience at rest. Finally, the great changes under Selim III and Mahmud II were not made in the name of a new ideology; they were not based on, or accompanied by, a novel set of values. On the contrary, all the important reforms were, as has been shown, presented as being required and sanctioned by Islam. Everything was done 'for the sake of religion and State'."[7]

It has often been observed that the ʿulema in various periods and different countries were more concerned with upholding the ideas and theoretical values of Islam than with fighting for the preservation of Muslim institutions in practice. "From far back they were accustomed to bowing to the will of the secular rulers and tolerating the violation of the holy law by

Muslim society," adds Heyd. "What mattered in their opinion were the divine doctrines of Islam, while reality was in any case temporary, fleeting and morally evil. . . ." It remains somewhat astonishing, nevertheless,

> that the leading ʿulema in Selim's and Mahmud's time were not far-sighted enough to realize that the Westernizing reforms supported by them would eventually destroy the Islamic character of the Ottoman state and society. This lack of perspicacity was, no doubt, due to their unbounded confidence in the superiority and eternal strength of their religion and, at the same time, to their limited knowledge and understanding of historical developments in the West. Even those among them who were aware of the decline of religion and the power of the clergy in contemporary Europe failed to draw the logical conclusion that modernization might lead to a similar result in the lands of Islam.[8]

Heyd concludes:

> By making the ʿulema an essential part of the Government, the Ottomans had largely succeeded in bridging the traditional gulf between the umaraʾ and the fuqahaʾ, between political-administrative reality and religious-legal theory. However, while thus preventing a clash of the European type between Church and State, they caused a deep split both within the ʿulema corps and in the minds of the leading ʿulema. The integration of the ʿulema in the ruling class of the Empire may have been beneficial for the unity of the Ottoman State but had most serious consequences for religion, at least in its official form. It caused the higher ʿulema to devote their main attention to politics and administration and, along with other factors, hampered the free spiritual development of Islam during the decisive period of its confrontation with Western civilization.[9]

The situation in our own time differs radically from that described by Heyd, conceivably because Muslims have learned the lessons that Heyd says their Ottoman predecessors failed to foresee. For years now, there has been a strong reaction in Muslim countries against secularizing tendencies, expressed in a number of Islamic radical movements, "loosely and inaccurately designated at the present time as fundamentalist," as Bernard Lewis has put it. "These movements," Lewis writes, "share the objective of undoing the secularizing reforms of the last century, abolishing the imported codes of law and the social customs that came with them, and returning to the holy law of Islam and the Islamic political order. That is what Islamic fundamentalism is primarily about."

In one country, Iran, these forces captured power. In several others they exercise growing influence. And a number of governments have begun to reintroduce shariᶜa law, either from conviction or as a preemptive strike against the fundamentalist challenge.

> Even nationalism and patriotism, which, after some initial opposition from pious Muslims, had begun to be generally accepted, are now once again being questioned and even denounced as anti-Islamic. After a long period in which, for example, Arab nationalism was sacrosanct, it is now under attack. In some Arab countries defenders of what has now become the old-style, so-called secular nationalism are accusing the Muslim fundamentalists of dividing the Arab nation, maintaining that these are setting Muslim against Christian. To this the fundamentalists say it's the nationalists who are being divisive, setting Turk against Persian against Arab within the larger community and brotherhood of Islam and that this division is the greater and more heinous offense.

In the literature of the Muslim radicals and militants, Lewis adds, "the primary enemy and immediate object of attack among many of these groups are the native secularizers, those who have tried to weaken and modify the Islamic base of the state by introducing secular schools and universities, secular laws and courts, and thus excluding Islam, and so also the professional exponents of Islam, from two major areas which they had previously dominated, education and justice." The fundamentalist demonology includes characters as diverse as King Faruq and Presidents Nasser and Sadat in Egypt, Hafiz al-Asad in Syria, Saddam Hussein in Iraq, the shah of Iran, and the kings of Arabia, "all lumped together as the most insidious of enemies, the enemy from within who wears a Muslim face and bears a Muslim name and is therefore much deadlier than the open enemies from outside."[10]

In recent years, what with the prevailing confusion as to an agreed definition of the term *fundamentalist*—and what with its being used interchangeably with *radical, resurgent, militant,* or *essentialist*—voices are heard protesting that it was wrong to lump all devout Muslims and those who advocate rule of the shariᶜa with Muslim militants of such groups as Jihad, al-Takfir wal-Hijra, or the radicals of the Islamic Salvation Front in Algeria. The well-known Moroccan scholar Abdallah Laroui, for one, has tried to affirm this distinction by coining the term *liberal Islam*. In an essay entitled "Western Orientalism and Liberal Islam: Mutual Distrust?" he writes that "liberal Islam" is "more than tolerant or moderate Islam," and that that is why "I cannot say in good faith that [liberal Islam] exists already or is imminent somewhere in the Islamic world."[11] Laroui then gives us his own definition of liberal Islam:

> I define as liberal a situation in which society is set free to operate according to its own rules; I don't say its specific rules because this is a trick familiar to traditionalists. I think that in circumstances of rapid change we need only to open our eyes to be convinced that society doesn't obey our orders, even when we believe that these come ultimately from God. Miracles just do not occur. To acknowledge the fact amounts to a mental revolution, what I call *qatiʿa* (rupture, divorce), which opens all doors. Everything becomes possible. I don't understand otherwise what occurred lately in Russia and before that in Spain. . . . Ideology is, in the long term, less powerful than sociology. As soon as this fact is recognized, the reforms just mentioned become inevitable because they serve the interests of all, including those who oppose them for ideological motives. From this standpoint I don't see in Islamic countries so much the preeminence of a *daʿwa* (religious message) or the ascendancy of a clerical elite, as the direct consequence of poverty and economic backwardness.[12]

"The collapse of the Berlin wall was not due to the policy of containment, blockade, propaganda as much as to a wise policy of easy-term loans, free trade and enhanced cultural exchanges," Laroui explains. The same strategy should secure the same results elsewhere.

> Sooner or later a developing society frees itself from ideas and ideals that no longer correspond to its new aspirations. For reasons I need not detail here, such an evolution will probably occur more easily in the countries of Asia than in the Arab Middle East and North Africa, not because the former are less religious but simply because the latter are on the whole less fortunate. Seeing that happening some time in the future, somewhere in the vast Islamic world, seeing that the law of society has at last prevailed over the orders of tradition or the commands of ideology, many will, I am sure, cry out, as they do now, facing the staggering performances of some Asian nations: Well, the seeds were always there; we failed to see them before, but now we take notice and we cheer.[13]

Readings

Islam in the Modern Era

Although nominally Islam is one religion, and although Muslims might be shocked to be told that under the roof of a single terminology very distinctive religious styles persisted, such was in fact the case. Islam traditionally was divided into a "high" form, the urban-based, strict, unitarian, nomocratic, puritan and scripturalist Islam of the scholars; and a "lower" form, the cult of personality-addicted, ecstatic, ritualistic, questionably literate, unpuritanical and rustic Islam of the dervishes and the marabouts. At times the two were at peace with one another; from time to time there would be a revivalist movement, such as the Wahabis or Usman dan Fodio's *jihad* in West Africa. But although the revivalist movement often won temporarily (the coming of new dynasties was usually associated with revivalist movements), there was no social base for any more permanent victory by the higher form of Islam over the lower. The rustic element of society had no role for the high Islam. It was not interested in abstract, unitarian theology, but in having mediators with the divine who could preside over the rustic rituals that were for it the essence of religion.

Under modern conditions, by contrast, the colonial and post-colonial state was sufficiently strong to destroy the rural self-administration units or tribes that had provided the social base for the personalized, ecstatic, questionably orthodox, low religion; and in this way it provided the base for a definitive, permanent victory by one of the two conceptions of Islam over the other. This, I think, is the great reformation that has taken place in Islam in the last 100 years, which the West has only recently noticed in connection with Ayatollah Khomeini in Iran and in the strength of fundamentalism more widely.

What I find so important about all this is that the presence of a genuinely indigenous tradition of high Islam—the scholarly, puritanical, relatively magic-free, sober and individualist Islam—has enabled the Islamic world to escape the dilemma that haunted other "underdeveloped" societies disturbed and humiliated by the impact of the West: the dilemma of whether to idealize and emulate the West (a humiliating option) or to idealize the local folk tradition and indulge in some form of populism, as exemplified recently by people like Solzhenitsyn, who repudiate the West in the name of an idealized and mystically conceived local tradition. Unlike many other societies, Islam had no need for this, because its own high variant has dignity in international terms and yet is genuinely local. As a result, the process of self-reform in response to modernity and the temporary domination of the West could take place in the name of the local faith. This is my main explanation for Islam's remarkable resistance to the secularization trend.

Ernest Gellner, "Islam and Marxism," *International Affairs* (London), January 1991, 5–6.

Attitude to Arabism

One leading Arab nationalist thinker of our own day, ʿAbd al-Rahman al-Bazzaz, bases his analysis on a premise identical to that of al-Kawakibi. For him, "the fact that the Prophet Muhammad was an Arab was not a matter of chance; a genius, he belonged to a nation of great abilities and qualities." In a booklet printed in Baghdad in 1952 titled *Islam and Arab Nationalism,* al-Bazzaz accuses the *shuʿubiyya* (non-Arab Muslim detractors of Arabs) of the desire to separate Muhammad from the Arab nation. The Arabs, he argues, were the backbone of Islam. "They were the first to be addressed in the verses of Revelation; they were the *Muhajirin* and the *Ansar;* their swords conquered countries and lands, and on the whole they are as Umar described them in a saying of his: "Do not attack the Arabs and humiliate them for they are the essence of Islam."

According to al-Bazzaz, after this "clear exposition of the intellectual problems and the factors that contribute to the mistaken belief that there is a contradiction between the principles of Islam and Arab nationalism, the factors and assumptions of nationalism are varied, and we do not intend to analyze them in this lecture. But we can assert that modern nationalism is based on language, history, literature, customs and qualities."

Language, then, "is the primary tenet of our nationalist creed; it is the soul of our nation and the primary aspect of its life. The nation that loses its language is destined to disappear and perish. It is the good fortune of the Arabs that their language is not only a national duty but also a religious one and the influence of Islam on its propagation and preservation is very great." Moreover, al-Bazzaz adds, "the Arabs had a glorious history before Islam, and their history is even more glorious and of great moment after Islam. The Muslim Arab, when he exalts his heroes, partakes of two emotions, that of the pious Muslim and that of the proud nationalist."

In fact, says al-Bazzaz, "the most glorious pages of Muslim history are the pages of Muslim Arab history, as the Western historians themselves admit." As for Arabic literature, "which is the result of Arab feeling and emotion all through the ages, its greatest and most venerable parts came from Islam, and indeed the Koran itself, in addition to being a book of direction, is the most awesome example of the elevated prose which the Arab . . . exalts." As for the pre-Islamic poetry, and especially descriptive and wisdom verse, there is in most of it nothing that contradicts the spirit of Islam.

So much for the first three foundations of Arab nationalism—language, history, and literature. The fourth, which consists of "the good Arab customs and qualities," again poses no problem. Here, too, there obtains "similarity, not to say complete identity, between the ethical ideal of Arab nationalism and that prescribed by Islam."

Turning from the cultural aspects of Arab nationalism to an examination of it "as a political movement striving to unite the Arabs and to give them self-government," al-Bazzaz again finds no discrepancy between Arabism and Islam. The Arab national movement, he writes, is democratic, socialist, popular, and cooperative. Islam, "although it did not lay down in detail the organization of government, requires consultation, and does, without any doubt, accept completely democratic organization." Its financial legislation and juristic principles are, in essence, socialist. It is enough to recall something of the life of the Prophet and the caliphs to realize the extent of the cooperative and popular spirit of Islam. This being the case, "the national movement for which we call does not in any way contradict Islam."

To say this, however, is not to imply a call for Pan-Islamism. "To say that Islam does not contradict the Arab national spirit is one thing. . . . It is not natural to expect the union of Iraq with Iran or Afghanistan, for instance, before Syria and Jordan are united."

It follows, al-Bazzaz concludes, that the call to unite the Arabs—and this is the clearest and most important objective of Arab nationalism—is the practical step that must precede the call for Pan-Islamism. "It is strange, therefore, to find that some of those who call themselves supporters of Pan-Islamism in the Arab countries are the most violent opponents of Pan-Arabism. . . . No fundamental contradiction or clear opposition exists between Arab nationalism and Islam."

In various versions and formulations this approach to the subject of Islam in relation to the Arab nationalist doctrine has also been advanced by conservative Muslim Arabs and even by some of the ʿulema in the Arab world. But only up to a point, and only rather equivocally and halfheartedly.

Nissim Rejwan, *Arabs Face the Modern World: Religious, Cultural, and Political Responses to the West* (Gainesville: University Press of Florida, 1998), 80–81.

Islam and Nationalism

In his book *al-Islam wa al-ʿuruba wa al-ʿilmaniyya* (Islam, Arabism, and secularism), Dr. Muhammad ʿImara attacked those who argue in favour of the contradiction between Islam and Arabism (Arab nationalism). Such an argument, he claims, has arisen only in the period of decline, ". . . when Mamlukes attained power in the Arab countries. As they were Muslims and not Arabs, they made the religious bond a substitute—in fact, a negation—of the Arab bond." Ottomans after them followed the same route. When the colonialists marched on Arab lands and the world of Islam, they played the same game, exploiting the presumed contradiction between the religious and the national bond in order to strike at Arabism and Islam and so conquer and occupy both the Arab countries and the Muslims. At one time these Europeans supported Muhammad Ali's "Arab project," and when he appeared close to succeeding in its implementation, they opposed him in conjunction with Ottoman Islam. Subsequently (e.g. in the Great War), they supported Arabism in the East against the Islam of the Ottomans. At the same time they divided (shared among themselves) the Arab nation that had emerged from the Great War, having managed to abolish the Islamic Caliphate (in Istanbul) and the project of the Arab nation-state. Then, in confronting Islamic thought, they sowed the seeds of secularism and Westernization among the Arabs. More recently, in combating the radical Nasserite Arab nationalist expansionist movement, they sought to set up regional alliances under the banner of Islam.

The thrust of ʿImara's argument is that non-Arab Muslims who controlled power for several centuries not only caused the decline of the Arabs, but also created the dichotomy between Islam and Arabism. The dichotomy surely dates from an earlier stage in the history of Islam. It was the Prophet Muhammad who offered Islam as the new bond holding the community of believers together and replacing the older bond of blood characteristic of Arab tribalism which prevailed before Islam. Furthermore, the strict orthodox Muslims, including the interpreters and upholders of the Sacred Law (the *shariʿa*), as well as the more militant exponents of radical Islam who now clamour for the return of religion to the centre of political life, insist on the incompatibility between Islam and the secular idea of Arab nationalism; for them, Islam is still the exclusive basis of national identity, the *umma,* or community of the faithful, the only nation to which a Muslim belongs. At the same time, such a Muslim does not deny the idea of patriotism, one's loyalty to one's own country: he does not think it undermines or contradicts loyalty to Islam. The fact remains that there has been, so far, no final resolution between all these several layers of loyalty. The matter remains part of the unresolved wider issue of Islam and politics, Islam and the state.

P. J. Vatikiotis, *Islam and the State* (London: Croom Helm, 1987), 82–83.

Nation, Nationality, and Islamic Principles

The very term "nationality," which is a derivation from "nation," implies a historic attachment to the distinctions of race, common descent, language, history or political institutions. All have entered into the legal definition of "nationality." That is why many principled thinkers, non-Muslim as well as Muslim, have warned us against confusing nationality, in the sense of ethnic or cultural or racial identity, and nationality as membership or citizenship in a particular nation. There is no such confusion in Islam. Of all this often confusing complex of sometimes conflicting meanings, Islam finds acceptable only the administrative concept of nationality. That concept refers to membership in an administrative or political identity, a membership which in Islam as in the modern world is open on an equal basis to people of differing ethnic identities or cultural background. Such a territorially-based political organization should be so administered that no prejudices and no considerations other than binding ideals and moral values are allowed to divide people, individual from individual or group from group.

"Nationality" should neither involve any separating barriers between human beings nor imply a narrow conception of nationalism based on any alleged supremacy of some people over others on linguistic, cultural or ethnological lines. In other words, the quality of people's membership in a particular nation or state can only be determined on the grounds of each member's basic allegiance to his or her own conscience: a conscience which is free of all prejudices. The political status and allegiance arising from membership in a national political community are to be based upon two fundamentals:

1. allegiance to one's own conscience, and
2. social allegiance to the society in which one lives.

Any deviation from either of these fundamentals constitutes a form of hypocrisy, individual or social, since sound membership of a society can only result from conscientious reciprocity. But once conscience is involved, religion enters with its claim to authority. This has happened throughout history. Whether one likes it or not, conscience and religion are intimately linked; indeed, they are one and the same in every religious conception and in every religion.

How, then, can social life be built up among people whose consciences are governed by different religions? An adequate answer to this question involves, however, ethical reasoning, and is therefore not altogether relevant to this present discussion. But the fundamental requirement is clear; that in any society religion should be given its proper place, so that every individual may act in accordance with his or her good conscience. This will enable all individuals to cooperate despite their adherence to different religions. . . .

This is particularly true of Islam, which, since its inception, not only discarded all artificial barriers between people—individually and as groups—but further introduced the objective conception of the ethnological oneness of all humankind as a matter of faith and of policy. In Islam, the ethnological plurality and the ontological unity of humankind are two sides of the one coin. Each entails and enriches the other.

Such a reconciliation of plurality and difference did not only occur among Muslims in the Islamic state. Under Islam in the age of historical glory, this same notion had a wider, all-embracing significance. It was actualised not simply among Muslims but also between Muslims and non-Muslims—among people of different religions who lived side by side as equals. In his history of Spain entitled *Histoire d'Espagne,* the Spanish historian [Miguel] Romera-Navarro observed that

> under [the Muslim] regime, the Hispano-Roman and Visigothic inhabitants of the peninsula preserved their property, their laws, their judges, their churches and their priests. The living conditions of the cultivators of the soil, of the slaves and of the Jews were much improved. The Jews, in particular, who had been cruelly persecuted during the period of Visigothic monarchy, enjoyed during the Arab epoch entire liberty; they were allowed to participate in the new government and to occupy positions in its administration. . . . There, men of all sects and of all races lived together in liberty. While in Christian Europe fanaticism reigned, here tolerance was practised.

K. Haridas, "Islamization of State and Society" in *Shari'a Law and the Modern Nation-State,* ed. Norani Othman (Kuala Lumpur: Sisters in Islam Forum [Malaysia] Berhad, 1994), 96–97.

Umma, Dawla, and the Islamic State

Since Islam brought with it a legal system, the *shariʿa*, it seems only logical to infer that Islam also proposes a government to enforce the *shariʿa*. Any government that is committed to enforcing the law of Islam, as this discussion will elaborate, may be termed Islamic. Supportive arguments for this theme are also found in the Qurʾanic concepts of *umma* and of human vicegerency or *khilafah*, in its injunction commanding good and forbidding evil, and in the Qurʾanic requirement of administering justice. The concept of *khilafah*, or the vicegerency of man, is by its nature rooted in the concept of trust (*amanah*) which is also a Qurʾanic principle and an attribute of political leadership in Islam. The basic unity of religion and state in Islam also represents a logical extension of *tawhid*, the oneness of Allah, which is a cardinal principle of the faith and a main feature of Islam's unitarian outlook on life.

The constitutional theory of Islam revolves around these concepts, namely *umma, shariʿa, khilafah, shura* (consultation) and *bayʿah* (pledge of allegiance). . . . The Arabic word for community, *umma*, is a derivative of *umm*, meaning "mother." *Umma* in Islam signifies more than the motherland. *Ummat al-Islam* comprises the entire collectivity of Muslims living anywhere regardless of their geographical location or the political boundaries separating them. *Umma* is a Qurʾanic concept which was initially applied to the Islamic community of Medina.

The Qurʾan highlights some of the attributes of *umma* as including belief in the truth of Islam, dedication to righteousness (by commanding good and forbidding evil), moderation and justice, and a single fraternity of equals. Pre-Islamic Arabia did not know or use the concept of *umma*; the only form of social organisation that it knew was the tribe. Afflicted with moral, social and economic bankruptcy, pre-Islamic Arabia was therefore impressed with the morally appealing and egalitarian call of the new *umma*.

With the emergence of the state of Medina, the term *umma* came to signify both religious and political unity under the leadership of the Prophet. *Umma* differed from any other preceding or succeeding community in one sense: it was an open-ended community under one universal God. This simply meant the creation for the first time in human history of a universal community based on complete equality, regardless of considerations of race, colour and ancestry. Islam became not only a religion but a unifying social bond. The Prophet's declaration "that there is no merit of an Arab over a non-Arab or of a red over a black except through piety" highlighted Islam's singleminded commitment to equality.

The unity that Islam proposed was meant to be for all, that is, the whole of mankind. Lacking the claim or notion of a chosen people, the community kept its door open to welcome all varieties of ethnic and cultural groups. Furthermore until the onset of rapid decline under Turkish rule, Muslims throughout their territorial expansion dealt with the people of the new territories not as subjects but as citizens. This was changed, however, under the Ottoman Turks who, by exploiting and degrading their citizens, made them second-class subjects. This marked the first phase of the decline of the Islamic polity. The second phase came with European colonialism which eventually dismembered the Muslim community. Only in recent decades has there emerged a renewed awareness among Muslims who envisage their strength through unity. The ideal of the *umma* offers that potential and continues to inspire Muslims to strive toward ultimate unity.

The *ummat al-Islam* may be distinguished from *dar al-Islam*. The first is centered on unity in faith, the second contemplates the legal and political aspects of a sovereign state with its territorial boundaries, population and government. A Muslim may consider himself a member of the *umma* even if he does not reside in *dar al-Islam*. This division between *dar al-Islam* and *dar al-kufr,* and the subdivision of the latter into *dar al-harb* (abode of war) and *dar al-ʿahd* (abode of treaty) is politically conceived and has become the focus of juristic writings, despite the absence of mention of such divisions in the *Qurʾan* or *sunna* (although there is recognition in these sources of other religions and their followers, the *ahl al-kitab*). In theory, *dar al-Islam*—which is a parallel concept to *dawlat al-Islam* (Islamic state)— comprises all territories that are totally or predominantly inhabited by Muslims and are governed by Muslim authorities. Another view, which is preferred here, maintains that it includes all territories where the *shariʿa* is implemented, regardless of the religious following of their inhabitants.

Umma is a Qurʾanic concept but state, or *dawlah,* is not. The word *dawlah* occurs in the *Qurʾan* only in the sense of material wealth. The nearest equivalent words with its political connotation that are found in the holy Book are *amr* and *hukm,* which signify a "command," or a "network of command." The nation-state is, of course, a Western concept representing a European phenomenon that developed between the sixteenth and seventeenth centuries C.E. It is natural therefore not to find such a concept in early Islamic political thought. Muslim jurists had much to say, however, about the body politic and the conduct of rulers and governors. If the concept of state in Europe cannot be understood in isolation from law, liberty and individualism, the Islamic concept of state cannot be understood in isolation from *umma* and *shari'a*. It thus appears that the state in Islam is neither normative nor the original locus of political authority. It is perceived as a vehicle of achieving order and security in the *umma* and implementing the basic mission of Islam, that is *amr bi'l ma'ruf wa nahy 'an al-munkar* (commanding good and forbidding evil). It is the *umma,* not the state, which is the locus of political authority and the principal bearer of the Qur'anic trust of vicegerency.

The population of *dawlah Islamiyyah* may include both Muslims and non-Muslims. Muslims who do not reside in the Islamic state are not necessarily or automatically citizens of that state, but residence is not a requirement of membership in the *umma*. The norm in the constitutional theory of caliphate is unity, not pluralism. This is stated in the writings of al-Mawardi (d. 450/1059) and others who maintained it to be unlawful to elect more than one *imam* at the same time. Only al-Baghdadi (d. 403/1012) has gone on record to say that electing more than one *imam* is permissible, but only if the localities in which they are elected are divided by sea. According to the classical doctrine of caliphate, any plurality of states in the Muslim lands is necessarily anomalous and contrary to the unitarian foundation of the *umma,* which should always be the ultimate goal.

The realities of the contemporary world are, however, such that proposing political unity under a unified leadership and state is impractical. But if *umma* is meant to embody a religious fraternity of all Muslims that transcends the political boundaries of national states, then this has always commanded support and continues to be a reality. Despite the plurality of states and nationalities among them, Muslims are still a single *umma*. An Egyptian Muslim is Egyptian by nationality as well as a member of the Muslim *umma*. That also applies to an American Muslim who is American by nationality but relates to the *umma* as a member of the Muslim fraternity. Political unity is not a reality at present, but the historical model of the caliphate may perhaps be revived in a modified form, either as a federation or else in looser unity as a commonwealth of nations.

Mohammad Hashim Kamali, "The State and Its Constitution," in Othman, ed., *Shari'a Law and the Modern Nation-State,* 46–47.

The Umma in History

Instead of speaking of the "Muslim world" we need a debate that refines our perception of the Qur'anic term *umma* and makes it more than an abstraction. *Umma* does not imply merely the community of all those who profess to be Muslims. The single most important implication of *umma* is that it is a moral conception of how Muslims should become a community in relation to each other, other communities and the natural world. It is manifesting in thought, action and openness a distinctive moral vision that is the *raison d'être* of the *umma*. It is an enduring commitment to the dynamism of a constant set of moral concepts and precepts that creates the contours and ultimate configuration of the *umma*. . . . The unifying force of the concept of *umma* is important in another respect, that of its underlying cultural precepts. The *umma* is not a cultural entity patterned on the norms of any one dominant group nor is it the product of cultural contingency. It does not embrace cultural relativism but exists within and is expressed through diverse cultural groups. As both concept and practice, the *umma* in history provides a demonstration of diversity within unity. This has enabled the history of the *umma* to be marked by an extremely rich interaction with other intellectual traditions.

Anwar Ibrahim, "The *Umma* and Tomorrow's World," *Futures: The Journal of Forecasting, Planning and Policy* 23, 3 (1991): 302–310.

Umma and Citizenry: A Modern Muslim Civil Society

Anwar Ibrahim's model of the new *umma* can only exist if there is first an understanding of the notion, and also the will to create and sustain a civil society in a modern Muslim state. What is meant here by "civil society" is a society in which there is scope and space for honest, reasoned and thoughtful discussion, within an atmosphere of principled openness. In this case, these features must be realised within, and characteristic of, a recognisably Muslim society, one which is not constrained by any authoritarian imposition of uniformity or conformism in the interpretation of civil and public Islamic law. . . .

The creation of this type of civil society is critical to the project of Islamic reformation and modernity. So long as we still seek to transplant the historical model of the premodern Islamic state in form—without recognising that Islam from its founding experience provides us not with a model of political structure but an imperative social ethic and moral vision—the problems of double-standards and discrimination within the Muslim state will not be resolved to the satisfaction of all constituents of that state.

Muslims today do not need nostalgic and imaginative reinvents of the classical Islamic state—the endless recycling of the same model of the pristine, even mythical, Islamic state that is the principal stock-in-trade of the fundamentalist ideologues. Rather, what we urgently require is a modern Ibn Khaldun or Montesquieu: a thinker who might explicate in modern terms, and appropriate to modern and still emerging circumstances, *l'esprit des lois Islamiques*—the enduring spirit and animating ethos of Muslim law, society and sociability. That would be a proper contribution towards understanding the constitution of a modern Muslim state.

There is, in other words, far more to what we must understand by the "constitution" of such a state—including everything that is suggested within such an expression as "the spirit of the laws"—than is contained in any written constitution or can be implied by a merely formal or legal constitutionalism. Beyond documents and lofty legal principles we must take account of what shapes the understanding and touches the hearts of everyday citizens. The structure of law and the constitution has a cultural content and a moral foundation; and even in modern times Islam, provided we understand its political message historically, can provide that cultural and moral foundation—not only for Muslims themselves but for non-Muslim citizens as well.

It can do so in a way that is not disingenuously self-serving. That is, it can provide such a foundation in a society comprised of both Muslims and non-Muslims, not by presenting as universal to non-Muslims values that are historically particular to Islam, but by providing persuasive Islamic grounds upon which Muslims may accept the cultural and religious pluralism that the presence of non-Muslims in their midst, or under Muslim majority rule, entails.

Islam will only achieve its truly universal aspirations when it becomes genuinely inclusive towards all humans, in their variety and cultural difference, as they actually are. It will only achieve that when, going beyond self-declared assertions of its own universality, its spokesmen and ideologues cease to pronounce upon the acceptability to non-Muslims—before they have freely spoken or been fully consulted—of its own historically specific cultural formulations of general, even universal, human values.

In his book *Toward an Islamic Reformation* (1990, see especially chapter 4) Abdullahi an-Na'im argues clearly and in great detail that an Islamic justification and support for constitutionalism is not only important but relevant to Muslims. Non-Muslims may have their own secular or other justifications for constitutionalism and for accepting the legitimacy of the state and its laws. Yet so long as all are agreed on the principle and on the specific rules of constitutionalism, including complete equality and non-discrimination on grounds of gender or religion, each may have his or her own reasons for coming to that agreement. But such agreement on the binding nature of constitutionalism, and the plurality or diversity of grounds upon which the citizens of a modern state may come to accept its legitimacy, both rest upon underlying values and commitments that no constitution can specify or require. This is, in fact, what is meant by "the spirit of the laws."

Islam, with its recognition that humankind is one but also plural, and plural because Allah wished it so even though we might have been made one and uniform in our ways (*al-Maʾidah* 5:48), provides precisely the kind of impressively principled grounds upon which Muslims may welcome such a pluralism of commitments towards and within the modern state—or, if they cannot accept it gladly, upon which they can be asked in Muslim conscience to accept it anyway.

If modern constitutionalism is the legal foundation for the implementation of a modern *shariʿa*, then a truly open and modern *umma* such as that which Anwar Ibrahim has conceptualised and advocates is only possible if it is grounded upon the institution of a democratic space for civil society to flourish.

Norani Othman, "*Umma* and Citizenry," in Othman, ed., *Shariʿa Law and the Modern Nation-State*, 83, 84–85.

The Democracy Debate

Many problems inhere in the debate about the exportability of democracy to the Arab Middle East. The Arabs will be divided well into the third millennium over how to be democratic while remaining sensitive to the Arabo-Islamic *turath* (cultural heritage)—how to be simultaneously genuinely democratic, genuinely Arab and genuinely Muslim. *What* and *how much* modernity and tradition will foster that hybrid democratic, Arab, and Muslim identity?

The current debate will also set Arab against non-Arab. Islamists represent one formidable political configuration for which the question of *what* and *how much* modernity and tradition are real issues for both the Islamization and democratization of Arab societies and polities. The notions of cultural specificity and exceptionalism encountered in certain Western discourses find resonance in the Islamist perspective. In both, the difference between the "self" and the "other" becomes the essence of identity and therefore a non-negotiable given. In both, specificity spells exclusion. Certain Western discourses claim democracy to be a Western cultural-civilizational byproduct unsuited to the "other" while others claim it to be a universal *telos*. Advancing discourses of cultural particularity and universalism of their own, Islamists reject exclusivist Western discourse by reading democracy into Islamic sources and retort to universalists in the West by upholding their right to borrow that kind and that amount of democracy that befits culture, history, and local values.

Contemporary Islamists follow the itinerary of earlier Islamist reformers, rejecting all Western political engineering in the AME. One obvious reason for this stance is the suspicion of Islamists harbored by many Western governments. . . . Other reasons derive from the reciprocal suspicion of Western intentions—the colonial experience, the fear that outside engineering of democracy could serve foreign interests and disseminate alien values, the view that such engineering will be undemocratic because it is not homegrown and dismissive of indigenous values, cultures, histories and, in particular, of Islam. . . .

As hinted at by [certain Islamist] leaders, democracy needs cultural reconstructing if it is to co-exist with Islamic values. Its individualism has to be balanced with Islam's emphasis on the community, and its secularism has to yield to the radically different precepts of temporal and spiritual oneness, and an imagining of political legitimacy in which the will of man is subordinate to the will of God.

Larbi Sadiki, "To Export or Not to Export Democracy to the Arab World: The Islamist Perspective," *Arab Studies Journal,* Spring 1998, 71–73.

Democracy and Shura

The debate about Islam and democracy is by no means new. Since the 1980s, it has witnessed some fresh thinking and considerable movement on the ground. A growing number of Muslims, including a good many Islamist activists, have called for pluralist democracy, or at least for some of its basic elements: the rule of law and the protection of human rights, political participation, government control, and accountability. The terms and concepts used are often rather vague or deliberately chosen so as to avoid non-Islamic notions. Many speak of *shura,* the idealized Islamic concept of participation-qua-consultation; others refer to "Islamic democracy," just as in the 1950s and 1960s they would have talked about "Arab" or "Islamic socialism"; still others do not hesitate to call for democracy.

The phenomenon raises serious questions, political as well as methodological. Are Islamist activists sincere when they declare their democratic convictions, or do they merely hope to gain popular support and reach power through democratic elections? In either case it is significant that they should think such pronouncements can help them. I have examined the question elsewhere. Here I would like to focus on the theoretical aspects of the issue: Assuming that they are acting in good faith and that they have adopted democracy as their "strategic option," is there an Islamic path to a pluralist democratic society? And how can it be analyzed?

There is among Muslims an explicit debate on the subject which directly compares Islamic modes of political organization to Western-style pluralist democracy, usually with the intent of proving Islam's superiority to Western concepts in moral as well as practical terms, indeed of proving that Islam served as the source and model from which democratic essentials such as the rule of law or the concept of the social contract were taken by European thinkers of the Middle Ages and the Enlightenment. There are in fact a sizable number of comparative studies looking at specific concepts such as sovereignty, the social contract, or the separation of powers "in Islam," in the West, and in contemporary Arab politics.

The fact that such studies are so numerous suggests that there is considerable demand. Yet, while of considerable interest, their apologetic thrust reduces their value to an outside observer. More rewarding is a look at the large body of books, pamphlets, draft constitutions, published talks, and conference proceedings that discuss the relationship of Islam, the state, and politics without direct reference to the West. Do these reflect basic notions, institutions, and procedures characteristic of pluralist democracy? To what extent have they been integrated into Islamic political thinking and thus been authenticated and rendered acceptable to a Muslim, or more specifically, an Islamist audience? . . .

There is general agreement among [Muslim] authors that Islam is comprehensive or, as the commonly used modern formula has it, that it is religion and state (*al-islam din wa-dawla*) or religion and world (*al-islam din wa-dunya*). This formulation signals the rejection of secularism as it was advocated by the Egyptian scholar ʿAli ʿAbd al-Raziq in his book *Islam and the Roots of Government (Al-Islam wa-usul al-hukm)*, published in 1925, shortly after the abolition of the caliphate. Almost three generations later, his claims—that Muhammad was a prophet and not a statesman, that Islam is a religion and not a state, and that the caliphate was from the beginning based on force—still provoke outrage. For these authors there can be no doubt that Islam comprises faith, ethics, and law as it was set forth in the Qurʾan, exemplified by the life of the Prophet Muhammad and his Companions (the *sunna*), and later developed by Muslim theologians and jurists (the *ʿulamaʾ* and *fuqahaʾ*) into the *shariʿa*.

The vocal denunciation of secularism, however, does not imply that these authors make no distinction between the spheres of religion proper and of worldly affairs, between the eternal and the temporal. In fact, this very distinction is reflected in modern Islamic legal theory (*fiqh*) which distinguishes between the *ibadat* involving a person's relation with his or her creator (essentially the five pillars of Islam—the profession of faith, prayer, fasting, almsgiving, and the pilgrimage) and the *mu'amalat*, covering all other aspects of economic, political, and family life. While the *ibadat* are eternal and immutable, the *mu'amalat* can be adapted to the changing requirements of time and locality, provided the results conform to the word (*nass*) and spirit (*maqasid*) of the *shari'a*. What they envisage, then, are two different spheres of human life and activity: one revolving around faith and worship and the other around worldly affairs, both subject to the precepts of Islam. . . .

Shared Assumptions

At the core of much of contemporary writing are a number of shared assumptions: that all people are born equal, having been installed as God's viceregents on earth (*istikhlaf*); that government exists to ensure an Islamic life and enforce Islamic law; that sovereignty (*siyada, hakimiyya*) ultimately rests with God alone, who has made the law and defined good and evil (*al-ma'ruf wa'l-munkar*), the licit and the illicit (*al-halal wa'l- haram*); that the authority (*sulta*) to apply God's law has been transferred to the community as a whole, which is therefore the source of all powers (*asl al-sultat*); and that the head of the community or state, no matter whether he (and they specifically exclude women from that function) be called imam, caliph, or president, is the mere representative, agent, or employee of the community that elects, supervises, and, if necessary, deposes him, either directly or via its representatives.

This simplified scheme of government does not constitute a sharp break with classic Sunni doctrines which, in contrast to Shi'i positions, declared that the caliphate was based on the consensus of the Muslim community (*ijma'*), not on any preordained divine order. But compared even to the widely quoted treatises of Ibn Taymiyya (d. 1328), with their emphasis on the centrality of the *shari'a*, modern positions mark a definite shift of emphasis away from the person of the ruler and the duty of obedience and acquiescence for the sake of peace and order, even under unjust rule, to the authority of the community and the responsibility of every individual believer. This shift no doubt reflects the impact of modern political ideas as well as the decline and final abolition of the historical caliphate. What emerges as a core concern of modern Muslims is the desire to check and limit arbitrary personal rule and to replace it with the rule of law.

Gudrun Kramer, "Islamist Notions of Democracy," in *Political Islam: Essays from* Middle East Report, ed. Joel Beinin and Joe Stork (Berkeley: University of California Press, 1997), 71–72, 73, 75–76.

Adapting Democracy

Democracy is not just a political system; above all it is a social phenomenon that eventually translates into a political system. Any attempt to liberalize or democratize a political system without paying close attention to the economic and social (including religious) factors of the Arab societies is putting the cart before the horse. Democracy is an evolving concept that does not exist in a vacuum; rather it expresses certain social values and economic conditions. Democratizing the political system without changing the reality it reflects will sooner or later backfire. We ought, therefore, to ask: Can a democracy, be it the most primitive or the most advanced type, succeed when conditions of enormous economic disparity prevail, as is the case within and among the various Arab countries? Can the Arabs really have Western-style democracy as their model when threatened with territorial divisions and when facing growing Islamic resurgence, partly in reaction to this very same Western orientation?

When we talk about "Western leverage," we should not understand it as being exercised to impose a new political system on client states. The maximum we can hope for at this stage is a change in attitude on questions such as human rights and freedom of speech as the first step toward tipping the balance in favor of the individual, who is currently swallowed up in the state apparatus. Like democracy, human rights and freedom of speech are broad and relative concepts. Yet perhaps they are easier to begin with as they are less abstract and more narrowly defined than democracy; indeed, they are components of it and therefore can serve as a point of departure. In the words of Giovanni Sartori:

> New states and developing nations cannot pretend to start from the level of achievement at which the Western democracies have arrived. In fact, no democracy would ever have materialized if it had set for itself the advanced goals that a number of modernizing states currently claim to be pursuing. In a world-wide perspective, the problem

is to minimize arbitrary and tyrannical rule and to maximize a pattern of civility rooted in respect and justice for each man—in short, to achieve a humane polity. Undue haste and overly ambitious goals are likely to lead to opposite results.

In light of such wise words, it would seem the Arabs are far more cognizant than their Western patrons of the pitfalls that strew the path to democracy for developing nations. The debates raging in the Arab world today over democracy and other Western notions signify a wealth of independent intellectual energy and a pluralism of opinion that must be the envy of any democratic society. Such debate ensures that if and when the Arab countries, singly or in groups, commit themselves to supporting democratization within their borders, the type of democracy implemented will be peculiarly Arab and therefore appropriate to the Arab societies. The West can only do the citizens of the Arab world irreparable harm by hurrying the process along and cutting short the debates of the Arabs before they have fully explored all the nuances of this immensely complex issue and settled on a type of government that is right for them.

Shukri B. Abed, "Democracy and the Arab World," in *Democracy, Peace, and the Israeli-Palestinian Conflict,* ed. Edy Kaufman, Shukri B. Abed, and Robert L. Rothstein (Boulder: Lynne Rienner, 1993), 206–207.

Shariʿa and Democracy Are Irreconcilable

. . . [L]ike the other ideologies current in the Arab world, pan-Arabism or Baʿthism, Islamic fundamentalism, as it has come to be generally called, has to be hostile to constitutional and representative government. It will be recalled that the same majority polled by *al-Ahram* which declared in favor of democracy also declared in favor of a *Sharia*-governed society, even though those who were polled did not see that the desire for democracy and the desire for rule by *Sharia* are utterly incompatible and irreconcilable. In modern society, constitutional and representative government is predicated on a society in which differences of outlook and belief are taken for granted, along with the potential disagreements and conflicts which it is precisely the function of representative government to mediate and reconcile. Hence, the irresistible logic of representative government entails the secularity of the state. Fundamentalism can have no truck with the variety of beliefs and opinions which characterize modern society. Muslim society, however, not being isolated from modern currents of thoughts, will, sooner or later, to some extent or another, exhibit the same variety of belief and opinion. Fundamentalism desires, on the contrary, uniformity of belief and works to enforce the truth at whatever cost to oneself and to others which may prove necessary.

Elie Kedourie, *Democracy and Arab Political Culture* (London: Frank Cass, 1994), 95–96.

6

Islam Misunderstood

Arthur J. Arberry, the noted British Orientalist who was born in 1905, has left us an eloquent portrait of the sort of creature his fellow-Westerners took the Muslim-Arab to be in recent times. In an autobiographical sketch published in 1960, Arberry writes that the average Englishman or American of the mid-twentieth century drew his idea of the Arab first and foremost from the *Arabian Nights*, "which he has read carefully expurgated in childhood, pruriently purveyed in youth, extravagantly rehashed by Hollywood for his mature amusement." To be sure, he will have heard of the Qur'an, and perhaps come to know that it is the Arabs' Bible; "but it is most unlikely that he will ever have glanced into it—or if he has, he will have been repelled by the most widely circulated travesties which masquerade as translations of that sacred and poetical book." Of the vast literature of the Arabs, ancient and modern, the contemporary Englishman or American is totally unaware. "For him, . . . the life, the manners, the ideals, the dreams of the Arabs down the ages are all contained within the pages of the *Arabian Nights*."

Arberry wrote in anger, with some resentment perhaps. But he could hardly have exaggerated. Our Englishman or American, he went on, "may by chance have made the equation between Arab and Saracen, and therefore looks upon the Arabs as the people who fought the Crusaders in their noble mission to free the Holy Land, cruel and treacherous dogs worshipping a monstrous image called Bahophet and sworn to destroy all relics of Christianity in the land of its birth." His picture of the Arab of the twentieth century, again, may have been taken from the novels of Robert Hitchens or the films of Rudolf Valentino: "He is a Sheik who rides a fierce Arab steed and carries a sharp Arab dagger and captivates to their serious undoing inexperienced but infinitely romantic and beautiful white maidens. These probably end their days in a harem, in the disagreeable company of numerous fellow wives and concubines of an Arab prince of inexhaustible virility."

But there is a less frivolous, though in no sense less false, image of the Muslim Arab in the minds of Westerners. "[He] is believed to be either a wealthy pasha whose son went to Harrow and who is very decent company at a duckshoot or at cards, or a greedy and rather stupid official who is nevertheless mercifully amenable to a bribe, or a low-down ruffian who robs you in a bargain, or a poor devil existing in incredible squalor in a mud-hut. He is either the natural ally of the British for various ill-analysed reasons, or their natural enemy for reasons equally ill-analysed. He is a good sportsman with a fine gift of repartee and a fabulously generous host, or else he is completely unreliable and treacherous and, above all, thoroughly ungrateful." Nor does the female of the species fare any better. "Arab girls are bints, mysteriously appealing in youth but very quickly growing fat and ugly."[1]

It is this image of the Muslim—more particularly of the Muslim *Arab*—that the organizers of the World of Islam Festival sought to rectify. It is difficult to see how such a feat could have been performed merely by affording a unique opportunity for viewing and studying so many aspects of Islam as a religion and as a culture, mainly such art objects as rugs, ceramics, miniatures, metalwork, and calligraphy; architectural models and slides; music, drama and folklore. With the picture of the Arab prevalent in the West—which Arberry summed up as "a man who understands only two things: money and force"—far more seems to be needed. As Akbar Ahmed related in *Postmodernism and Islam,* late in the year 1990, at the height of the Gulf crisis, London's tabloids were "distorting anything on Islam, even a straightforward academic lecture on the subject." This was illustrated, he adds, by a lecture he gave at the Royal Anthropological Institute in London on September 13, 1990, arranged for the Princess of Wales. "The *Sun*'s headline averred that the Princess 'takes Islam books home after war lesson,' that she 'was swept up in the Gulf crisis' and given 'a lecture on holy war'." The *Daily Express*'s headline said: "I'm not Diana's guru says top academic." "For the record," writes Ahmed, "I had neither talked of a holy war, nor given a war lesson, nor claimed to be the guru of the Princess, nor indeed anyone. The *Sun* chided me with some petulance: 'newspapers were accused of "distorting" the religion that holds thousands of Britons hostage'. Islam was thus reduced to nothing more than a religion of hostage-takers in the reference to Saddam Hussein's detention of Western visitors in Iraq."[2]

At one point in the introduction to his *Islam and the State,* Vatikiotis remarks on the curious fact that a self-proclaimed, militant Islamic regime in Tehran had fought a typical war *as a nation-state* against another nation-state, Iraq. The deadly war, fought over a territorial dispute, developed into a Sunni-versus-Shi'ite sectarian conflict and into an Arab-versus-Persian ethnic one. "It has given rise to other manifestations of disarray in the *umma*," he writes, "especially in the ranks of the Arab states. . . . The Islamic rationalization of it is the objective of overthrowing a 'heretical, infidel, deviant, usurping, tyrannical regime' in Baghdad for the greater glory of Islam."[3]

Two Iranian scholars, both professors of economics at the American University in Paris, have produced an excellent and detailed account of the 1978–79 Islamic revolution which swept Iran and disposed of its shah with such apparent ease and swiftness that everyone was taken by surprise, not excluding some of the best intelligence agencies in the world. In writing their book *The Secular Miracle,* Ali Rahnema and Farhad Nomani have of course the great advantage of being native Iranians as well as close observers of the Iranian scene—and in their book they use their knowledge of the country and the language to great advantage.

The central theme of *The Secular Miracle* is closely if somewhat indirectly related to the subject of Islam's predicament in the modern world. The "secular miracle" of the title has to do with the transformation the authors perceive the Islamic Revolution to have undergone in the first ten years of the regime—up to Iran's defeat in its war with Iraq and the death shortly afterward of Ayatollah Khomeini. The "transformation," the authors maintain, had started rather early in the proceedings, when Khomeini, while applying terror against those who questioned his leadership, tolerated dissent among those who publicly announced their allegiance to his leadership.

This state of affairs resulted in the clerical leadership falling prey to a great deal of vacillation, pragmatism, and backpedaling—so much so that its foremost aim, the creation of the New Islamic Man, became well-nigh impossible to attain. What compounded matters further was that Khomeini himself, confronted by at least four factions or schools of thought *within his own camp,* refused to identify with any of them, so that, when things went wrong, he was able in turn to blame any one of the factions for the failure.

Basically, argue Rahnema and Nomani, what will make the secular miracle increasingly real are the pressures brought to bear on the regime in the postwar, post-Khomeini era, especially in the economic sphere. Wondering whether "the fragile Islamic system of values and life-style now in place will stand the pressure of billions of dollars which will flow through the economy in times of peace," the authors venture the thought that the new social relations permeating the areas and sectors in which the money will be spent "will necessitate a cultural and value system different from that which the Islamic Republic has sought to impose." Their answer to this question is clear enough. Postwar prosperity, they suggest, may breed consumerism, idleness, moral laxity, and a love of leisure, and the Iranian bourgeoisie may demand "a value system compatible with that of their international counterparts."

The clerics' dilemma here is a ponderous one—and it has a direct bearing on the broader subject of the dilemmas which contemporary Muslims face in trying to catch up with modernity and the modern world. To quote the authors of *The Secular Miracle,* "Should the clerical leadership become pragmatic enough to allow the re-emergence of a non-Muslim value system, while maintaining the 'Islamic Order' as the basis for their own power, a coalition of democratic social forces may well dethrone them and impose the sovereignty of the people—the as yet unfulfilled objective of the Iranian revolution."[4]

In many ways, the fundamentalist wave which the world is now witnessing—and not only among Muslims—can be described as "a last-ditch stand." If the appraisal offered by Rahnema and Nomani is valid, the present state of the Muslim fundamentalists in Iran offers a classic example of the phenomenon.

A novel view of the subject of Islamic fundamentalism comes from a somewhat unexpected source. Habib Boularès is a former Tunisian minister of culture who now lives and works in Paris as a university lecturer and journalist. In *Islam: The Fear and the Hope,* he is concerned with one crucial aspect of Muslim fundamentalism—or Islamism, as he calls it in this book—namely the degree to which its rise has occasioned an assault on traditional Islamic moral values.

In Boularès's opinion, the Islamic faith itself, though the fundamentalists claim they represent it in its most pristine form, need not inspire fear. Admitting that, today, "Islam is very frightening," he cites the case of an Orientalist of renown, a man "who has devoted his life to making Islamic civilization comprehensible to the European public," who once told him: "Do not speak to me any more of Islam. I see in Islam a daily tragedy. Each time I begin to explain to my students the human import of this religion, I give the impression of nonsense."

In his own way, Boularès comments, his Orientalist friend "was describing the trauma lived by millions of Muslims." After giving a brief comparative picture of Islamic fundamentalism in Egypt, Syria, Jordan, Iran, and other Muslim countries, he examines in a chapter entitled "The Many Paths of Reformism" the difficulties confronted by Muslim reformers and modernists in some of these countries, covering movements like Kemalism in Turkey, the reformism of Afghani and ʿAbduh in late-nineteenth-century Egypt, and others. He also takes notice of the difficult issue of the position of women in Islam, Islam's attitude to science, and the subject of religion and state in Islam.

Boularès concludes on a fairly optimistic note. "Islam," he writes toward the end of his analysis, "can make a new start, thanks to a return to the Quran that should go hand in hand with an understanding of the text according to the needs of the present century." Earlier in the book, he asserts that "the only path that will not end in disaster is for Muslims to readapt their religion to present circumstances."[5]

One could hardly agree with this more. The problem, however, is that attempts at such readapting have been made with impressive regularity for more than a century now—so far with no noticeable success. In fact, the rise of a fundamentalist wave in contemporary Islam offers an eloquent proof of the failure of these attempts.

Mutual Misconceptions

The way in which the West and Islam perceive each other brims with mutual misconceptions. Akbar Ahmed quotes recent opinion polls in the West that confirm the impression that Islam is seen as "the major 'next' enemy after communism." The general Muslim response to the West, on the other side, "confirms the impression that it is widely perceived as attempting to dominate and subvert Muslim societies through economic and cultural power." The result, adds Ahmed, is that Muslims "fall back on and reinforce their own identity." Of course there is no such thing as a monolithic West; there are hostile, indifferent and even friendly individuals who people it. "But, just as there has grown a media stereotype of Muslims in the West so there is a Western stereotype in Muslim minds. In particular, America, the powerful dynamo of the contemporary dominant world culture, repels as it fascinates Muslims. For some it is Utopia, which has attracted about 5 million Muslims; for others it is the embodiment of evil, indeed the Great Satan."[6]

The derision of and antipathy towards Islam in the Western media cannot be blamed on the media alone. Many factors mingle, juxtapose and fuse. Some are rooted in history, others are contemporary: blame for the oil crisis, atavistic memory of the Crusades, anti-Semitism (Muslims now take the place of Jews as alien, repugnant orientals), plain Western jingoism, the collapse of the communist states and the revival of the Christian heritage, the ire of those who dislike the holier-than-thou attitude of Muslims and the incapacity of Muslims to explain themselves effectively, have all helped to focus on Islam as the new enemy of the West. . . . In the face of this mutual hostility, especially the unsavoury and terrible onslaught of negative media images, the prognosis for the coming years is of culture clash and political tension. The pattern of the relationship between Muslims and non-Muslims appears to be forming. The more we are interlocked with each other, in our times, through technology, the more intolerant of and distant from each other we become. Instant, atavistic responses create instant misunderstandings.[7]

Edward Said, in what has become something of a standard work on the subject, presents a more sophisticated case against Western Orientalists. Quoting Duncan MacDonald's assertion that "*inability* . . . to see life steadily, and see it whole, to understand that a theory of life must cover all the facts, and *liability* to be stampeded by a single idea and blinded to everything else [are what constitutes] the difference between the East and the West," Said finds in it nothing especially new:

From Schlegel to Renan, from Robertson Smith to T. E. Lawrence, these ideas get repeated and re-repeated. They represent a decision about the Orient, not by any means a fact of nature. Anyone who, like MacDonald and Gibb, consciously entered a profession called Orientalism did so on the basis of a decision made: that the Orient was the Orient, that it was different, and so forth. The elaborations, refinements, consequent articulations of the field therefore sustain and prolong the decision to confine the Orient. There is no perceivable irony in MacDonald's (or Gibb's) views about Oriental liability to be stampeded by a single idea; neither man seems able to recognize the extent of *Orientalism*'s liability to be stampeded by the single idea of Oriental difference. And neither man is concerned by such wholesale designations as "Islam" or "the Orient" being used as proper nouns, with adjectives attached and verbs streaming forth, as if they referred to persons and not to Platonic ideas.[8]

Citing Gibb's works as samples, Said speaks of

the now traditional Orientalist ability to reconstruct and reformulate the Orient, given the Orient's inability to do so for itself. In part Gibb's Islam exists *ahead* of Islam as it is practiced, studied, or preached in the Orient. Yet this prospective Islam is no mere Orientalist fiction, spun out of his ideas: it is based on an "Islam" that—since it cannot truly exist—*appeals* to a whole community of believers. The reason that "Islam" can exist in some more or less future Orientalist formulation of it is that in the Orient Islam is usurped and traduced by the language of its clergy, whose claim is upon the community's mind. So long as it is silent in its appeal, Islam is safe; the moment the reforming clergy takes on its (legitimate) role of reformulating Islam in order for it to be able to enter modernity, the trouble starts. And that trouble, of course, is dislocation.[9]

From the beginning of Western speculation about the Orient, Said concludes, "the one thing the Orient could not do was to represent itself. Evidence of the Orient was credible only after it had passed through and been made firm by the refining fire of the Orientalist's work."[10]

One of the topics about which Islam can justly be said by its defenders as having been misunderstood is that of its alleged affinity to communism. Apart from Arab political thinkers of the Nasserist era who argued that there was no real conflict between the teachings of Islam and Marxist socialism, a number of Western students of Arabic Islam held similar though by no means equally explicit appraisals. Concluding a well-argued essay published in 1958—to give one example—Bernard Lewis writes: "The political experience and traditions of Islam, though very different from those of eastern Europe, do nevertheless contain elements which might, in certain circumstances, prepare the way for Communism."[11]

This was written at a time when Nasser's Arab Socialism was the order of the day in Egypt and when intellectuals of the left in the Arab world were trying very hard to convince their Muslim audiences that there was no conflict between their religious beliefs and practices on the one hand and Arab socialism on the other.

The fact, however, is that, while Islam's basic opposition to Marxist ideas continued to be extremely strong, relations between the Muslim world and communism passed through considerable changes between the 1920s and 1980s. In the early 1920s, a number of Egyptian nationalists began to show some interest in communism and a certain flirtation started between Lenin and leaders of the Egyptian National Party. In an attempt to counter this, a number of public-spirited Egyptian citizens—later alleged to have been none other than "the British occupation authorities" in disguise—sent a query to the grand mufti of Egypt. "What is your opinion, may your bounty be everlasting," the rather loaded query started, "of a doctrine called Bolshevism which permits a man to cohabit with his mother or sister?" The mufti's *fatwa* came promptly: "If the situation is as [stated in] the question, then the doctrine is utterly anathema."

Despite the passage of some fifty years, and although many dozens of volumes have been written propounding an opposite thesis, this stand of the Muslim religious establishment did not change. A book published in Cairo in 1975 by Mustafa Mahmud, an observant though thoroughly modernized Muslim scholar, is worth mentioning here. The book, *Al-Marksiyya wal-Islam* (Marxism and Islam) appeared at a time when the subject of socialism and Marxism became part of the controversy over the question of Nasser and Nasserism, and what many observers perceived as a systematic campaign aimed at discrediting the late Egyptian leader's legacy. "De-Nasserization," as it was commonly called, was often aided and reinforced by ostensibly purely theoretical debates on Marxism and communism. This was usually done through a device bordering on sheer sophistry: Nasserism's main socioeconomic doctrine was Arab Socialism; Arab Socialism was once described by Nasser as "scientific socialism"; in Marxist terminology, "scientific socialism" is just another name for Marxism and, by inference, communism!

Parallel to his harsh critique of Marxism, Mahmud gives a rather idealized view of Islam as a code of conduct and a way of life, arguing that it embodies most of the progressive, forward-looking ideas of our own day. These include equality of opportunity, social security, freedom from hunger, a delicate balance between individual liberty and the requirements of public order, private ownership, and public ownership, state interference in the economy, and so on. In fact, he argues, Islam combines the best in both capitalism and socialism and safeguards the interests both of the individual and of society.[12]

Christendom and Islam Compared

A far more balanced assessment of the subject of modern Islam and the way it has been treated by its various students comes from the pen of Bernard Lewis—a renowned Orientalist who, it is worth mentioning here, is one of those who feature in Said's dock. In an article written in 1997, Lewis draws a highly instructive analogy. Christendom and Islam, he writes, both claimed a universal mission, "but the Islamic oecumene extending over large parts of Asia, Africa, and Europe was the first to create a civilization that was multiracial, multicultural, in a sense intercontinental." Islamic civilization, he explains, extended far beyond the utmost limits of Roman and Hellenistic culture, and was thus able to borrow, adapt, and incorporate significant elements from the remoter civilizations of Asia. To these, Middle Easterners added their own rich contribution, which helped to form the nascent civilization of the West. "A late medieval Indian, African, or European might well have asked—is modernity Islamic?"

Lewis then proceeds to offer a few examples which he says may suffice to show they would have asked with good reason. "Experimental science, Westerners like to persuade themselves, is peculiarly and exclusively Western. In fact, it was developed in medieval Islam much more than in the ancient world. The Greek genius lay in theory and philosophy. The Muslims developed experimental science and bequeathed a rich legacy which helped to start the modernization of the West."

> Nowadays, we Westerners claim diversity as a characteristic merit of our Western societies. This is a fairly recent development, as Western societies for most of their history were totally intolerant of diversity. The Islamic societies of the Middle East, on the other hand, were enormously diverse, and people of different religions, races, and ways of life developed the capacity to live side by side, I will not say in full equality, but in reasonable, mutual tolerance. That has changed for the worse in the Middle East, as the strains grew greater and the opportunities fewer. It is much more difficult to be tolerant when you are under threat than when you feel yourself to be on top of the world. Meanwhile, in the Western world, tolerance of diversity has increased markedly.[13]

A fitting footnote to this interesting comparative appraisal is provided by a passage from Muhammad Iqbal, a Muslim philosopher who is himself accused of having been influenced by European ideas. As quoted by Ahmed, Iqbal, comparing Greek thought to the Qur'an—and finding the former wanting—wrote:

> As we all know, Greek philosophy has been a great cultural force in the history of Islam. Yet a careful study of the Quran and the various schools of scholastic theology that arose under the inspiration of Greek thought disclose the remarkable fact that while Greek philosophy very much broadened the outlook of Muslim thinkers, it, on the whole,

obscured their vision of the Quran. Socrates concentrated his attention on the human world alone. To him the proper study of man was man and not the world of plants, insects, and stars. How unlike the spirit of the Quran, which sees in the humble bee a recipient of Divine inspiration and constantly calls upon the reader to observe the perpetual change of the winds, the alternation of the day and night, the clouds, the starry heavens, and the planets swimming through infinite space.[14]

In the concluding part of *The Islamic Threat,* Esposito poses the question: Is there an Islamic threat? While he admits that, "in one sense," the answer is in the affirmative, Esposito in fact argues that Islam today and its various revivalist movements pose a challenge rather than a threat—"a challenge to the established order of things, to the presuppositions that have guided many governments and policymakers."

The ways in which this challenge manifests itself are briefly but effectively reviewed by Esposito. The political strength and durability of Islamic movements and their ideological impact are reflected in a variety of ways, he writes. "They have forced government changes and, where permitted, have successfully contested elections. Rulers from Morocco to Malaysia have become more Islamically sensitive and sought to coopt religion or suppress Islamic organizations. Many have employed Islamic rhetoric and symbols more often, expanded support for Islamic mosques and schools, increased religious programming in the media, and become more attentive to public religious observances such as the fast of Ramadan or restrictions on alcohol and gambling."

When free from government repression, moreover, "Islamic candidates and organizations have worked within the political system and participated in elections in Algeria, Tunisia, Turkey, Jordan, the Sudan, Egypt, Kuwait, Pakistan, and Malaysia; activists have even held cabinet-level positions in the Sudan, Pakistan, Jordan and Malaysia." In countries such as Algeria, Tunisia, Egypt, Jordan, and Pakistan, too, Islamic organizations have been "among the best-organized opposition forces, and are often willing to form alliances or cooperate with political parties, professional syndicates, and voluntary associations to achieve shared political and socioeconomic reforms. Islamic student organizations successfully compete in student elections in the universities and lead student strikes and demonstrations."[15]

Summing up his central thesis, Esposito speaks of two types of Muslim revivalist. For many Muslims, he writes, revivalism is "a social rather than

a political movement whose goal is a more Islamically minded and oriented society, but not necessarily the creation of an Islamic state." For others, however, the establishment of an Islamic order requires the creation of
an Islamic state. "In either case, Islam and most Islamic movements are not
necessarily anti-Western, anti-American, or anti-democratic," Esposito explains. "While they are a challenge to the outdated assumptions of the
established order and to autocratic regimes, they do not necessarily threaten
American interests. Our challenge is to better understand the history and
realities of the Muslim world."[16]

Quoting the Qur'anic edict, "Let there be no compulsion in religion,"
Muhammad Mohaddessin draws our attention to what he considers the
profound antagonism between the two opposing interpretations of Islamic
ideology and the message of revelation—"a conflict," he adds, "which has
persisted for fourteen centuries, since the founding of the Islamic community in the 7th century by Prophet Muhammad."

On one side is the dogmatic outlook, "which is unable to comprehend
the true essence of the teachings of the Quran and the Prophet of Islam, i.e.
mercy, liberty, and guidance of the individual and society toward moral
and material evolution. . . ." On the other, those Muslims "who followed
Muhammad's genuine message of mercy and liberty from the Quran, rejecting dogmatism and fanaticism despite threats of excommunication or
charges of heresy." This ideological clash has persisted to varying degrees
within all Islamic communities. "Conflicting ideological interpretations are
common to all religions. With Islam, however, the issues have immediate
political overtones more volatile than theoretical discussions or academic
disputes. The conflicts may last for centuries, because Islam's distinctive
characteristic is a model of life, not just of worship. Hence, differing interpretations of the teachings of Islam directly and immediately translate into
political conflicts."

Mohaddessin concludes:

> A closer look at this linkage of politics and religious sentiments of the
> Muslim masses is essential to understanding how religious demagogues
> and fundamentalists—chief among them Khomeini—have exploited
> this bond to usurp power, and why Marxism, nationalism, and liber-
> alism (especially in their antireligious form) have failed to serve as an
> alternative to the religious forces in the Islamic world. The only alter-
> native capable of countering fundamentalism is modern, democratic
> Islam, which opposes the union of church and state, for both political
> and religious reasons.[17]

Readings

Self-Image

The Koran says: "We have made you a people in the middle." This, al-Baidawi (d. 1282) explains, is to say that the Muslims are fair-minded and purified in thought and action. They will strike the golden means between avarice and profligacy, temerity and cowardice, etc. Their character being as it is, the koranic line implies that their *ijma*ᶜ is authoritative, for, were they to agree on something vain, it would reflect upon their sense of balance. More conclusive is the second part of the koranic verse where it is stated that this was done to make them witnesses in regard to the people. Elsewhere the Book assails the separatist. "But him who splits from the messenger after the Guidance has become clear to him, and follows any other way than that of the believers, We shall consign to what he has turned to, and roast in Gehenna—a bad place to go to!"

By asserting that "never will my community be united in an error," the Prophet eliminated the uneasiness that the consensus might, on occasion, be misguided and thence misguiding. In the beginning the consensus of the Companions was considered authoritative. Malik thought the consensus of the holy places, Mecca and Medina, decisive. Gradually *ijma*ᶜ came to be interpreted as the agreement of those competent to judge in religious matters; it became the agreement of the learned. There being no organization of the learned, it is not possible to poll them and to obtain a decision on a moot question.

The *ijma*ᶜ, then, cannot be determined by resolutions of any kind regarding future settlement of this or the other problem. It rather is to be determined by retrospection. At any given moment one is in a position to realize that such and such opinions, such and such institutions, have become accepted through *ijma*ᶜ. Deviation from the *ijma*ᶜ is unbelief, *kufr*.

The doctrinal area covered by decision of *ijma*ᶜ—these decisions may be expressed in statements, actions, or silence—constantly widens as the scope of what is left to its decision steadily narrows. The questions to be settled by future *ijma*ᶜ will tend to become ever more minute and insignificant. This natural development diminishes considerably the potentialities of *ijma*ᶜ in reforming Islam. It may, of course, develop that, at some future time, the agreement will lend the *ijma*ᶜ wider scope so as to allow it to sanction far-reaching changes concerning validity and content of the *fiqh*.

The consensus has, in former times, compelled the admission of the cult of the saints as well as that of the infallibility, *ᶜisma*, of the Prophet, in both cases disregarding koranic statements and the early *sunna*. Thus, the *ijma^c* could, for instance, by shifting its stand on *ijtihad*, remove one of the main obstacles to the modernization of the Islamic structure. A tradition of the Prophet has it that he who applies himself to form his own opinion through his personal exertion (*mujtahid*) will receive a reward even though he reach the wrong conclusion. The fallible *ijtihad* of the individual would always be corrected by the inerrant *ijma^c* of the community. However, the view has been held, and sanctioned by *ijma^c*, that with the passing of the founders of the great law schools the *ijtihad mutlaq*, the absolute, i.e., unrestricted *ijtihad*, had disappeared. Their successors were entitled to *ijtihad* only within the framework of their respective schools, and the subsequent generations of jurisconsults possess an even more reduced authority in that they may answer specific legal questions on the basis of their knowledge of precedent. This commonly accepted theory was, from time to time, contested by theologians who claimed farther-reaching rights of *ijtihad* for themselves. The *ijma^c* has, so far, sided against their claim. But a reversal of popular sentiment could and would reopen the "door of personal exertion" and thereby possibly pave the way for a thorough overhauling of the *shari^ca*.

Gustave E. von Grunebaum, *Medieval Islam* (Chicago: University of Chicago Press, 1961), 150–151.

European Misconceptions

Christians could not distinguish between God speaking (in the Qur'an) and Muhammad speaking (as reported in the Lives of him and in the Traditions). They would not even distinguish in purely Christian terms between Muhammad speaking *in propria persona* in the Traditions and *in persona Dei* in the Qur'an. It is very remarkable that Europeans who knew enough to distinguish between Qur'an and Traditions and other sources of information about Muhammad, more or less authentic, very generally failed to do so. They always argued "Muhammad said . . . " when, in conversation with Muslims, it would surely have been more effective to say "You believe that God said. . . ." It would certainly have been more courteous. Thus Oliver of Paderborn used the phrase, "Muhammad says in his Qur'an," when he was supposed to be writing a friendly and encouraging letter to the Ayyubid Sultan in Cairo. Peter the Venerable thought to disprove the truth of a prophecy, attributed to Muhammad in a weak tradition, by the supposed assertion of the Qur'an that what did not conform to it was untrue; but he did so, not on the ground that the

Qurɔan claimed to be revealed, but on the grounds that it was most authentically Muhammad's. . . .

The failure to distinguish between the authority of the Qurɔan, of the Prophet's reported utterances, and of the Arabic commentators, may have been deliberate, intended to make it clear that all three were equally human artifacts; but, if so, this makes it impossible for us to tell now whether the Islamic attitude was clearly understood.

On the other hand it is at least certain that the Qurɔan was very widely understood to be without equal in the eyes of Muslims. Writers who spoke of parts of the Qurɔan as sent by God might also speak, at another time, as though they knew that the whole was claimed to have been revealed. Peter the Venerable did so when he said, "your law, which you are wont to boast was sent from heaven." Again, in his phrase, *falsum est ergo oraculum tuum,* he seemed to stress the divine claim which he had "proved" to be false. The phrase was borrowed by William of Auvergne, to use less ambiguously: ". . . the Muslim people holds and adores those lunacies which we read in its Laws, as divine oracles sent to it through the Prophet of God; and obeys them as commands of God."

N. A. Daniel, *Islam and the West: The Making of an Image* (Edinburgh: University Press, 1958), 36–37.

Terminology and Precedent

. . . many sociopolitical terms which play a genuine—that is, historically warranted—role in Western thought . . . are extremely equivocal with reference to Islamic ideology. One could, for example, assert (as some modern Muslim writers do) that Islam is "socialistic" in its tendencies because it aims at a state of affairs which would ensure to all citizens equality of opportunity, economic security, and an equitable distribution of national wealth; however, one could maintain with the same degree of assurance that Islam is opposed to socialism if it is taken to imply (as Marxian socialism undoubtedly does) a rigid regimentation of all social life, the supremacy of economics over ethics, and the reduction of the individual to the status of a mere economic factor. Even the question as to whether Islam aims at "theocracy" cannot be answered with a simple "yes" or "no." We might say "yes" if by theocracy we mean a social system in which all temporal legislation flows, in the last resort, from what the community considers to be a Divine Law. But the answer must be an emphatic "no" if one identifies theocracy with the endeavor—so well known from the history of medieval

Europe—to invest a priestly hierarchy with supreme political power: for the simple reason that in Islam there is no priesthood or clergy and, consequently, no institution equivalent to the Christian Church (that is, in an organized body of doctrine and sacramental functions). Since every adult Muslim has the right to perform each and every religious function, no person or group can legitimately claim to possess any special sanctity by virtue of the religious functions entrusted to them. Thus, the term "theocracy" as commonly understood in the West is entirely meaningless within the Islamic environment.

In brief, it is extremely misleading to apply non-Islamic terms to Islamic concepts and institutions. The ideology of Islam has a social orientation peculiar to itself, different in many respects from that of the modern West, and can be successfully interpreted only within its own context and in its own terminology. Any departure from this principle invariably tends to obscure the attitude of Islamic Law toward many of the burning issues of our time. The application of non-Islamic terminologies to Islamic concepts of state and government is . . . not the only pitfall in the way of a student of Islamic political law. Perhaps an even greater danger is the reliance of so many Muslims on "historical precedents" as possible guides for our future development. . . .

If we examine objectively the political ordinances of Qur³an and Sunnah, we find that they do not lay down any *specific* form of state: that is to say, the *shari͗ah* does not prescribe any definite pattern to which an Islamic state must conform, nor does it elaborate in detail a constitutional theory. The political law emerging from the contest of Qur³an and Sunnah is, nevertheless, not an illusion. It is very vivid and concrete inasmuch as it gives us the clear outline of a political scheme capable of realization at all times and under all conditions of human life. But precisely because it was meant to be realized at all times and under all conditions, that scheme has been offered in outline only and not in detail. Man's political, social, and economic needs are time-bound and, therefore, extremely variable. Rigidly fixed enactments and institutions could not possibly do justice to this natural trend toward variation; and so the shari͗ah does not attempt the impossible. Being a Divine Ordinance, it duly anticipates the fact of historical evolution, and confronts the believer with no more than a very limited number of broad political principles; beyond that, it leaves a vast field of constitution-making activity, of governmental methods, and of day-to-day legislation to the *ijtihad* of the time concerned.

With reference to the problem before us, one may safely say that there is not only one form of the Islamic state, but many; and it is for the Muslims of every period to discover the form most suitable to their needs—on the condition, of course, that the form and the institutions they choose are in full agreement with the explicit, unequivocal *shari'ah* laws relating to communal life.

Muhammad Asad, *The Principles of State and Government in Islam* (Berkeley: University of California Press, 1961), 21–23.

The Myth of Monolithic Islam

Monolithic Islam has been a recurrent Western myth which has never been borne out by the reality of Muslim history. When convenient, Western commentators waste little time on the divisions and fratricidal relations of the Arab and Muslim world so as to underscore its intractable instability. Sen. Albert Gore, speaking of Syrian-Iraqi relations, noted; "Baathite Syrians are Alawites, a Shiite heresy, while the Iraqis are Sunnis. Reason enough in this part of the world for hatred and murder." Yet when equally convenient, Islam, the Arabs, and the Muslim world are represented as a unified bloc poised against the West. However much the ideals of Arab nationalism or Islam speak of the unity and identity of a transnational community, history has proven otherwise. At best, some Muslims, as in the Iranian Revolution, have achieved a transient unity in face of a common threat, a solidarity which dissipates as easily as it was formed, once the danger has subsided and competing interests again prevail. The inability of Arab nationalism, Arab socialism, Iran's Islamic Republic, or Muslim opposition to the Soviet Union's invasion of Afghanistan to produce a transnational or regional unity, as well as the disintegration of the Arab coalition (Iraq and the Gulf states) against Iran after the Iran-Iraq war, are but several modern examples. As James Piscatori has observed, "The problem with assuming a unified response is that it conceals the reality of . . . entrenched national differences and national interests among Muslims."

Diversity rather than Pan-Islamic political unity is also reflected in foreign policy. The common "Islamic" orientation or claim of some governments reveals little unity of purpose in interstate and international relations because of conflicting national interests or priorities. Qaddafi was a bitter enemy of Sadat and Nimeiri at the very time when all three were projecting an "Islamic" image. Khomeini's Islamic Iran consistently called for the overthrow of the house of Saud on Islamic grounds, their rivalry even erupting during the annual pilgrimage to Mecca. Islamically identified governments also reflect differing relationships with the West. While Libya and Iran's relationship with the West, and with the United States in particular, has often been confrontational at the same time, the United States has had strong allies in Saudi Arabia, Egypt, Kuwait, Pakistan, and Bahrain. National interest and regional politics rather than ideology or religion remain the major determinants in the formulation of foreign policy. . . .

Islam and Democracy

Many argue that Islamic values and democratic values are inherently antithetical, as seen in the inequality of believers and unbelievers as well as of men and women.

History has shown that nations and religious traditions are capable of having multiple and major ideological interpretations or reorientations. The transformation of European principalities, whose rule was often justified in terms of divine right, into modern Western democratic states was accompanied by a process of reinterpretation or reform. The Judaeo-Christian tradition, while once supportive of political absolutism, was reinterpreted to accommodate the democratic ideal. Islam also lends itself to multiple interpretations; it has been used to support democracy and dictatorship, republicanism and monarchy. The twentieth century has witnessed both tendencies. . . .

Democracy has become an integral part of modern Islamic political thought and practice. It has become accepted in many Muslim countries as a litmus test by which both the openness of governments and the relevance of Islamic groups are certified. It is a powerful symbol of legitimacy, legitimizing and delegitimizing precisely because it is seen to be a universal good. However, questions as to the specific nature and degree of popular participation remain unanswered. In the new Muslim world order, Muslim political traditions and institutions, like social conditions and class structures, continue to evolve and are critical to the future of democracy in the Middle East.

A major issue facing Islamic movements is their ability, if in power, to tolerate diversity. The status of minorities in Muslim-majority areas and freedom of speech remain serious issues. The record of Islamic experiments in Pakistan, Iran, and the Sudan raises serious questions about the rights of women and minorities under Islamically oriented governments. The extent to which the growth of Islamic revivalism has been accompanied in some countries by attempts to restrict women's rights, to enforce the separation of women and men in public, to require veiling, and to restrict their public roles in society strikes fear in some segments of Muslim society and challenges the credibility of those who call for Islamization of state and society. The record of discrimination against the Bahai in Iran and the Ahmadi in Pakistan as "deviant" groups (heretical offshoots of Islam), against Christians in the Sudan, and Arab Jews in some countries, as well as increased sectarian conflict between Muslims and Christians in Egypt and Nigeria, pose similar questions of religious pluralism and tolerance.

If many Muslims ignore these issues or facilely talk of tolerance and human rights in Islam, discussion of these questions in the West is often reduced to two contrasting blocs; the West which preaches and practices freedom and tolerance, and the Muslim world which does not. Muslim attitudes toward Christian minorities and the case of Salman Rushdie are marshaled to support the indictment that Islam is intolerant and antidemocratic.

John L. Esposito, *The Islamic Threat: Myth or Reality?* (New York: Oxford University Press, 1992), 183–184, 186–188.

Anger, Powerlessness, Confrontation

In recent decades Muslim cities have been captured (Jerusalem), Muslim states have been divided (Pakistan) and invaded by foreign forces (Afghanistan) and have disappeared altogether (Kuwait—in this case to reappear a few months later). Muslim struggle and sacrifice pass almost unnoticed in the world media (on the West Bank, in Kashmir and in Central Asia). But the villain in the drama is not necessarily a non-Muslim. . . .

In this period many Muslim leaders, heads of government, right across the Muslim world, have met a violent end by shooting (Sadat, Faisal, Mujib, and, starting with Daud, too many to name in Afghanistan). They have been hanged (Bhutto) or even blown up in the air (Zia). What Muslims have done to their leaders is more than matched by what the leaders did to their Muslim followers. . . .

Furthermore, large proportions of the unprecedented wealth from oil revenues have been squandered on an unprecedented scale, in an unprecedented style. Call-girls in London and casinos in the south of France, ranches in the United States and chalets in Switzerland diverted money which could have gone into health-care provision, education and the closing of the vast gaps between the rich and poor. Oil money created an arrogance among some Muslims who have cherished a sense of special destiny around their family or clan. These antics provided legitimate ammunition for the Western satirists wishing to lampoon Muslims; they became the caricature of a civilization. Ordinary Muslims, therefore, have good cause to complain.

The main Muslim responses appear to be chauvinism and withdrawal; this is both dangerous and doomed. The self-imposed isolation, the deliberate retreat, is culturally determined. It is not Islamic in spirit or content. Muslims who are isolated and self-centered sense triumph in their aggressive assertion of faith. . . .

Because orthodox Muslims claim that Islam is an all-pervasive, all-embracing system, this affects the way in which Muslim writers and academics think. The increasing stridency in their tone is thus linked to the larger Muslim sense of anger and powerlessness. They advocate confrontation and violence, an eye for an eye, a tooth for a tooth; this attitude confirms the stereotypes of Muslims in the West. They argue that moderation has failed and that extremism will draw attention to their problems. Perhaps in the atmosphere of violence and blind hatred, of injustice and inequality, they have a certain logic in their position. At least they will be heard. They will force Muslim problems onto the agenda where more sober voices have failed and because we live in an interconnected world, no country can isolate itself from—or immunise itself against—Muslim wrath. Nevertheless, violence and cruelty are not in the spirit of the Quran, nor are they found in the life of the Prophet, nor in the lives of saintly Muslims.

Locating the Essence of Islam

The Muslim voices of learning and balance—whether in politics or among academics—are being drowned by those advocating violence and hatred. Two vital questions arise with wide-ranging, short-and long-term implications: in the short term, has one of the world's greatest civilizations lost its ability to deal with problems except through violent force? In the long term, would Muslims replace the central Quranic concepts of *adl* and *ahsan*, balance and compassion, of *ilm*, knowledge, and *sabr*, patience, with the bullet and the bomb?

Balance is essential to Islam and never more so than in society; and the crucial balance is between *din* (religion), and *dunya* (world); it is a balance, not a separation, between the two. The Muslim lives in the now, in the real world, but within the frame of his religion, with a mind to the future afterlife. So, whether he is a business man, an academic or a politician, he must not forget the moral laws of Islam. In the postmodern world *dunya* is upsetting the balance, invading and appropriating *din*.

Islam is essentially the religion of equilibrium and tolerance; suggesting and encouraging breadth of vision, global positions and the fulfilment of human destiny in the universe. Yet the non-Muslim media, by their consistently hammer-headed onslaught, have succeeded in portraying a negative image of it. They may even succeed in changing Muslim character. Muslims, because of their gut response to the attack—both vehement and vitriolic—are failing to maintain the essential features of Islam. Muslim leaders have pushed themselves into a hole dug by themselves in viewing the present upsurge simplistically as a confrontation with the West. They are in danger of rejecting features central to Islam—such as love of knowledge, egalitarianism, tolerance—because they are visibly associated with the West. In locating anti-Islamic animosity firmly in the West they also implicitly reject the universalism of human nature. But Allah is everywhere. The universal nature of humanity is the main topos in the Quran. God's purview and compassion take in everyone, "all creatures." The world is not divided into an East and a West: "To Allah belong the East and the West: whithersoever Ye turn, there is Allah's countenance" (Surah 2:115). Again and again God points to the wonders of creation, the diversity of races and languages in the world. Such a God cannot be parochial or xenophobic. Neither can a religion which acknowledges the wisdom and piety of over 124,000 "prophets" in its folklore be isolationist or intolerant. With its references to the "heavens" above, the Quran encourages us to lift up our heads and look beyond our planet, to the stars. . . . Islam has always shown the capacity to emerge in unexpected places and in unexpected times. The true understanding of Islam will therefore be critical in the coming years—and not only for Muslims.

Akbar S. Ahmed, *Postmodernism and Islam: Predicament and Promise* (London: Routledge, 1992), 46–49.

The Cultural Content

. . . Once again, we are faced with similarly structured arguments about the essential cultural content of Islam, its incompatibility with modernity and hence the failure of the modern nation-state to strike roots in the Middle East. In the contemporary context, this argument comes in two rather different forms. In the first place, a number of writers conform to the culturalist style of analysis. . . . Thus Fouad Ajami writes of *The Arab Predicament* in the following terms: the Arab world is a "defeated civilization," which because of Islam is "stubbornly impermeable to any democratic stirrings." Viewed in this way, 1967 represents a defeat of Oriental despotism and tribalism by the modern state, leaving a space for Islamist forces to occupy. A second version of the argument also asserts the continuity of Islam but argues for its compatibility with the main features of modernity understood as an industrial division of labour. This is the argument of Ernest Gellner:

> The trauma of the Western impact (appearing in diverse Muslim countries at different points in time, stretching from the late eighteenth to the twentieth centuries) did not, amongst Muslim thinkers, provoke that intense polarization between Westerners and Populists, *a la Russe* . . . the dominant and persuasive answer recommended neither emulation of the West, nor idealization of some folk virtue and wisdom. It recommended a *return* to, or a more rigorous observance of, *High* Islam.

Against these kinds of analysis, a number of preliminary points should be noted. There is a strong tendency in culturalist and essentialist arguments to, in Sami Zubaida's helpful characterization, "read history backwards," "seeing the current 'revival' as the culmination of a line of development of Islamic politics, rather than as the product of recent combinations of forces and events." Rather than be seduced by the apparent piety of High Islam we should also pay attention to the ideological mobilization of Islamic purity in blatantly hypocritical ways. Political Islam is by no means the only force in play in contemporary Middle East politics, as secular nationalist and leftist forces remain strong, and Islamic movements therefore compete in a political field not entirely of their own making. This means that political Islam cannot simply represent the religious elements of popular culture, but must instead constitute *new* forms of political mobilization. Moreover, the so-called religious revival in the region is not confined to Islam, but also can be seen in aspects of the politics of the Jewish and Christian communities. In all these cases, a number of general socio-economic and political events appear to have a significant bearing on the politicization of religion, including the trauma of 1967, the worsening economic crisis, the failure of secular nationalist and leftist regimes, and the demonstration effect of the Iranian revolution. Political Islam is itself a thoroughly heterogeneous formation with no pre-given unity: the role played by Islamist forces has varied with the social location of Islamic elements in the process of state formation. And finally, we must remember that Islamist groups are competing *for* (access to) state power and they therefore seek to oppose the configuration of specific regimes rather than the state *per se*.

Simon Bromley, *Rethinking Middle East Politics: State Formation and Development* (Cambridge: Polity Press, 1994), 177–179.

Essence of the West's Attitude

The Western attitude [toward Islam] is not one of indifferent dislike as in the case of all other "foreign" religions and cultures; it is one of deep-rooted and almost fanatical aversion; and it is not only intellectual but bears an intensely emotional tint. Europe may not accept the doctrines of Buddhist or Hindu philosophy, but it will always preserve a balanced, reflective attitude of mind with regard to those systems. As soon, however, as it turns towards Islam, the balance is disturbed and an emotional bias creeps in. With very few exceptions, even the most eminent of European orientalists are guilty of an unscientific partiality in their writings on Islam. In their investigations, it almost appears as if Islam could not be treated as a mere object of scientific research but as an accused standing before his judges. Some of these orientalists play the part of the public prosecutor bent on securing a conviction; others are like a counsel for defence who, being personally convinced that his client is guilty, can only half-heartedly plead for "mitigating circumstances." All in all, the technique of the deductions and conclusions adopted by most of the European orientalists reminds us of the proceedings of those notorious Courts of Inquisition set up by the Catholic Church against its opponents in the Middle Ages; that is to say, they hardly ever investigate historical facts with an open mind, but start, almost in every case, from a foregone conclusion dictated by prejudice.

Muhammad Asad, quoted in Rafiq Zakaria, *Muhammad and the Quran* (London: Penguin, 1989), xii.

Downgrading Islam

The most concerted effort to paint Islam and Muslims in hostile terms in the West has come from two sources. One is the need of the anti-Communist Cold Warriors and the military-industrial complex to find a continued source of threats, adversaries, and dangers that will supply them with arguments for ceaseless vigilance accompanied by appropriate military expenditures to protect Western interests that are immensely elastic. The other source is Israel and its phalanx of supporters, Zionists or otherwise, in the West. Israel, as America's closest strategic ally in the Middle East, not unlike Britain at the end of World War Two, is engaged in an effort at the end of the anti-Communist struggle to assure itself that the United States continues to remain the guarantor of the Middle East state system, and hence of the status quo in historic Palestine, by casting the world of Islam as an enemy of the West.

Only at its own peril can the Muslim world remain indifferent to developments in the non-Muslim world and to the views of those who have shaped the political destiny of the West. For Muslims, a new century, the fifteenth since the *hijrah* of Prophet Muhammad (pbuh) marking year one in the Islamic calendar, began in November of 1979. Hence from the Muslim perspective we are already well advanced into a new Islamic century, and the year 2000 A.D. (*anno Domini*) will be the year 1421 A.H. (*anno Hegirae*). A brief comparison of the state of the *ummah* in the year 1300 A.H. with the state of the *ummah* in the year 1400 A.H. can show us to what extent the condition of Muslims has changed over the past one hundred years and what this change in condition suggests about the future for Muslims in the 21st century of the Western calendar.

The beginning of the 15th Islamic century coincided with the Islamic revolution in Iran and the invasion of Afghanistan by the former Soviet Union. The Islamic revolution symbolized in a very profound sense the renewal of Muslim civilization and culture after more than two hundred years of continuous decline and fragmentation of the *ummah*. The Soviet invasion of Afghanistan in December 1979, however, revealed the continuing vulnerability of the *ummah* to external powers and the developmental gap in terms of economic-military-technological capabilities that separates the Muslim countries of Asia and Africa as part of the Third World from the West.

Salim Mansur, "Muslims in the Year 2000 and Beyond," *Middle East Affairs Journal* (Annandale, Va.), Winter–Spring 1997/1417, 21.

7

Islam and the Dhimmis

Islam, a monotheistic religion founded by Muhammad in the seventh century, is the system of beliefs and rituals based on the Qurʾan. The term *Islam* is derived from the Arabic verb *aslama* (submit), denoting the attitude of the Muslim to God. Although the creed in its barest outline consists of the declaration "There is no god but God (*Allah*) and Muhammad is His prophet," Islam is a religion of both faith and works, faith being but one of the five pillars (*arkan*; singular, *rukn*) that a believer should observe. In addition to faith, or *iman*, which consists of a recital of the creed, are *salat*, divine worship five times a day; *zakat*, payment of the legal alms; *sawm*, the month-long fast of Ramadan, and *hajj*, pilgrimage to Mecca.

Like Judaism, Islam stresses the unity of God, and the Qurʾan specifically rejects the concept of the Christian Trinity. God has revealed himself to man through prophets, starting with Adam and including Noah, Abraham, and others; but he has given books only to three of them—the Law (*tawrat*) to Moses, the Gospel (*injil*) to Jesus, and the Qurʾan to Muhammad. Muhammad, however, is the last of the prophets, the chosen instrument by which God sent the eternal message in its last and definitive form.

The Jewish and Christian presence in Arabia, where Muhammad was born and grew up, and his travels, first with the uncle who raised him after he was orphaned and then on behalf of his wife Khadija, are generally considered the most crucial influences on Muhammad's life and on his mission. At the age of about forty, in the year 610 A.D., Muhammad received a divine call through the archangel Gabriel commanding him to assume the role of prophet, bearing a new message embodied in an Arabic Scripture. But the notables of Mecca, where he resided, looked askance at the man and his message, while the following he had managed to command there was too small to fulfill his expectations. The turning point came in 622, when Muhammad accepted an invitation to come to Yathrib (later to be known as Medina). He arrived there with a number of followers, and this migration (*hijra*) marks the beginning of the Islamic era and the first year in the Muslim calendar. Establishing himself in Yathrib as a political as well as a spiritual leader, Muhammad soon became master of the situation, extending his control to Mecca itself, which he purged of idols and "infidels." Jewish and Christian tribes in and around Medina were brought under tribute and delegations from Arab tribes came to declare allegiance and pay zakat. Indeed, at the time of his death in 632, Muhammad was the undisputed ruler of all Arabia.

At the time of Muhammad's appearance a great number of Jews lived in Arabia; large-scale commercial relations between Arabia and Palestine had existed already in the days of Solomon. The Hebrew Bible contains a number of references to the close relationship between Arabs and Jews, and the books of Job and Proverbs contain many Arabic words. Moreover, some paragraphs in the Mishnah refer specifically to the Jews of the Arabian Peninsula. While considering himself the Messenger of God and "the Seal of all the Prophets," Muhammad did not intend to establish Islam as a new religion. Rather, he regarded himself as sent by Allah to confirm the Scriptures. His basic contention was that God could not have omitted the Arabs from the revelations with which he had favored the Jews and the Christians, and subsequently he accused the Jews of deliberately deleting from the Bible predictions of his advent.

The expansion of Islam following the great Arab conquests later in the seventh century placed the victorious Muslims from Arabia in a position of rulers where the teachings of the Qur'an regarding followers of these two faiths and the way they were to be treated are to be put into practice. For non-Muslim populations in Byzantine and Persian territories already subjugated to foreign rulers, writes John Esposito,

> Islamic rule meant an exchange of rulers, the new ones often more flexible and tolerant, rather than a loss of independence. Many of these populations now enjoyed greater local autonomy and often paid lower taxes. The Arab lands lost by Byzantium exchanged Graeco-Roman rule for new Arab masters, fellow Semites with whom the populace had closer linguistic and cultural affinities. Religiously, Islam proved a more tolerant religion, providing greater religious freedom for Jews and indigenous Christians. Most of the local Christian churches had been persecuted as schismatics and heretics by a "foreign" Christian orthodoxy. For these reasons, some Jewish and Christian communities had actually aided the invading Muslim armies. . . .

Just as Muslim rulers tended to leave the government institutions and bureaucracy intact, so too religious communities were free to practice their faith and be governed in their internal affairs by their religious laws and leaders; . . . religious communities were required to pay a poll or head tax, in exchange for which they were entitled to peace and security; thus they were known as "protected people." The Islamic ideal was to fashion a world in which, under Muslim rule, idolatry and paganism would be eliminated, and all people of the book could live in a society guided and protected by Muslim power. While Islam was regarded as the final and perfect religion of God, others were to be invited, through persuasion first rather than the sword, to convert to Islam. Thus non-Muslims were offered three choices: (1) conversion to Islam and full membership in the community; (2) retention of one's faith and payment of a poll tax; or (3), if they refused Islam or "protected" status, warfare until Islamic rule was accepted.[1]

Relations between Islam and Judaism can be dealt with under two main headings: Islam's indebtedness to Judaism and Muslim attitudes toward Jews living in the realm of Islam. As for Judaic influences in Islam, there is a wealth of evidence to show the extent to which they have been deep and lasting. The very name for Islam's Scripture, *Qur'an,* while it may be a genuine Arabic word meaning "reading" or "reciting," is thought to be borrowed from the Hebrew or Aramaic *mikra,* used by the rabbis to designate the Scripture, or Torah. Muhammad's principal Jewish source, however, was not the Bible but the later Haggadah, which was communicated to him by word of mouth. This is especially apparent in the numerous references in the Qur'an to "prophets" preceding Moses. Noteworthy among these is the exceptional position allotted to Abraham. Abraham is "the friend of God"; he is neither Jew nor Christian but, as a true believer in one God, is considered to be the first Muslim, the first to have submitted unquestioningly to the will of Allah. According to Erwin Rosenthal, Muhammad saw his mission as consisting of restoring the pure religion of Abraham. This change took place in Medina, and the exaltation of Abraham was the direct result of Muhammad's alienation from the Jews.

Halakhah and Shari'a

The Qur'an is the Holy Book of Islam in exactly the same way as the Hebrew Bible is the Holy Book of Judaism. In the same fashion, however, as

Judaism created an enormous exegetic literature after the conclusion of the biblical period, so Islam after the death of Muhammad created an exhaustive literature based on its own Scriptures. While Judaism is a religion of *halakhah*, Islam is a religion of shariᶜa, both words denoting the same thing, namely, a God-given law minutely regulating all aspects of a believer's life: law, worship, ethics, social behavior. Halakhah and shariᶜa are both grounded on oral tradition, called in Arabic *hadith* and in Hebrew *torah she-be-ᶜal peh*. As S. D. Goitein has observed, these authoritatively interpret and supplement the written law—*kitab* in Arabic and *torah she-bikhtav* in Hebrew, which are again similar terms. In Muslim and in Jewish literature the oral tradition falls into two parts, one legal and the other moral, and in both cases they assume the same form of loosely connected maxims and short anecdotes. Again, the logical reasoning applied to the development of the religious law is largely identical in Islam and Judaism, and this is seen by Goitein not as mere coincidence inherent in the nature of things but, as the similar terms used in both traditions show, the result of direct contact. Finally, in both religions the study of even purely legal matters is regarded as worship, the holy men of Islam and Judaism being not priests or monks but students of the divinely revealed law. Scholars have also remarked on the fact that Muslim religious law developed mainly in Iraq, which at the time was the leading center of rabbinic learning.

One of the manifestations of this close interaction between Islam and Judaism is the laws governing *taharah*, ritual purity and cleanliness, which are the same in both religions, as is the term itself. These laws concern forbidden food and drink, touching the sexual organs, bodily discharge, and contact with a corpse or a carcass—all of which cause ritual impurity and bar the affected from fulfilling religious duties such as prayer, presence in a place of worship, and recitation of Scripture. Prayer is another shared feature of these sister faiths: in Islam the first essential in prayer is *niyya*, intent, literally corresponding to the Jewish *kavvanah*, without which prayer is incomplete. According to Rosenthal, taharah and niyya are obviously imitations of the conditions for Jewish prayer as laid down in the talmudic treatise Berakhot. As far as dietary laws are concerned, while Muhammad came to reject most of these (which he considered a punishment for the Jews), he retained the prohibition against eating pig, blood, and carcasses, and decreed ritual slaughtering of all animals permitted for human consumption. Of social obligations and duties—which in both Islam and Judaism are considered religious duties incumbent upon every believer—zakat in Islam corresponds to *zedakah* (the giving of charity) in Judaism. The care of widows and orphans is also a religious duty in both religions, and visiting the sick is commended in Islam in terms identical to haggadic recommendations.

Akbar Ahmed touches on this subject in his *Postmodernism and Islam:*

> In spite of the general cultural antipathy, for most serious Muslim scholars the larger continuities and unity between the three religions outweigh the differences. The Islamic spiritual and social legacy derives from and acknowledges the Judaic-Christian traditions. The main figures are the same: Abraham, Moses, Jesus. The eponymous ancestor is Adam. Rituals, dietary laws and the vision of life and the hereafter are reflected in the earlier religious traditions. The notion of an all-powerful, all-knowing, eternal God is similar. In particular, several Islamic and Jewish traditions are alike: the prohibition of pork, the circumcision of boys, the prohibition of pictorial representations of God, the patriarchal family, the headgear for prayers, the religious rites for slaughter of animals and even the greeting, Jewish *shalom* or Muslim *salam,* which expresses the yearning for peace. Most important, the holy books of the earlier religions entitle their adherents to be placed in the category of *ahl-el-kitab,* those of the acknowledged Book. The Quran speaks favorably of the people of the Book. For example, Surah 3, verse 199, carries a universal message of goodwill and hope to all those who believe, the people of the Book irrespective of their religious label Christian, Jew or Muslim.[2]

Muslims can also marry with the people of the Book.

> Between Jewish and Muslim culture a remarkable harmony and symbiosis are recorded. It is a fact which those locked in the terrible confrontation in the Middle East today would do well to recall. On the whole, Jewish culture and thought thrived under the Muslims: "The caliphs, once their original missionary zeal abated, showed themselves willing to accord an almost boundless toleration in return for a slender poll tax," notes the *Encyclopedia Britannica.* Thus the dignity of the exilarch, which existed from remote antiquity, was maintained with renewed magnificence. Intellectual leadership resided in the *gaon,* head of the academy, who developed the principles of the Talmud. The *gaon* Saadiah (882–942) exemplified the fruitful combination of Helleno-Arabic and Jewish culture. In particular the synthesis of cultures was to flourish in Muslim Spain: "In Spain there came about a remarkable revival. The Jews knew no

restriction upon their activities. . . . It was the Arab invasion that brought salvation" (ibid.).[3]

In the lands dominated by Ottoman Islam, which by the beginning of the sixteenth century included Syria and Egypt, the conditions under which the Jews were permitted to live contrasted so strikingly with those imposed on their coreligionists in the various parts of Christendom that the fifteenth century witnessed a large influx of European Jews into the sultan's domain. The measures taken against the Jews in Spain, culminating in their expulsion in 1492, gave the greatest momentum to this migration. Istanbul soon came to host the largest Jewish community in the whole of Europe, while Salonika became a predominantly Jewish city. The degree of the Jews' integration into the life of Ottoman Islam was such that H. A. R. Gibb and Harold Bowen, two notable students of modern Islam, find that there has been "something sympathetic to the Jewish nature in the culture of Islam," since "from the rise of the caliphate till the abolition of the ghettos in Europe the most flourishing centers of Jewish life were to be found in Muslim countries—in Iraq during the Abbasid period, in Spain throughout the period of Moorish domination, and thereafter in the Ottoman Empire."[4]

In this connection it is of interest that, as far as Palestine is concerned, the right of Jews to "return" to live as a religious community in this strip of land was accepted by all the successive Muslim rulers from the Muslim conquest to the end of the nineteenth century, when Zionist settlement, entangled as it was in European *Weltpolitik*, was viewed as a threat to the integrity of the Ottoman Empire.

Relations with Ahl al-Kitab

The main point to be made about Islam's attitude toward Jews and Judaism is that, as people of the Book, Jews are not regarded as nonbelievers, since they share with Muslims the belief in the one and only God. Jews, however, are not regarded as true believers because they have failed to believe in the Qur'an and the mission of Muhammad. Consequently, these "scripturaries" (*ahl al-kitab*), while allowed to live in the Islamic state unmolested, were granted this right on condition that they pay a poll tax, *jizya*, and accept the status defined in treaties and charters concluded with the Muslim community. As a protected minority, however, the Jews, along with the Christians and other "people of the covenant" (*dhimmis*), were exempted from payment of zakat, the alms tax imposed on Muslims as a religious precept. In this way the imposition of the jizya may be seen not as a penalty for religious nonconformity but as a kind of substitute for zakat. No less important was the fact that the tolerated non-Muslims were supposed to pay this special tax also as a levy on their exemption from taking part in the wars of the Muslims.

The rules and regulations governing relations between the Muslims and ahl al-kitab derive from the Qur'an, the oral tradition, and to a certain extent from local traditions and practices. These regulations included a number of disabilities, but practice differed considerably from the jurist's exposition of the law, the degree of tolerance depending largely on the whims of the rulers and their officials. Both sides, at times, tended to ignore and even violate the law with regard to the employment of non-Muslims in government, the payment of jizya, and the building of synagogues and churches. Jews and Christians were granted a large measure of self-rule, and each community was left to be governed by its own religious head, who was responsible to the Muslim ruler of the day.

Not that there were no exceptions to these rules. However, as Mohammed Arkoun has pointed out, "On the tolerance scale Islam surely does not rank last." Without falling into the sort of self-indulgence that seeks to absolve Islam of practices and conceptions characteristic of certain periods of history, he adds, "Westerners must follow the lead of historians in recognizing that Muslim ethics demonstrated a concern both for rendering the fate of slaves more tolerable and for respecting the religious dignity of 'people of the Book' (*ahl al-kitab*) above and beyond legal regulations." Although they recognized freedom of religion, however, these regulations "also stressed the social and political inferiority of unmistakable rivals to the 'true religion' (*din al-haqq* in the Qur'an), which, transformed into historic Islam, was obliged to cohabit with peoples of the Book. Jews and Christians, even when reduced to the status of *dhimmi*, never ceased to proclaim in a copious and polemical literature their callings as ideal communities enjoying the promise of salvation. We must interpret all the relationships of domination and, now and then, communication among the three monotheistic families in this context of mimetic rivalry to incarnate, live, and defend 'true religion'. The idea of tolerance would emerge slowly, with great difficulty, and in ever precarious fashion through the excesses of the inquisition, persecution, and wars of religion, as they are called in the West."

This, adds Arkoun, applies to the whole set of human rights.

Revelation as collected in the sacred writings contains starting points, strong roots, and carrier concepts for the emergence of the person as a subject equipped with rights and as an agent responsible for the observance of obligations toward God and peers in the political community. The idea of peers does not coincide, of course, with the modern idea of citizens, abstracted as it is from religious beliefs and philosophical positions. I have just shown that the person postulated by revelation is the believer who adheres to a set of dogmas and who translates this adherence into strict observance of the "rights of God." The rights of "peers" thus defined comes to be incorporated as duty insofar as each believer respects the rights of God in the first place. The rights/duties pair reacquires in effectiveness and spiritual content that which is lost by extension sociologically: The nonbeliever must be reduced to an inferior status and even fought.[5]

And, indeed, as the power of Islam spread, and as it began to come in contact with more peoples and civilizations, the degree of its religious tolerance became more pronounced. During the Abbasid period, from the eighth to the thirteenth centuries, Jews and Christians held important financial, clerical, and professional positions. In 985, the Arab chronicler al-Maqdisi found that most of the money changers and bankers in Syria were Jews, while most of the clerks and physicians were Christians. Under several caliphs we read of more than one Jew in the capital of the caliphate and the provinces assuming responsible state positions. In Baghdad, the capital, the Jews maintained a large, prosperous community. Rabbi Benjamin of Tudela, who visited the city in 1169, found the community in possession of ten rabbinical schools and twenty-three synagogues; he depicts in glowing colors the high esteem in which the head of the Babylonian Jews was held as a descendant of David and as Prince of the Exile, *Ras el-Jalut* (in rabbinic Aramaic, *Resh Galuta*).

There is a good deal of ambiguity about Islam's attitude toward non-Muslims. Goitein points out that the Qur'an contains two diametrically opposed views on adherents of other faiths, as it does on several other vital matters, a fact that—Goitein says—can be explained by the spiritual and political history of Muhammad and his young community:

Unlike Christianity, which originated in opposition to its mother religion [Judaism] and therefore negated its right of existence, Islam came into being in defiance of paganism and through self-identification with the People of the Book, that is, Jews and Christians. This is the root of that primitive universalism—the belief that monotheistic religions were essentially one—which pervades the early parts of the Quran, and as a consequence of which Islamic law recognized in principle the right of existence of other monotheistic religions.[6]

Subsequently, however, Muhammad discovered that he could not maintain his claim to prophethood without establishing a church of his own, demanding for itself exclusive authority just as the synagogue and the various Christian denominations had done before. Moreover, Muhammad obtained by military and political means what he had failed to obtain by his powers of persuasion, with the result that the last ten years of his life were marked by incessant warfare. As the larger part of the Qur'an originated during this latter period, the imprint left on the character of Islam by these events is such that toward the end of his life Muhammad was exhorting his followers: "Fight until religion everywhere belongs to God," that is, fight until all the world worships the one true God of Islam. Consequently, Islamic law divided the world into two domains—dar al-Islam and dar al-harb, the domains of Islam and of war, respectively.

Thus, in theory, no Islamic state can make peace with a non-Muslim power; the most that is religiously permissible is an armistice of short duration. As far as Christians and Jews living in the domain of Islam are concerned, they have to pay the jizya and are to be kept in submission in order to demonstrate that Islam is the true and dominant religion. However, while Muslim scholars and lawmakers laid down a long list of discriminatory laws to give expression to submission, the actual application of these laws differed from time to time and place to place depending on the existing socioeconomic and religious situation.

The subject of Islam's attitude toward the Jews, and of relations between Muslims and Jews generally, has been studied and analyzed by scholars of such caliber as Goitein, Erwin Rosenthal, Salo Baron, Leon Poliakov, and, more recently, Mark Cohen and Norman A. Stillman. The latter, in a well-researched and very readable paper published in 1997 under the title, "The Commensality of Islamic and Jewish Civilizations," contrasts the Judeo-Christian historical encounter with that between Judaism and Islam. While the former, Stillman writes, "began with the breakaway of a sect from within the Jewish fold, and developed early on into a fiercely competitive, highly inimical, and ultimately destructive relationship," the Judeo-Muslim encounter, in contrast, "though not without its stresses and tensions, was marked from the very beginning and for long periods of time thereafter by cultural intercourse within a common civilizational context: Islamic civilization."[7]

Readings

Muhammad and the Jews

The Apostle [Muhammad] wrote to the Jews: In the name of Allah the Compassionate the Merciful from Muhammad the Apostle of Allah, *friend and brother of Moses who confirms what Moses brought*. Allah says to you, O people of the Book, and you will find it in your Book, "Muhammad is the Apostle of Allah, and those with him are hard against the disbelievers, compassionate among themselves. Thou seest them bowing and prostrating themselves seeking grace and acceptance from Allah. The mark of their prostrations is on their foreheads. That is their description in the Torah. And their description in the gospel is like a seed which sends forth its shoot and strengthens it, and it becomes thick and rises straight upon its stalk, delighting the sowers, that he may cause the disbelievers to burn with rage at (the sight of) them. Allah has promised those who believe and do good works forgiveness and a great reward." I adjure by Allah, and by what he has sent down to you, by the *manna* and the quails He gave as food to your tribes before you, and by His drying the sea for your fathers when He delivered them from Pharaoh and his works, that you tell me, do you find in what he has sent down to you that you believe in Muhammad? *If you do not find that in your Book then "there is no compulsion upon you*. The right path has become plainly distinguished from error" so I call you to Allah and His Apostle. . . .

The frequent references to the Jews in the Qur'an, as interpreted by the classical interpreters of the Qur'an, the unfolding of the Muslim practice, the development of the *Shariʿah* and the garbled accounts of the controversy with the Jews of Yathrib have created a picture of religious controversy which is both distorted and distorting. Almost all the modern historians have taken the view that when the Apostle left Mecca he looked forward to his acceptance by the Jews of Yathrib. On arrival he tried to win them over by adopting the fast of "Ashura," by turning towards Jerusalem for prayers, etc. The Apostle was, however, soon disappointed by the Jewish rejection, so he broke with them and crushed them.

This picture represents a contorted reflection of events. There is no evidence for [the] assumption that the Apostle at one time had considered the Jews of Medina as "converts to Islam." Two early Meccan *surah*s, the *Bani Israʾil* and the *Yunus*, show that the Apostle from the very beginning had an idea of the Jewish reaction to his claim. The seventeenth chapter of the Qur'an, the *Bani Isra'il,* has the following verses warning the Jews of their future:

> And we revealed to the children of Israel in the Book, (saying) you will surely do mischief in the land twice, and you will surely become excessively overbearing. So when the time for the first of the two warnings came, we sent against you (some) servants of Ours possessed of great might in war, and they penetrated (the innermost parts of your) houses and it was a warning that was bound to be carried out. Then We gave you back the power against them, and aided you with wealth and children, and made you larger in numbers.
>
> Now if you do well, you will do well for your own souls; and if you do evil, it will (only) be against them. So when the time for the latter warning came, (We raised a people against you) to cover your faces with grief, and to enter the mosque (The Temple) as they entered it the first time, and to destroy all they conquered with their destruction.
>
> It may be that your Lord will now have mercy on you; but if you return (to your previous state), We too will return and We have made hell a prison for the disbelievers.
>
> Surely, this Qur'an guides to what is most right; and gives to the believers who do good deeds the glad tidings that they shall have a great reward. And that for those who do not believe in what is to come later We have prepared a grievous punishment.

In these verses of the *Bani Isra'il* the use of the personal pronoun in the second person is highly significant. [Henri] Lammens, after an examination of early sources, has rightly pointed out that there were no Jews in Mecca, and there is general consensus that the verses are definitely Meccan. These verses do not point towards an Apostle looking forward to be accepted by the Jews. They also do not indicate an active controversy between the Apostle and the Jews. It is a general statement without polemics. A later verse on the subject is clear: "And We prepared for the children of Israel a blessed abode, and We provided them with all manner of good things. They differed not in anything till true knowledge came to them. Surely thy Lord will judge between them on the day of Judgment concerning that in which they differed."

. . . The Apostle knew before his arrival in Medina that he would be rejected by the Jews and yet offered them the terms of the *Sahifah* on the basis of the Unity of God. But the Jews considered him not even a false Messiah, but an outright usurper; being a gentile (*ummi*) he could not be a prophet unto them, and as a prophet to the Arabs he could endanger their already declining position of influence. Two of their major allies in Medina had already accepted this refugee prophet; the Meccans were unable to crush him alone, and their own efforts in Medina to dislodge him had rebounded. The decline was rapid and they were unable to do anything to stop it.

Barakat Ahmad, *Muhammad and the Jews: A Re-Examination* (New Delhi: Vikas Publishing House 1979), 114, 117–119; emphasis in original.

Non-Muslims under Muslim Rule: Qurʾanic Imperatives

The *Qurʾan* requires that "if ye (O Muhammad) judge between mankind, judge justly. Lo! Comely is this which god admonisheth you. Lo! God is ever Hearer, Seer" (*an-Nisaʾ* 4:58). All moral values, such as justice, equality, honest dealing and the like are here held sacred. They are to be practised, irrespective of differences of religion. Their authority is dependent only on their equity, which recognises no barrier between people. In other words, they are the human standards of an honest attachment to religion and to human sociability itself. In consequence, the more truly "Islamic" in their behaviour and attitudes Muslims become, the better is the guarantee to non-Muslims that these moral values will be practised.

Like any other human being, however, a Muslim may fail to live up to those high standards. But he has no right to attribute his deviation to any Islamic principle. . . . Nor has he the right to justify that deviation on any political or economic pretext. For, according to the Islamic concept, moral values are absolute and concrete: they are meant to be realised in action and not merely accepted in theory. They are alive only when people live according to them.

Said Ramadan . . . acknowledges that the *de facto* status of non-Muslim subjects might entail unfair discrimination, as occasionally happened in the course of history. But their *de jure* status remains upheld in both the *Qurʾan* and the *sunna*. It is a status meeting the highest standards of equity and equality. As an absolute moral imperative, it should be made concrete. This *de jure* status is as securely grounded and binding as any Qurʾanic or Prophetic text could be. Every struggle to establish it in practice in an Islamic state is accordingly not merely legal and constitutional; it is also religiously enjoined, and therefore mandatory upon the Islamic state itself and its leaders.

Religious conscience is therefore not only not opposed to such struggle, but absolutely demands and supports it. It was in accordance with this principle that Muslim jurists led the Muslim public in a strong protest against the caliph Walid ibn Yazid when, fearing a Roman attack, he exiled the non-Muslim citizens of Cyprus to Syria. Not until they were brought back to Cyprus was the caliph allowed to rest.

"This is an eternal and universal injunction," Said Ramadan maintains, "and the best advice, therefore, that I can give to you is to remind you of one of the directives of God's Prophet, that he himself will stand up as plaintiff against all such Muslims, who are unkind to those non-Muslims who have entered into an agreement with them, and who tax them beyond endurance."

The *Qur'an* is quite clear that ultimately everybody will have to account for his or her own actions. Nobody shall be held responsible for, or may assume the moral burden of, anybody else's actions. This obligation here is the obligation upon Muslims of ensuring justice to non-Muslims living among them.

Stressing a spirit of humanity, Said Ramadan says that the authority of moral values, in the name of Islam, does not merely transcend every difference of religion. It goes far beyond that. One of Islam's moral principles is the conception that human beings, wherever they live, are fundamentally one and the same. As the *Qur'an* urges, "O men, revere your Lord, Who created you from a single mould and made out of it a pair, and thereupon brought forth multitudes of men and women" (*an-Nisa* 4:1).

The goal of human life, then, is for people to come closer together and to know each other better, not to become estranged from and hostile to one another. The *Qur'an* declares,

> O people! Behold, We have created you from a male and a female and made out of you nations and tribes so that you may know one another (and be good to one another). The noblest among you before God is the best in conduct. Behold God is the Knower, the Aware (al-Hujurat 49:13).

This, Said Ramadan says, implies that the Muslim, by virtue of his faith, should be deeply attached to humankind as a whole and conscious of the fact that geographical borders, political divisions and differences in appearance, race or language must not become a barrier between people. Or as Canon Taylor put it,

> Islam thrust aside the artificial virtues, the religious frauds and follies, the perverted moral sentiments, and the verbal subtleties of theo-

logical disputants. It replaced monkishness by manliness. It gave hope to the slave, brotherhood to mankind, and recognition to the fundamental facts of human nature.

K. Haridas, "Islamization of State and Society," in *Shariᶜa Law and the Modern Nation-State,* ed. Norani Othman (Kuala Lumpur: Sisters in Islam Forum [Malaysia] Berhad, 1994), 93–95.

Ahl al-Kitab

As is well known, the encounter between Judaism and Islam goes back to the very birth of the latter in Arabia in the seventh century. I do not wish to get involved here in what has become overall an arid and futile debate that began with Abraham Geiger in the last century and was followed in this one by Charles Torrey, Richard Bell, Tor Andrae and S. D. Goitein, as to who were the primary sources of inspiration for Muhammad's religious message. I would simply say that a considerable body of religious concepts, ethical notions, homiletic lore and scriptural topoi were disseminated among the pagan Arabs by Jews, Christians, and various sectarians, including, perhaps, Judeo-Christians and Gnostics. Taking into account Julian Obermann's caveat that seemingly Jewish material could have come to Muhammad's attention from Christians and vice versa, there is still much that is specifically and identifiably of Jewish origin in early Islam. A great body of extra-Qurʾanic lore which comprises an important part of scriptural exegesis (*tafsir al- qurʾan*) and prophetic hagiography (*qisas al-anbiyaʾ*) is actually called *israʾiliyyat,* or Israelite narratives.

But more significant than any borrowed or shared elements in Judaism and Islam are: 1) the attitude of Islam toward Judaism, Christianity and Zoroastrianism, and 2) the very structural model of Islam itself as a religion.

Islam's attitude toward Judaism is particularly significant, because it provided the psychological framework for later commensality. Unlike Christianity, Islam did not begin as a sect within Judaism and did not claim to be *Verus Israel,* but merely the last and best of a series of divine revelations. There is nothing in either the Qurʾan or later Muslim theological writings that is comparable to the overwhelming preoccupation with Jews and Judaism that one finds in the New Testament, Patristic literature and other Christian writings.

In the Islamic view, Jews shared the status of *ahl al-kitab* (scriptural people) with the far more numerous Christians and Zoroastrians. As long as they submitted to the suzerainty of the Islamic state, paid tribute, and comported themselves with the humble demeanor of subjects, they were entitled to the protection of the Muslim community, and hence their legal designation as *ahl al-dhimma* (protégés). Despite certain restrictions, they enjoyed freedom of cult (within discreet limits), freedom of economic endeavor, and a great measure of internal communal autonomy.

The second factor which helped to lay the groundwork for the later commensality was the structural model of Islam itself, which was far closer to that of Judaism than Christianity. Both Islam and Judaism share an uncompromising, iconoclastic monotheism. Both possess the notion of religious polity governed by divine law. Thus, Islam was not perceived by Judaism as idolatrous (*ʿavoda zara*), as Christianity was perceived. Indeed, when Islam burst upon the scene of history as the Arab armies poured out of the Arabian desert into the surrounding lands, Jewish apocalyptic literature depicted the conquests as a divine visitation upon wicked Edom, the code word for Byzantine Christendom.

The three hundred years following the Islamic conquests witnessed the transformation of much of world Jewry that now lived within the Dar al-Islam into an essentially urban population. The process whereby Jews went over from an agrarian way of life to a cosmopolitan one had begun in late antiquity, but was now completed in the wave of urbanism that occurred as a direct result of the conquests.

This was also the period when Jews from Spain in the west to Iraq in the east went over to speaking Arabic, the lingua franca of the new *oikoumene*. But more important than merely adopting Arabic in speech, by the tenth century Jews were using Arabic for nearly all forms of written expression, including in the religious domain. Queries and responsa, scriptural exegesis, legal documents, and treatises of all sorts were written in Arabic, albeit normally in Hebrew characters. One reason for this thorough linguistic assimilation, as Joshua Blau has pointed out, is that in the Jewish heartlands of Palestine, Syria, and Iraq (Bavel), Arabic supplanted Aramaic, the previous lingua franca of both Jews and Gentiles. Aramaic had already been used for all purposes, religious and profane. Therefore, the transition to Arabic seemed a natural process affecting everyone, irrespective of nationality or confession.

To this I would add three other reasons. First, there was the recognized familial kinship of Arabic to Aramaic—and of course to Hebrew—that mitigated against any feeling of foreignness. Second, there was the prestige of Arabic within Islamic society, a veritable cult of language, which did have its own psychological impact on Islamicate Jewry. Third, there was a secular aspect of general culture for which Arabic was the medium and that could be safely shared. By contrast, no such parallel existed in Christendom at the time, where Latin was the language of a thoroughly clerical culture and the vernaculars enjoyed no comparable prestige.

Norman A. Stillman, "The Commensality of Jewish and Islamic Civilizations," in *Middle East Lectures* 2 (Tel Aviv: Moshe Dayan Center for Middle Eastern and African Studies, 1997), 82–84.

Khatami's Version

. . . Anti-Semitism is . . . a Western phenomenon. It has no precedence in Islam or in the East. Jews and Muslims have lived harmoniously together for centuries. In the East, we have had despotism and dictatorship, but never had fascism or nazism. These, too, are also Western phenomena, and the West has paid dearly to combat them. What concerns me is that, first, this Western anti-Semitism has turned into a tool for the imposition of a whole range of improper policies and practices on the people of the Middle East and Muslims in general. Secondly, I am concerned that this Western dilemma may be projected elsewhere, that as fascism and nazism are suppressed in the West, they may resurface in another form in Western policies elsewhere. Obviously, Washington is the U.S. capital where policy decisions on U.S. national interests must be made. However, the impression of the people of the Middle East and Muslims in general is that certain foreign policy decisions of the U.S. are in fact made in Tel Aviv and not in Washington. And I regret to say that the improper American policy of unbridled support for the aggressions of a racist terrorist regime does not serve U.S. interests, nor does it even serve that of the Jewish people. Zionists constitute a small portion of the Jewish people and have openly declared and proven in practice that they are expansionist. The Israeli intransigence in the course of the current peace process, and its failure to honor its own undertakings has enraged even U.S. allies in the region. In my view, peace can come to the Middle East when all Palestinians, Jews and Muslims alike, can determine the future of the land. That should include those living in Palestine as well as those refugees living elsewhere. Only then can a stable and lasting peace be established. Many in the world might share our view, and many may differ with us. We simply present our opinion, and have the greatest respect for all Palestinians who are concerned about the future of Palestine. Meanwhile, we believe the United States should not risk the substantial prestige and credibility of the American people on supporting a racist regime which does not even have the backing of the Jewish people. The subject of Middle East peace is one that needs a sober and pragmatic analysis. We believe that it will not succeed because it is not just and it does not address the rights of all parties in an equitable manner. We are prepared to contribute to an international effort to bring about a just and lasting peace in the Middle East.

Iranian President Muhammad Khatami, interview on CNN, January 7, 1998.

A Framework for the Coexistence of Judaism, Christianity, and Islam: Common Thread of Salvation

I advocate a new humanistic base for the cooperation and coexistence among all the sects, doctrines and paths of the three religious cultures: Judaism, Christianity and Islam.

In Judaism, the Old Testament, or Torah, is based on the ten commandments and other rules and regulations that govern the life of the individual and community. In time, the rabbis offered new interpretations and new legal rules, which were set down in the Talmud. Torah, which originally meant "the way of guidance," was expanded to mean all of the juridical rules in the Hebrew Bible, and then further extended to mean the new rules and interpretations developed by the rabbis in the Talmud. Because the Talmudic law is considered all-comprehending, it is not easy for such a system to cooperate with or to accept any other system of laws.

In Christianity, Jesus Christ never spoke about law in any great detail. However, the church, after him, felt obliged to establish laws to regulate the activities of the individual and community. These laws came to be known as ecclesiastical law and are considered sacred. Thus it is very difficult for such a system to cooperate with or to accept any other system of laws.

In Islam, there are many legal rules in the Qurʾan and in the traditions of the Prophets. Muslim scholars interpreted these rules and created other rules, which comprise jurisprudence. Jurisprudence is wrongly called Islamic law—Shariʿa—and is considered to be part of the faith. The word *Shariʿa*, however, does not mean law at all. Its meaning in Qurʾanic terminology and in the Arabic language is "the path, the way, the method," and the like. However, the term was extended by scholars to mean the entire Islamic system of law. Hence, this, too, is an isolated system that finds it very difficult to cooperate with or to accept any other system of laws.

These three systems, then—Judaism, Christianity and Islam—are closed systems. Each system considers itself an absolute and revealed system and refuses to recognize the other systems, which are, in its view, relative, were not revealed, or were falsified. How then shall we find a framework for creative coexistence among these juridical systems?

The solution, I am convinced, can be found in the authentic concept of Islam. The authentic concept of Islam—as mentioned above—is that there is only one religion revealed by God to all the teachers, messengers and prophets throughout history and to all peoples all over the world. This religion simply put is to have faith in God and to be straight in conduct. All the faithful throughout history and all over the world are one community. Those who believe (in the Qurʾan), and those who follow the Jewish scriptures, and the Christians and the Sabians—any who believe in God and the last day, and righteousness, shall have their reward with their Lord: "on them shall be no fear, nor shall they grieve" (Sura 2:62).

Thus, in the authentic concept of Islam we all have one religion and we are all one community of the faithful. But every teacher, messenger or prophet had or has his own Shariʿa—path, method or way—in teaching the people how faith and righteousness should be lived in accordance with their state of mind, culture and customs. There is a verse in the Qurʿan that reads, "We [God] gave you [teachers, messengers and prophets] one religion, but we gave every one of you his own Shariʿa: path, method or way" (Sura 4:84).

If we analyze the disagreements between the different forms of religion we will find that they are mainly verbal disagreements, linguistic interpretations and philosophical attitudes. People believe in words and differ about words, without having a precise definition of words and without keeping the faith away from words.

Instead of highlighting the differences, we should consider the common base shared by Judaism, Christianity and Islam, which is to have faith in God and to be straight in conduct. What differs is the path, the method or the way of each culture, or the interpretations of its scholars and faithful ones. We have to consider ourselves the faithful of one religion and to consider the interpretations and jurisprudence as man's effort to realize his faith and to promote humanity. The absolute is a combination of all paths, interpretations and cultures. In the light of this, and in this way only, can we state a juridical coexistence for the three cultures and other cultures as well.

One religion, many paths, several interpretations, changeable law and flexible jurisprudence to suit man's activities without disturbing him or harming his spirit, his mind, activities, freedom and ambitions. Humanity must not neglect anyone because no person has been created in vain or without meaning. Every woman and man is the prophecy of the future and they were created to express a particular meaning, perhaps the one that no one else could express. Each woman and man's perfection and salvation can be attained only if no one is left out.

Along with the similar goals shared by Jewish, Christian and Islamic belief, these faiths also share the universal belief in salvation. Salvation, in religion, is the deliverance or redemption of man from fundamentally negative or disabling conditions, such as suffering evil, finitude and death. In some faiths, salvation is the restoration or raising up of the natural world to a higher realm or state. Salvation is a universal religious notion. Salvation may be referred to as deliverance or growth, and the concept includes (1) the basic goal of salvation, (2) the means of achieving salvation, (3) the cosmic situation which elicits the striving for salvation, (4) the notion of the soul, and (5) the ascription of decay and death to a primordial misdeed or to human sin.

Muhammad Sa'id al-'Ashmawi, in *Against Islamic Extremism: The Writings of Muhammad Sa'id al-'Ashmawi,* ed. Carolyn Fluehr-Lobban (Gainesville: University Press of Florida, 1998), 55–57.

Muslim Anti-Semitism

What has come to be known as the peace process—the developing dialogue between the state of Israel on the one hand and the Palestinians and some Arab governments on the other—raised hopes that it would lead to a lessening of hostility and more specifically of anti-Semitism. In some quarters this did indeed occur. But in others the peace process itself has aroused a new Arab hostility to Jews, among both those frustrated by its slowness and those alarmed by its rapidity. As a result, anti-Semitism in recent years has conquered new territory and risen to a new intensity.

European anti-Semitism, in both its theological and racist versions, was essentially alien to Islamic traditions, culture, and modes of thought. But to an astonishing degree, the ideas, the literature, even the crudest of inventions of the Nazis and their predecessors have been internalized and Islamized. The major themes—poisoning the wells, the invented Talmud quotations, ritual murder, the hatred of mankind, the Masonic and other conspiracy theories, taking over the world—remain; but with an Islamic, even a Qur'anic twist.

The classical Islamic accusation, that the Old and New Testaments are superseded because Jews and Christians falsified the revelations vouchsafed to them, is given a new slant: the Bible in its present form is not authentic but a version distorted and corrupted by the Jews to show that they are God's chosen people and that Palestine belongs to them. (*Ash-Sha^b,* Jan. 3, 1997; *Al-Watan* [Muscat], Feb. 12, 1997) Various current news items—the scandal over Swiss banks accepting Nazi gold stolen from Jews, the appointment of Madeleine Albright as secretary of state, even the collapse of the Bank of Credit and Commerce International (BCCI)—are given an anti-Semitic slant. Jewish world plots—against mankind in general, against Islam, against the Arabs—have become commonplace.

One of the crimes of Israel and of the Zionists in these writings is that they are a bridgehead or instrument of American or, more generally, of Western penetration. For such, America is the Great Satan, Israel the Little Satan, Israel is dangerous as a spearhead of Western corruption. The more consistent European-type anti-Semites offer an alternative view; that America is the tool of Israel, rather than the reverse, an argument backed by a good deal of Nazi-style or original Nazi documentation. In much of the literature produced by the Islamic organizations, the enemy is no longer defined as the Israeli or the Zionist; he is simply the Jew, and his evil is innate and genetic, going back to remote antiquity. A preacher from Al-Azhar University explains in an Egyptian newspaper that he hates the Jews because they are the worst enemies of the Muslims and have no moral standards, but have chosen evil and villainy. He concludes: "I hate the Jews so as to earn a reward from God." (*Al-Ittihad,* Dec. 20, 1996).

The argument that "we cannot be anti-Semitic because we ourselves are Semites" may still occasionally be heard in Arab countries, though of course not in Turkey or Iran. But some of the more sophisticated spokesmen have become aware that to most outsiders this argument sounds silly or disingenuous. Some writers make a serious effort to maintain the distinction between hostility to Israel and Zionism and hostility to Jews as such. But not all. President Khatami of Iran, in his interview on CNN, pointed out—correctly—that "anti-Semitism is indeed a Western phenomenon. It has no precedents in Islam or in the East. Jews and Muslims have lived harmoniously together for centuries." A newspaper known to express the views of the "Supreme Guide" Khomenei rejected this statement as untrue: "The history of the beginnings of Islam is full of Jewish plots against the Prophet Muhammad and of murderous attacks by Jews. . . . unequivocal verses in the Qur^an speak of the hatred and hostility of the Jewish people against Muslims. One must indeed distinguish between the Jews and the Zionist regime, but to speak in the manner we heard was exaggerated and there was no need for such a presentation." The Egyptian director of a film about President Nasser reports a similar complaint by the late president's daughter. She objected to a passage in his film indicating that "Nasser was not against the Jews, but against Zionism, because she wanted to portray her father as a hero of the anti-Jewish struggle."

Bernard Lewis, "Muslim Anti-Semitism," *Middle East Quarterly,* June 1998, 43–44.

"Muslim Anti-Semitism"?

Dear Editor:

Writing about what he calls "Muslim Anti-Semitism" [*MEQ*, June 1998], Professor Bernard Lewis engages, as too often, in selective scholarship. He approaches his subject in a total vacuum. Sporadic phenomenon of so-called Arab or Muslim anti-Semitism is not related to any wrongdoing by Israel or its supporters, or to the universally acknowledged fact of Palestinian victimization by an ethnic and a religious group that has suffered greatly at the hands of Hitler and other European anti-Semites.

Professor Lewis's sweep of accusations is really too wide, perhaps on purpose in order to obfuscate. No one could deny the existence, though very limited, of verbal manifestations of anti-Semitism in the Muslim world. Such manifestations, however, should be unequivocally condemned. But how much of this is really anti-Semitism in the well-established sense of the word, and how much of it is an expansion of indignation and frustrations against an Israeli policy of occupation, ethnic cleansing (1948 and 1967), settlers' behavior etc.? The list is really very long.

Professor Lewis could have asked himself if Palestinian, Arab, and Muslim reaction would have been different if the occupier was Great Britain, Russia, or America. The professor of Islamic studies has never told us how Jewish extremists in Israel or in the United States perceive the Palestinians, the Arabs, and Muslims. The favorite slogans of these extremists, as is well known, are: "Death to the Arabs" and "The only good Arab is a dead Arab."

Allow me, Professor, to ask how you would describe the Jewish advocates of "transfer," which is a euphemism for ethnic cleansing. And Professor, which is really more nefarious, crude verbal expression of bias toward the enemy, or a consistent policy of annexations and total violation of human rights in the occupied territories?

I don't think there is enough space to respond to every piece of disinformation in Professor Lewis's piece. But I will refer to two examples he has given because they reflect on the cast of his scholarship. Professor Lewis is very proud of the fact that after the massacre of Shatilla and Sabra in Lebanon, there was an inquiry in Israel to determine Mr. Ariel Sharon's responsibility, something the professor is telling us could not happen in any Arab country.

As we recall, the massacre—it is true—was carried out with extreme brutality by Lebanese Phalangists who were trained and reviewed by then General Sharon's troops before they were set loose to do their mayhem. Incidentally, Professor, in this unprovoked invasion of Lebanon, 20,000 hapless Lebanese and Palestinians were murdered by Israel.

Another example touted by Professor Lewis is the banning of *Schindler's List* in many Arab countries. Personally, I'm against the banning. But the banning of this film could also be viewed against the very effective censorship exercised by Jewish activists of any film or television documentary sympathetic to the plight of Palestinians. In the 1960s and 1970s when I used to live in New York City, all Soviet-bloc artistic shows, including classical operas, were banned from the city. The Soviets were perceived as pro-Arab. Cultural boycott remains a constant feature among Jewish activists to this day. We have a saying in Arabic which roughly translated means: "If you have no sense of shame, then every thing is possible."

The Egypt you have vilified in this article is the same Egypt that had provided a sanctuary to Sephardic Jews escaping the Inquisition and Jewish settlers in Palestine fleeing German and Turkish persecution during 1914, World War I, etc. The Egyptian-Jewish community was part of the socio-economic elite, well-respected and highly trusted until Zionists started to foment disloyalty to Egypt among its members. The rest is well known.

Finally, Islam need not be apologetic about how it has treated its Jews. I thought you knew.

Abdelaleem El-Abyad, Press and Information Bureau, Embassy of the Arab Republic of Egypt, Washington, D.C., *Middle East Quarterly,* September 1998, 91–92.

The French King, the Muslim Ambassador, and the Blood Libel

A fictitious story about a blood libel related in the sixteenth-century chronicle *Shevet yehuda,* by Solomon ibn Verga, illustrates a fundamental Jewish perception of the difference between Islamic and Christian attitudes toward the Jews. The tale (which Ibn Verga says he found in a chronicle from France) concerns two Christians who accused a Jew of killing a Christian "on the eve of their holiday"—Passover (when Jews were believed to reenact the crucifixion). The king, realizing its erroneous nature, vigorously dismissed the charge. Embarrassed, the Christian accusers enlisted the support of the common folk. Two witnesses came forth and reported that they had gone to the house of the Jew, "to borrow from him at interest"; there they "found the Jew coming out of the room with a blood-soaked knife in his hand."

Brought before the king, the Jew claimed that he had been using the knife to slaughter poultry according to Jewish ritual for the holiday. Nonetheless, at the king's command, he was subjected to judicial torture. Under duress, the Jew confessed to the murder, stating that fifty prominent Jews had conspired with him and joined in the deed. All were arrested, but the co-conspirators talked their way out of prosecution by reminding the king that his own law disallowed testimony about third parties that had been extracted by torture.

Present at court was a "Muslim ambassador," to whom the king posed the question: "Do things like this happen in your kingdom?" The Muslim ambassador replied:

> We have never heard nor seen this, thanks to our rulers, who will not be degraded by such childish matters that, moreover, have no basis either in rational thinking or in religion. How could a Jew dare to murder a Christian when he is subjugated to the latter's rule; certainly regarding such an abhorrent deed as performing a sacrifice with the blood of a human, concerning which we have never heard about any people on earth, even though they may be attracted to [other] irrational, abhorrent matters. This sort of thing would not occur to them, since it is completely foreign to human rationality. You adhere to in your land and heed in your courts—the courts of kings—things which one is forbidden to believe.

> The king became angry at this and said; "But the perpetrator confessed. According to the law, what else can I do? What does it matter if it is irrational, given that he confessed?"

> The Muslim replied: "In our realm, a confession extracted by torture will do as an excuse when it is accompanied by other inculpations, but it will not do [by itself] for pronouncing judgment."

> One of the Christians present then said to the Muslim: "Honored sir, if this does not exist in your realm, that is because the Jews have no gripe . . . against the Muslims. But they have one against the

Christians on account of Jesus. That is why they take a Christian and give him the name Jesus and eat his blood to take vengeance upon him."

More deeply convinced of the prevarication, the Muslim questioned the logic of the Christians in the matter—for according to their belief that the Jews killed Jesus ("whereas in our belief the Jews did not kill Jesus [see Sura 4:157], who, rather, ascended alive to heaven"), the Jews had already taken ample and cruel revenge on him. "Jesus ought to have asked his Father to take vengeance on the Jews! Praised be the Creator who separated us from such lies and cast our lot among the believers of truth."

The Christians replied: "You say that Jesus ought to have sought vengeance against the Jews. He already has! Real life circumstances prove it. Why would they be living in exile, cast aside, belittled, repressed, and having their hair torn out, if not to avenge the blood of Jesus?"

Responded the Muslim: "If the Father takes such vengeance on behalf of his son, should the Jews take vengeance yet again in order to exact a second payment? This is absurd. Moreover, if God exacts punishment against the Jews, why do you need to pursue separate justice? At any rate, I have not come to save the Jews, for they are not my coreligionists, nor do they come from my realm, nor do I love them, for I know what they did to some of the prophets. I came, however, to say the truth, since the king asked my opinion."

In the continuation of the story, the Christian commonfold produce fresh "false witnesses" that the accused Jew and his alleged accomplices admitted their guilt in their earshot. In the end, the alleged co-conspirators are saved by a divine miracle, and the Jew initially accused of the deed is saved from punishment when new Christian witnesses are found who testify that they had seen "so and so" (plainly, a Christian) throw the corpse into the Jew's house. The culprit is condemned to have his hands and feet cut off.

Mark R. Cohen, *Under Crescent and Cross: The Jews in the Middle Ages* (Princeton: Princeton University Press, 1994), 189–191.

8

Fundamentalism Strikes Back

Bilal X, the black muezzin in Salman Rushdie's controversial novel *The Satanic Verses*, advises the faithful: "Burn the books; trust the Book." The Book, of course, is the Qurʾan, which Muslims are taught is the Word of God, dictated by the Archangel Gabriel and written down, *unaltered*, by the Prophet Muhammad's scribes. Rushdie's major heresy was that his character Salman the Persian mistranscribes a portion of the Qurʾan. The idea is based on an episode recorded by early Muslim chroniclers, in which Satan is supposed to have introduced verses into the Prophet's mind permitting a modified version of polytheism, allegedly to placate the skeptics.

A more glaring variation on the same theme is the episode in which a character named Gibreel Farishta, supposed to be India's most popular movie star, suffers from a schizophrenic breakdown and discovers in the process that there is no God. He develops a halo around his head and lives a cinematic dream in which he is cast as the Archangel Gibreel, and is subsequently asked by a number of petitioners to deliver God's word. One of these is a businessman named Mahound, cast as a prophet, and in the course of their exchanges, Gibreel dreams of a brothel where prostitutes take on the roles of Prophet Mahound's wives.

What the few believing Muslims who read Rushdie's novel found so offensive in this scene is that it, too, is based on an episode in the Prophet's biography. Early in his mission, the story goes, Muhammad was willing to include in the Qurʾan an acknowledgment of three female deities, but later he repudiated these verses as satanically inspired. This obviously tends to undermine the orthodox position that the Qurʾan was dictated by God without any human interference.

This strict orthodox attitude to the Qurʾan, which amounts to what has been described as "a cult of the text," is not new. What is new about the uproar that surrounded the publication of Rushdie's novel was that this was the first time in which a book written in a Western language and published in a non-Muslim country was represented virtually as a casus belli. Equally novel is the fact that the anti-Rushdie campaign originated in Britain, where soon after its publication a special action committee was set up to coordinate the campaign. The chairman of the committee, who was also the head of the Islamic Cultural Center in Regent's Park, characterized the novel as "the most offensive, filthy and abusive book ever written by any hostile enemy of Islam." The secretary-general of the Islamic Council of Europe urged the Islamic Conference in Jidda, Saudi Arabia, to have all Muslim states ban the book, to bar its author from entry, and to blacklist all Viking-Penguin publications should the firm fail to withdraw the book and pulp it.

But the most interesting comment came, ironically enough, from the chairman of an organization calling itself The Islamic Society for the Promotion of Tolerance in the United Kingdom. This luminary, a Dr. Hesham al-Essawy, wrote to the managing director of Viking, saying: "To sanction such a work is to invite agonies and disasters from which none of us will be safe; we might as well knight muggers and give mass murderers the Nobel prize."[1]

On the pros and cons in the Rushdie controversy a great deal has been written. One of the more articulate cases for a more balanced view of the affair was made by John Esposito of Georgetown University. "Just as tolerance and freedom are equated with the West," Esposito writes, "so too is liberalism, while illiberalism is imputed to Islam." The Salman Rushdie case is often cited to illustrate that Muslims have little use for the liberalism of J. S. Mill. "Such judgments reduce the complexity of the Rushdie uproar to the issue of Islam's incompatibility with Western liberalism, rather than the question of whether religious belief places limits on free speech; it also implies that all Muslims hold a single position or speak with one voice." Any discussion of the Rushdie affair, Esposito adds, "must be seen against the background of the past, must recognize the historical and international context in which the debate occurred."

> Muslims were offended by passages in the book which questioned the authenticity of the Koran, ridiculed the Prophet and the contents of Islam's holy book, and referred to Muhammad as "Mahound"—a term used in the past by Christian authors to vilify Muhammad. The book also had prostitutes assuming the identity and names of Muhammad's wives, and the very Quranic symbol for their seclusion and protection, "The Curtain," is transformed into the image of a brothel, which men circumambulate as worshippers do the sacred shrine (*Kaaba*) during the pilgrimage to Mecca.[2]

On February 14, 1989, the Ayatollah Khomeini issued a fatwa condemning Rushdie, who was born a Muslim, to death and calling for his execution. The mufti of Sokoto (Nigeria) also called for Rushdie's death. In contrast, religious scholars at Cairo's al-Azhar University stated that, according to Islamic law, Rushdie must first have a trial and be given an opportunity to repent. The warrant drove Rushdie into hiding, where he still is, and Viking-Penguin into a siege mentality and a tight security system which cost a fortune to maintain. Moreover, the Pearson group, which includes Penguin as a subsidiary, was threatened with economic boycott by forty-six Muslim countries.

Does Rushdie's plight tell us something of significance about the strength of what has come to be called Islamic fundamentalism? Can we speak of Islam—and of Islamic fundamentalism—as one of a piece, regardless of time and place? How does Shi'ite fundamentalism compare to Sunni fundamentalism—Iran's version, say, to the Egyptian, Saudi, or Jordanian one?

These and many other related questions are difficult to answer because there is quite a variety of ways in which Islam has been perceived by Muslims. One of the more interesting aspects of contemporary Islam is the many different and often opposing ways in which its own adherents view it. Thus, while Khomeini was calling openly for Rushdie's murder, the sheikh of al-Azhar, Sunni Islam's leading religious authority, flatly rejected the Iranian ruler's edict. "This is not our way," he declared, and suggested instead that Rushdie be put on trial and his book banned.

It is worth noting here, too, the number of past and recent cases in which authors of Arabic books deemed blasphemous or in other ways offensive to Islam and to Muslims were punished by the religious establishment of the day. In Egypt in the 1920s, for example, two books by two well-known Islamic scholars, 'Ali 'Abd al-Raziq and Taha Husain, were banned—Raziq's for treating the institution of the caliphate in a manner perceived by the author's fellow Azharites as blasphemous, Husain's for casting doubts on the authenticity of the pre-Islamic poets, whose works were the source for rules of grammar and syntax used in Qur'anic exegesis.

In 1959, again, an allegory by Egypt's leading novelist and the 1987 Nobel laureate for literature, Naguib Mahfouz, *Children of the Alley*, was banned because it was thought to suggest—which it did, as an allegory—that the God of Adam, Moses, Jesus, and Muhammad might be "dead." No measures, legal or otherwise, were taken against any of the three "heretics," while all three books in question have been available in numerous printings published mainly in Beirut and often sold openly in many Cairo bookshops, the bans notwithstanding!

Muslim Establishment Disowns Fundamentalists

Does this, then, mean that "Islamic fundamentalism" has been on the ascendant? Has the Islamic religious establishment become more rigid, more "hardline"? Hardly. Where the Arab countries are concerned, at least, what can be termed official Islam has come out openly against the fundamentalists. The fundamentalists themselves, those who are calling for a return to pristine Islam as the only way out of the present predicament, can boast of no substantial or meaningful progress anywhere in the Arab countries of the Middle East and Africa.

Except for Algeria, a few groups of fanatics in Egypt, and a group of activists within the Islamic coalition in Jordan, fundamentalist Islam is nowhere near the helm in the Arab world. Colonel Gaddafi of Libya keeps talking about the necessity of a return to authentic Islam and its precepts and traditions but fails to do anything of consequence about it; in the Sudan Ja'afar Numeiri staked his rule on it—and lost; and the Saudis do not even pretend to strict Islamic orthodoxy or religious practices. Even Iran's ayatollahs, before as well as after Khomeini's demise, chose to continue to have daily intercourse and dealings with the "infidels" of the real world, rather than literally follow Islam's precept, which calls on the faithful to fight and subdue them.

Attacks launched by the Islamists on secularists have generally been more rhetorical and argumentative than scholarly or well balanced. But there are exceptions. Writing on developments preceding Khomeini's rise to power in Iran, Salim Mansur of the University of Western Ontario says much change took place within the Muslim world in those decades. Following World War II, he writes, practically all Muslim countries under European control gained political independence, and governments of all stripes pledged to their peoples the promise of modernization, to bring technologically backward Muslim societies into the modern age of science and technology as represented by the West.

It is clear that despite some material progress, decline and decay of the umma have been neither halted nor reversed. In some ways the situation is even more desperate, because the illusion of independence provides a false impression of progress. What did go wrong? Mansur asks. Apart from technology, he answers, another element facilitated the West's hegemony.

> Democracy, without any need here of making qualifications, is the other element that makes the West vibrant, dynamic, and powerful. . . . [Now,] while leaders in the Muslim world continuously pay lip service to making knowledge accessible to the population, Muslim

societies almost without exception remain retarded because of their lack of democracy. . . . [Al-Afghani] would point out that democracy and Islam are inseparable just as he pointed out that science and Islam are inseparable, and that it is the enemies of Islam within the Muslim world and outside who are joined together in defeating Muslims by denying them the fruits of democracy.

The tenets of democracy, Mansur explains,

are Islamic in their nature and function, including the principles that those who govern must represent the people and hold office only as long as they enjoy the support of the people, that all authority must be limited by a higher authority or principle, that laws bind both the governors and the governed, that accountability is the condition of electability, that obligations and duties are greatest on the shoulders of those who hold office in the name of the people, and that the voice of the people is more authoritative than the voice of the governors. Nothing of democracy is alien to the principles enshrined in the Quran and the Tradition of our noble Prophet. . . .[3]

The absence of democracy is at the heart of the contemporary malaise in the Muslim world, Mansur asserts. The lack of democracy is accompanied by the prevalence of nationalism, which he calls "the most corrosive ideology imported into the Muslim world from Europe." Al-Afghani, he adds,

did not fully comprehend the meaning and consequence of this European poison in Muslim homes, because the meaning of nationalism was not entirely revealed or understood at the time that he wandered across the Muslim world. . . . Eventually nationalism would set Muslims against Muslims, Arabs against Turks, Indians against Indians. After fully serving the interest of European powers in dividing the *ummah*, nationalism would weaken it from within, provide an opening for Zionists to penetrate the Arab-Islamic lands, and set the stage where territoriality of states engineered by European interests in the Middle East, North Africa, Central Asia, and South Asia would become the basis of new rivalries, wars, alliances, and exploitations.

Muslims now know this, says Mansur.

They also recognize today more clearly than ever before that progress in science, in acquiring knowledge of the material and the non-material world, presupposes democracy, for science and learning cannot exist in the absence of freedom to think, to question, and to freely associate and exchange ideas. The present-day ruling class in the Muslim world by being an obstacle to democracy is also the guarantor of bigotry, ignorance, and sectarianism. Thus we come full circle. "Political Islam," and "Muslim fundamentalists" are the swear words today in the language of those in the West and their allies who are opposed to democratic developments in the Muslim world. "Political Islam" and "Muslim fundamentalists," terms that in themselves are meaningless, threaten the negative status quo that was designed and imposed by Western powers when the Muslim world had reached the depths of its decline and decay. If al-Afghani were present today he would have been hounded by the label of "Muslim fundamentalist."

If Muslims are to convince the rest of the world to take them seriously, Mansur adds, "they have to show this capacity to build by respecting those values that we seem to have forgotten, the values of tolerance, respect, and large-heartedness that were once the mark of Muslims in the Classical Age. The decline and decay of Muslim societies were directly related to the hardening of the political system, which was becoming transformed into power-oriented states dominated by a military caste, and to the subordination of knowledge to the service of monarchs who constrained the language of Islam to legitimate their own narrow interests." By way of a conclusion Mansur writes:

A great distance in time separates us from the era when the Mediterranean basin was the most dynamic center of world trade, commerce, science, and learning, and when Muslims played a role second to none. The Muslim world stretches between the Atlantic and the Pacific, and can be the natural link between the West and the East across the continents. Just as by geography the Muslim world is in the middle, so by temperament, history, and culture the Muslims are the people of the middle. The Quran states, "Thus we have appointed you a middle nation." It remains for Muslims to show that as the people of the middle they can be once again the stabilizing force of moderation, which is what democracy is all about and what Islam stands for.[4]

Violence and Repression

Writing on the current conflict between the Islamic movements and the secular state, Rashid al-Ghanuchi, leader of the Tunisian Al-Nahda Islamic movement, starts with an optimistic note.

Islam is progressing forcefully while secularism is falling rapidly. While Islam attracts people who are looking for justice, secularism is losing major footholds and has lost its ability to defend itself except by violence. When you see a secular state using more and more violence, know that it is bankrupt. The secular state has lost its legitimacy. Instead of being based on popular support, these states are based on international support and on violence. Meanwhile, Islam is progressing vertically and horizontally. Its idea deepens daily while spreading from fields such as politics and economics to art, human resource development (including women) and institution-building.[5]

On the current conflict between the Islamic movement and the secular state, al-Ghanuchi states that the movement "is being subjected to horrific amounts of violence and suppression." The question is: How should the movement respond to oppression by the secular state? Is state violence a justification for popular violence? There are many religious replies to these questions, he answers.

Pragmatically speaking, . . . all of the episodes where Islamists responded violently to state violence have been negative. Popular violence, whether Islamic or otherwise, has not been able to damage any regime's standing. Leftists and Islamists have carried out violence, and it has led to nothing but disaster, as in Syria. The Islamic movement must abide by peaceful methods. It must refuse all forms of military activity. This is the lesson we can learn from the Rafah Party in Turkey. . . . The arena of the Islamists is thought, and that is where the rulers are bankrupt. We should not be pulled into a field where they will surely win.

On the subject of democracy, al-Ghanuchi has this to say:

Many Islamists associate democracy with foreign intervention and non-belief. But democracy is a set of mechanisms to guarantee freedom of thought and assembly and peaceful competition for governmental authority through ballot boxes. The Islamic movement's negative attitude toward democracy is holding it back. We have no modern experience in Islamic activity that can replace democracy. The Islamization of democracy is the closest thing to implementing *shura* (consultation). Those who reject this thought have not produced anything different than the one-party system of rule. The Islamists have two examples: Iran and Sudan. Both are searching . . . for a modern Islamic form of government. We have no modern example for implementing Islamic government. . . . The Islamists must realize that, despite the achievements of the Islamic movement, the balance of power is simply not in their favor. The balance is in the secularists' favor. Governance might be something the Islamic movement cannot do alone. Maybe the better option is to participate in government as long as the balance of power is what it is.[6]

Hasan Turabi, the man who is generally considered the dynamic force behind the Islamist regime in Sudan, writes as quietly and persuasively as Mansur does. In a short survey of the state of the Islamic movements in the Arab world, he asserts that only in "countries like Yemen and Jordan" is there "a certain degree of freedom." Turning to his own country, Sudan, Turabi writes:

At the present time Sudan may be considered an Islamic state in which the following issues are being studied: the form of government, the electoral system, the constitution, *shura,* the improvement of the economy by Islamic means, and the establishment of suitable institutions for that purpose. The role of Islamic banks and insurance companies is being debated, as is the nature of Islamic justice, the ways in which music and the arts may be encouraged, and how the system of education may be improved. All of this is going on at present in Sudan. Still, there are other countries in which there is no possibility of progress except by the means of revolution, as happened in Iran. History teaches us that sometimes revolution is the only way that change may be brought about. The revolutions of France, America, Russia, and China are good examples.[7]

Turning to the West's attitude to these movements, Turabi describes as "unfortunate" the West's failure "to understand this new wave of Islamic revivalism or, as they prefer to call it, 'fundamentalism'. In the United States, the media has labeled this revival 'fundamentalism' because they suppose it to resemble their own Christian fundamentalist movements. As a result, they have treated Islamic revivalism as if it were another reactionary and backward movement. In fact, they know very little about the true content of Islamic revivalism because popular Orientalism is concerned in the main with the history of classical rather than contemporary times in the Islamic world."

The West is democratic, Turabi concedes. However, "whenever it believes that democracy is leading to the appearance of an Islamic state in any part of the world, it wastes no time in attempting to bring it down."

It appears, lamentably, that the West is not serious in its belief that democracy is an absolute universal value. Whenever it seems that democracy and Islam are going to work together, the West is ready to stage an overthrow. This is what has happened time and again in Turkey, and so recently in Algeria. In fact, I have little doubt that the same will happen in other places in the Islamic world. So what about human rights? It appears to me that the definition of human rights in the West is not inclusive of all human beings. If there are hundreds, or thousands, or tens of thousands of Muslim political prisoners in the world, the West has closed its eyes to their plight.[8]

The reason why Turabi advocates a democratic interpretation of Islam based on popular consensus (ijmaᶜ), says Haifa University professor and Sudan specialist Gabriel R. Warburg, is his belief that "individual freedom was the most basic principle of Islam." In the past, Warburg explains, a select learned elite was shouldered with the task of interpreting Islam due to the ignorance of the people. "Education and learning had made this elitist approach unnecessary and even the *shura*, the Islamic way of consensual decision making, could now become an open popular process which, unlike secular democracy, would be based on the sovereignty of God and Islamic morality and thus is free from secular distortions." Islam, through a process of renewal, "would overcome the sectarian divisiveness inherent in its history, and establish the just society based on its tenets. As Turabi put it: 'The correct method is to guide men gently from darkness to light, instead of standing apart and waiting for some miracle to achieve this for you'."[9]

Warburg quotes one of the movement's spokesmen, Abdelwahab el-Affendi:

The modern Islamist movement looks like the only hope for rescuing modern Muslim societies from the endemic cycle of instability caused by the inherent illegitimacy of the secular political systems ruling over them. . . . For a worldview that remains unchallenged theoretically, that places its adherents at the center of the universe as the divinely-sanctioned leaders of humanity, replacements are hard to find, especially if they all entailed third-or fourth-class membership in the community of nations.[10]

"Another argument used by the Islamists to justify their willingness to achieve their goal through collaboration with the military," Warburg adds, "was that in abiding by Western democratic principles, they would have to accept secularism as a framework in which to act in the political arena."

Furthermore, they argued that even were the Islamists to gain power democratically, they would not be granted legal recognition or power, as illustrated both in the Sudan and in Algeria. Alternatively they could act by force, stage their revolution and impose their Islamic norms on society. El-Affendi observes that "when your opponents do not play by the rules, the temptation to reciprocate is hard to resist." As for Turabi himself, he advocated the use of force quite openly, saying that the Islamic movement had the full right to assume power by all means, including military force.[11]

Readings

The Muslim Brothers

... It is remarkable how elaborate and comprehensive the Muslim Brethren's methods and general principles are. Pointing out that the Brethren "will always prefer gradual progress and development," Hasan al-Banna in 1945 explained that this gradual development must pass through three distinct stages:

1. A stage of propaganda—the promulgation and inculcation of the idea and its dissemination among the broad masses of people.
2. A stage of attracting and selecting supporters, the drilling of recruits, and the mobilization of those who answer the call.
3. A stage of implementation, action, and fulfillment. . . .

On various occasions, al-Banna laid it down that Islam has an all-inclusive meaning, regulating all the affairs of life and interpreting all matters, for which it lays down exact and precise rules. He claims that the peoples of the Islamic East will never find a decent life based on noble ideals except in Islam. He believes that nationalism in Islam is more complete, purer, nobler, and higher than it is on the lips of the Europeans and in their writings. In everything related to the issues worrying the world's politicians and sociologists—internationalism, nationalism, socialism, capitalism, Bolshevism, war, the distribution of wealth, relations between producer and consumer— in all of these, al-Banna says, Islam has immersed itself and laid down for the world rules which will secure for it all the benefits therein. He believes that the movement is a universal and all-embracing one. It has not passed by anything worthy in any other movement without acquainting itself thoroughly with it and reaching conclusions.

The principles of the Brethren, which are thus said to embrace every religious, political, social, and economic aspect of life, are usually summed by in six broad aims:

1. Scientific: To explain the Holy Koran in precise terms, interpreting it and referring back to its origins and universal elements, completely revealing it in the spirit of the age, and defending it from falsehoods and suspicions. . . .
2. Practical: To rally the Egyptian nation and all the Islamic nations around these Koranic principles, to imbue the peoples with the spirit of the Koran, and to bridge differences between the viewpoints of the various Islamic sects.
3. Economic: To increase the national wealth, liberating and protecting it; to raise the standard of living; to achieve social justice between individuals and classes, social security for all citizens, and equal opportunity for all. This principle is aimed to serve the workers, who had been the backbone of the movement, put a limit to foreign influence in the economy, animate local industries, and enable the workers to organize themselves in trade unions.
4. Social work: Social welfare and social service; the fight against ignorance, disease, poverty, and vice; and the encouragement of useful, benevolent, and charitable works.
5. Patriotic: To liberate the Nile valley and all other Arab countries and parts of the Islamic fatherland from all foreign domination; provision of assistance to Islamic minorities everywhere to secure their rights; unqualified support for Arab unity and working for an Islamic league; sincere furtherance of world cooperation based on high and worthy ideals; and institution of a sound state that can put the rules and injunctions of Islam into practice.
6. Universal: The promotion of universal peace and a humanitarian civilization, both material and spiritual, on the basis of Islamic principles, proclaiming fraternity for all and providing the practical means to its attainment in a world yearning for a virtuous and spiritual life. . . .

The [Brotherhood's] memorandum *Toward the Light* concludes with the following words: "We place ourselves, our talents, and all we possess at the disposal of any organization or government which would step forward with the Islamic nation to advancement and progress. We shall answer the call and we shall be the redemption."

Nissim Rejwan, *Arabs Face the Modern World: Religious, Cultural, and Political Responses to the West* (Gainesville: University Press of Florida, 1998), 71–72, 73.

The Brotherhood's Political Theory

Political theory in Islam rests on the basis of justice on the part of the rulers, obedience on the part of the ruled, and collaboration between ruler and ruled. These are the great fundamental features from which all the other features take their rise.

There must first be justice on the part of the rulers. "Verily Allah commands justice." "And when you judge between the people, you must do so with justice." "And when you speak, act justly, even though the matter concerns a relative." "And be not driven by hatred of any people to unjust action; to act justly is closer to piety." "Verily on the Day of Resurrection he who is dearest of all men to Allah, and he who is nearest to Him will be the just leader; but he who is most hated by Allah on that Day, and he who is most bitterly punished will be the tyrannical leader."

Secondly, there must be obedience on the part of those who are ruled. "O you who have believed, obey Allah, and obey the Messenger of Allah and those who hold authority among you." The fact that this verse groups together Allah, the Messenger, and those who hold authority means that it clarifies the nature and the limits of this obedience. Obedience to one who holds authority is derived from obedience to Allah and the Messenger. The ruler in Islamic law is not to be obeyed because of his own person; he is to be obeyed only by virtue of holding his position through the law of Allah and His Messenger; his right to obedience is derived from his observance of that law, and from no other thing. If he departs from the law, he is no longer entitled to obedience, and his orders need no longer be obeyed. Thus one authority says that, "There can be no obedience to any creature which involves disobedience to the Creator." Or again: "Hear and obey—even if your ruler is an Abyssinian slave with a head like a raisin, so long as he observes the Book of Allah the Exalted." It is made very clear by this tradition that to hear and obey is conditioned by the observance by the ruler of the Book of Allah the Exalted. An absolute obedience such as this is not to be accorded to the will of the ruler himself, nor can it be a binding thing if he abandons the law of Allah and of His Messenger. "If anyone sees a tyrannical power which is contrary to the will of Allah, which violates the compact of Allah, and which produces evil or enmity among the servants of Allah, and if he does not try to change it by deed or by word, then it is Allah who must supply the initiative. . . ."

Thirdly, there must be collaboration between ruler and ruled. "Take counsel with them in the matter." "And their affair is a matter for collaboration between them." Collaboration is one of the fundamentals of Islamic politics, although no specific method of administering it has ever been laid down; its application has been left to the exigencies of individual situations. The Messenger used to take the advice of the Muslim community in matters which did not pertain to the spiritual; thus he would ask their opinion in worldly affairs in which they had some skill, such as positions on a field of battle. . . .

Sayed Kotb, *Social Justice in Islam*, trans. John B. Hardie (Washington, D.C.: American Council of Learned Societies, 1953), 93–96.

The Principles of Islamic Government

. . . Power comes only through union, and merely symbolic union will not invest [Muslim states] with even an atom of respect or awe. Indeed the Arab League is not far from our memory. This League, which was compelled to flee before a gang of homeless Jews in Palestine, which proved impotent in the numerous questions affecting the Arab states and which has filled the waste-paper baskets to overflowing! It is true union founded on the true Islamic creed which will be of service and which will rally the Muslims of the West and of the East. The Arabs have not drawn even one atom of benefit from the Arab League because it was a kind of forum for the Arab leaders to spend in it pleasant and merry times. The Arab League is a league of politicians and leaders and nothing more. The people know nothing about it except what is written in newspapers and magazines. This is the secret of its failure. If the Muslims could perchance have an Islamic League, then the ideal of this league would be amalgamated with the beliefs of all the Muslim peoples and they would sacrifice themselves and their most precious things for its sake.

We are not preaching such a rejection of nationalism that will bring with it derision of the fatherland and its neglect. The Muslim has a smaller fatherland, which is the state where he was born and bred; Islam requires him to defend it and glorify it. But the Muslim has also a greater fatherland: this is the Muslim state towards which he is attracted by a creed anchored in the depths of his soul and Islam obliges him to struggle for the sake of this greater fatherland and towards its greater glory. The nationalism which we reject is that which requires the Muslim to become fanatical in the cause of the state in which he grew up, and to ignore that he has a vast Muslim fatherland and a great Muslim nation, because this stupid fanaticism perpetuates the dismemberment of the Muslim state and its weakness, and encourages the great powers to swallow it statelet by statelet. We repeat once again: Islamic union will not arise unless true Muslim rule prepares for it in the Muslim states a rule which aims at the good of Islam, its fatherlands and its peoples. Muslim rule however will not come into being unless the Muslim peoples have a union to preserve their existence. And the Muslim peoples will not have a corporate existence unless they are ruled in the true Muslim way and thereby attain internal stability, and unless they have an Islamic union strong enough to provide them with power and a voice which counts in the world. First and last, responsibility lies on the shoulder of the Muslim peoples who are trying to live cut off from Life.

Muhammad ʿAbdullah as-Samman, *The Principles of Islamic Government* (Cairo, 1953), trans. Sylvia G. Haim, *World of Islam*, n.s. vol. 5 (1958): 252–253.

Islamic Government: A Contemporary Muslim's Prognosis

Whether by faith, tradition, religious reflection or practice, Islamic government, whether the Caliphate or the Imamate, has been centered in a specific race, tribe and family; the ruler (Caliph, Imam, Sultan, or whatever) has been made infallible; and this ruler has been given a free hand, full power and absolute authority over the people, the national income and the destiny of the nation. In domestic affairs, the people were almost always (with few exceptions) treated as members of a herd rather than as citizens; as subjects rather than as brothers in Islam. For example, the Caliphate sometimes demanded tribute from Muslims rather than the taxes they should pay as Muslims, as happened when the Ottomans demanded tribute from Egypt. Any sharing in decision making, any consultation, was completely optional and left to the whim of the Caliph. No opposition was allowed, and when it arose, it was called heresy and damned as atheism.

The result is a sorry history of plots and intrigues, massacres and civil wars as those who had power struggled with those who aspired to it; for example, consider ʿAli (the fourth rightly guided Caliph) and Muʾawiyya, the Umayyids and the Shiʿites, the Umayyids and the Abbasids, the Abbasids and the Shiʿites, and so on.

As for foreign affairs, it must be remembered that after the period of the four rightly guided Caliphs, the Islamic state became, in fact, an empire. The Caliphs, in their capacity as emperors, invaded other countries to protect their empire, increased their power, gained new subjects and gathered new fortunes. Many ethical questions remain, especially when we observe that these invasions were undertaken for temporal purposes and earthly concerns but carried out under the flag of religion and in the name of God.

Some would object that the main motivation of the Caliphs' war was to spread Islam, but this is not accurate. For example, the Egyptian people were not converted to Islam until about three or four centuries after the Muslim conquest. In Andalusia, despite about eight centuries of Islamic rule, most of the native population remained Christian. While these are excellent examples of Muslim tolerance, they also show either that the spread of Islam was not the goal of these conquests or that Muslims were lax in their mission, and, in some instances, failed in it.

To give the Caliphs' religious support for their policies, Islamic scholars came to divide the world into the abode of peace, which is that part of the world under Islamic rule, and the abode of war, which is everywhere else. It is important to note that this well-known distinction does not come from genuine Islamic religion but is entirely an invention devised to give religious legitimation to the Caliphs' foreign policy. Thus, this division can and must be abolished to preserve Islam's true image, a religion of tolerance, equality and peace.

The Muslim invasions of Andalusia, Eastern Europe (by the Turks) and India (by the Moguls) left deep and hurtful effects. Many historians and non-Muslim intellectuals consider the rule of the invaders to have been cruel, arrogant and (especially in Andalusia) sometimes degenerate. They say that non-Muslims under Muslim rule were, if not persecuted, discriminated against, in that they were allowed to practice their religious rituals (under Muslim supervision) but not to exercise equal political or social rights.

The Caliphs and political leaders were wary of education and high culture, and often prohibited real education and limited teaching for Muslims to the memorization of verses from the Qur'an, memorization of the traditions of the Prophet and memorization of scattered quotations from the jurists. The result was a high illiteracy rate, and the Islamic world's being left behind as the West steadily advanced with the industrial revolution and the development of modern technology.

Authentic Islam is aware of the consequences of using religion for political purposes and of using the people to secure personal and family interests. For there is not a single verse in the Qur'an that directs Muslims to any specific political form or that ordains for them any specific kind of government. Were the Caliphate or the Imamate (or any other form of government) part of the religion of Islam, we should expect that it would have been mentioned and sketched out in general outlines in the Qurʾan. Nor are these forms of governments mentioned in the prophetic tradition. The clear conclusion to be drawn is that systems of political power and leadership are socially and historically conditioned structures, which ought to be developed according to the needs of the people and the spirit of the age and in keeping with the demands of Islamic ethics: justice, equality, humanity and mercy.

True Islamic government—after the Prophet—is a government of the people, a government in which the people freely elect, a government in which the people share, a government in which they control and supervise, and in which they may change peaceably, without bloodshed and without being denounced as heretics.

It was mentioned previously that in Qurʾanic terminology, *government* means the administration of justice. It is only by distorting the Qurʾanic meaning of the word and by understanding it as referring to political authority that Qurʾanic verses using the word *government* are used to support the call for an Islamic government like those which have appeared in history. What Muslims should in fact be calling for is not an Islamic government but a government that will serve Islam rather than use it, a government based on facts rather than slogans, on realities rather than dreams, on clarity rather than confusion. Islam does not recommend any single form of government and is absolutely against religious government. Islam is concerned with people, not with systems; with the conscience, not with legal rules; with the spirit, not with the letter of the law. A truly Islamic government will be one based on justice. This government, best described as a civil government, will come from the people and will be ruled by the people for the benefit of all the people. This government will gather everyone into one community and will exclude no one. This government will care about education, culture, science, art, history, literature and civilization. It will encourage cooperation, understanding, work, planning, constructive labor and self-sacrifice. It will understand Islam as mercy rather than as a sword, amity rather than enmity. It will offer Islam to all humankind as a way to God, a method for progress and a path for mercy. This is the new and true Islamic government. . . .

Everyone uses the term "Islamic" according to his or her own interpretation, hopes and understanding. Many people in the West see in the term a sword being raised up against non-Muslims. For many in the Islamic world the term excites an emotional reaction compounded of wishful thinking, great respect for the era of the Prophet and the rightly guided Caliphs, a tendency to hallow the past and a general lack of knowledge of the history of humanity. A clear understanding is lacking, and the words are frequently misused. But most will agree that the term refers to a system in which Islamic law, Shariᶜa, is applied, and in which, whether in fulfillment of doctrine or simply in fact, a religious leadership controls the government.

We may now ask the following questions.

If an Islamic government is based on justice and morality and aims to spread faith, what may be said of other governments with the same base and the same aims?

If a government is based on equity and practices justice, is it Islamic? Or against Islam?

If a government aims to spread faith, is it Islamic? Or against Islam?

In fact, no government can rule unless it calls for justice, is consonant with some kind of ethical system and, apart from the atheist countries, respects faith of some kind.

A saying of the Prophet is: A kingdom may be built on heresy, but never on injustice. In other words, any government that lasts must be based on justice. In every nation of the world throughout history, constitutions and legal rules aim at providing justice. The problem, of course, is in the application. Actually political systems should be evaluated on the basis of facts, not on the basis of ethical claims that were never considered in the application and never made effective in history.

If the goal of an Islamic government can be defined as the application of Shariᶜa, serious academic studies must take place in order to explain Shariᶜa in a precise way: What does Shariᶜa mean? It is important to note that the way the term Shariᶜa is used today is not the way the word is used in the Qurʾan and does not correspond to its original Arabic meaning.

1. *Shariᶜa* (Islamic law) means the path, the method or the way.
2. The path of Islam is mercy.
3. To restrict Islam as a nationalism is to leave the absolute for the relative and abandon religion for chauvinism.
4. To limit the path in legal rules and jurisprudence is to localize it in place and fix it in time.
5. To confine the method in some texts and opinions is to fossilize it in words and nothing but words.
6. Mercy is to have no confrontation with any country or enmity with any people.
7. Mercy is to recognize and respect any other path: Judaism, Christianity, Buddhism, Hinduism and so on.

8. Mercy is to cooperate with everyone regardless of faith, color, language or origin.
9. Mercy is to establish a new method of comprehension, to understand and to respect each other.
10. Mercy is to care for humankind and to gather the past, the present and the future in one humanistic vision.
11. Mercy is to look for what is human, not for the text, to look for the spirit of the text, not the letter of the text.
12. Mercy is to spread prosperity, liberty, equality, justice and love, not only for Muslims but also for everyone, anytime and anywhere.

Today Shariᶜa has come to include the whole body of legal rules developed in Islamic history, with all interpretations and opinions of the legal scholars, that is, jurisprudence. Therefore, in reality, to apply Shariᶜa means to codify Islamic jurisprudence. Muslims who call for applying Shariᶜa justify their call for this application with examples from the period of the Prophet (610–632 C.E.) or of ᶜUmar, the second Caliph (634–644 C.E.), often confusing legal and judicial systems with the pure Islamic ethics of the early period or with particular events that are narrated about this period, in order to prove that Islamic government is just and ethical.

Muhammad Saᶜid al-ᶜAshmawi in *Against Islamic Extremism,* ed.
Carolyn Fluehr-Lobban (Gainesville: University Press of Florida, 1998),
77–78, 88–89.

The Three Components of Islamist Movements

The mid-1970s was a watershed period for the Muslim world. The sky-rocketing oil prices brought about tremendous change in the distribution of wealth within Muslim countries—many of which export it, while most others benefit from the indirect effect of this bounty. This wealth, however, was unevenly distributed, and it created long-term social disruption. As new wealth boosted consumption, it made inequality not only more visible but also more difficult to accept, as was the case in Iran, where the upper class close to the palace had ostensibly creamed off oil revenues. . . .

The Young Urban Poor

Apart from the many changes linked to oil prices, the mid-1970s in the Muslim world witnessed a structural and dramatic transformation in demographics and in related variables such as age distribution, urban versus rural distribution, literacy, and modes of access to the political system. The demographic explosion of the post–World War II period gave birth to an unparalleled youth cohort—with more than 50 percent of the population below the age of twenty. They came of adult age from the 1970s. Among the most salient characteristics of these new youths was their mass migration from a countryside that could feed them no longer toward cities where they expected a better life. Those newcomers could not reach the heart of the cities and became foreign to their traditional social networks and political culture. They dwelled in a new space between the urban and the rural worlds, jamming shantytowns, informal neighborhoods, or housing projects in the outskirts of the cities.

This young "rurban" population epitomizes the major social breakdown of the current quarter century. Though spatially, politically, and socially "marginalized," they have become the actual demographic "center" of contemporary Muslim societies. They shared three unique characteristics: they were generally poor, significantly more literate than their parents, and had no memory of the struggles for independence on which most of the ruling elites in the Muslim world had built their legitimacy. At the time these youths were reaching adulthood, they usually had scarce job opportunities.

Finally, the Young Urban Poor remained impervious to the ruling elites' rhetoric of legitimization, tracing back to the 1950s or early sixties. They did not consider the incumbent rulers legitimate—all the more because they never had a say in choosing them. In their view, the ruling class was accountable for today's problems rather than yesterday's glory; and as far as the most burning of these problems were concerned—jobs, housing, and respect—the state simply did not deliver. The Young Urban Poor were not politically integrated, they did not relate to the state system: they were out. Their social protest was expressed in cyclical waves of riots, usually targeting the city centers from which they were excluded, and focusing on symbols of state authority such as official buildings, public means of transportation, and traffic signs. . . .

The Intellectual Counterelites

Within this "new youth" of the 1970s, a sizable minority acquired modern education, whether at high school, college, or university levels, in local institutions of learning and, for some of them, in foreign universities. Modern education was a top priority for governments of independent countries in the Muslim world. The number of graduates, however, far exceeded the available corresponding employment opportunities. Many of the degrees obtained locally were below international standards because of understaffing in schools, poor infrastructure, and obsolete instruction techniques that still relied heavily on rote learning. Hence, the better openings were provided to U.S. or European graduates whenever competence made the difference. As for key positions of power in the state bureaucracy, in the army, or any structure linked to the preservation of the prevalent social order, kinship, lineage, and connections often took precedence over merit.

It is within this "relatively deprived" group that the intellectual Islamist counterelites are to be found. This group has played a pivotal role in the emergence of the movement because its members both coined the new Islamist ideology of the 1970s and attempted to reach the bulk of the disfranchised youth, mobilizing them and "conscientizing" them through a network of benevolent associations funded by the Pious Bourgeoisie.

Throughout their opposition to the state, the young Intellectual Counterelites used the language of Islam for a number of converging reasons: its intellectual categories could be understood easily by the masses of the Young Urban Poor that they wished to mobilize, they themselves came from "traditional" backgrounds where they had been accustomed to such worldviews, and, above all, they saw Islam as the means par excellence to demonize the "secular" state, to create the "other" to be fought against. . . .

The Intellectual Counterelites were crucial for giving the Islamist movements of the 1970s and 1980s their ideological character. The resource they possessed was "cultural capital," but they were not, by themselves, sufficiently strong to pose a social threat to the regimes they opposed, and they attempted to mobilize the Young Urban Poor to that effect. For the sake of efficiency, the clerics' cooperation proved crucial, not only in mobilizing the urban poor but also, and especially, to reach to the social group that possessed the financial resources to fund the movement: the Pious Bourgeoisie.

The Pious Bourgeoisie

The third component of Islamist movements is somewhat more heterogeneous than the first two. The Pious Bourgeoisie does not belong solely to the social cohort of the youths. Some of its members are old enough to remember how the ruling class actually came to power. They recall how they were excluded from participation in the power system after independence, as was the case in Egypt and Algeria in the 1960s, when socialist policies were implemented and a nomenclature, which would evolve later into a state bourgeoisie, was formed. In Iran, they had memories of the events of 1953 and 1963, which paved the way for the absolute power of the shah and of a privileged upper class of cronies who creamed off the oil revenues, to which the traditional middle class, symbolized by the bazaar merchants, had little access. This older segment of the Pious Bourgeoisie had close links to the ulema, most of whom came from traditional families. In Egypt and Algeria many of them had been close to political-religious movements of the pre-independence period such as the Muslim Brotherhood and the Association des Oulemas, founded in 1931 by Sheikh Abdel Hamid Ben Badis in Constantine.

These organizations advocated moral reform and the advent of an Islamic state to replace colonial domination, but their conservative social agenda did not challenge the class structure or private property. They had hoped to play a major role in the independent states, but they were marginalized by Nasser (who violently crushed them in October 1954) and Ben Bella, who resented the fact that they had waited some two years before joining the FLN in the war it had waged against the French since November 1954. They were bashed as "enemies of progress," while the Pious Bourgeoisie, whose interests the Muslim Brothers and Algerian ulema advocated, saw their properties sequestered or nationalized and their economic positions hampered by legal procedures.

The Pious Bourgeoisie was to gain new prominence after the failure of socialist policies was acknowledged by state authorities—in Egypt in the mid-1970s with Sadat's *infitah* ("open-door economic policy") and in Algeria with Chadli Bendjedid's liberalization in the mid-1980s. Though they were courted by and, for some, co-opted into the power structures, they would not identify with the ruling groups, whom they considered parasites constantly levying taxes while proving increasingly incapable of equipping the country with an infrastructure that could match the population growth, or even maintain law and order. . . .

The Iranian Pious Bourgeoisie, which was neither uprooted nor impoverished, as opposed to the young urban disfranchised, nevertheless participated, by 1978, in a movement whose final aim was the overthrow of a regime that had alienated it. They portrayed their movement as Islamic, not only because the mosques were the only remaining venues for political mobilization that had managed to resist SAVAK repression, but also because most bazaaris remained traditionally religious, paying their tithe and alms taxes to the mullahs. To them, reference to Islam was a clear-cut means of differentiation from the imperial regime, which they demonized as "impious." It would also prove an efficient way to join forces with other social groups within the movement.

Each of the three components of Islamist movements possesses its own peculiar resource: the Young Urban Poor are a potential social threat that can play a decisive role in taking to the streets to bring down those in power. But they will do so only if organized, otherwise their revolt would remain short lived and would be crushed by the state security forces. The Intellectual Counterelites provide cultural capital as their own resource: they can articulate the *dawla Islamiyya* (Islamic state) project that sets the political goal of social mobilization. But they are more of an age cohort with a common cultural capital than a cohesive social group. They represent no major social threat by themselves, and they have no direct access to sources of funding. They exist as long as they can provide the potential ideological substratum that will bridge the gap between the differentiated social agendas of the Young Urban Poor and the Pious Bourgeoisie. They are likely to be disintegrating as a group in the case of a successful revolutionary takeover (as in Iran) or of a major split in the movement (as in Algeria). Their members might then side, according to each individual's preferences, with either one of the two social groups. As for the Pious Bourgeoisie, they possess financial capital, but they lack the ideological resources for mobilization, and they constitute no potent social threat by themselves.

Giles Kepel, "Toward a Social Analysis of Islamist Movements," in *Ethnic Conflict and International Politics in the Middle East,* ed. Leonard Binder (Gainesville: University Press of Florida, 1999), 184–185, 186–187, 190–191.

The Status of Muslim Minorities

Muslim minorities are 45 percent of the entire world population of Muslims. They are a major value for Islam, and they are the pioneers of Islamic propagation. Either they help open the path or else they become extinct. . . .

The role I suggest for Muslim minorities is to reinforce the Islamic presence in the countries they live in. There is a big difference between maintaining a presence and working to establish an Islamic government. The most a minority can hope for is participation in politics. In fact, their entry into the realm of politics is sometimes a major reason for the attention minorities get. So they better focus on social work. Politics is a grinding arena. The race for government is the race for wealth and influence.

Sometimes we find Muslim minorities asking for independence or a separate state. Of course this is allowed from a legal point of view, but in reality

it must not be allowed. We can ask: is the quest for independence necessary? Or can we accept a lesser arrangement, like self-rule, in preparation
for the return to Islam? That goes for the Chechnyans, where the Muslim
minority is demanding independence from Russia. Russia is a decaying
empire; Islam can get to it in time. So why should we prevent that by split-
ting from it, especially if independence is simply not viable and would lead
to the annihilation of the Muslim minority? Also, the incessant demand for
independence might damage the relationship between the Muslim world
and the nation that the Muslim minority wants independence from. If the
Muslim minority in China adopts the demand for independence one day,
and the Muslims find an interest in allying with China against some mutual enemy, the Muslims will be faced with a major dilemma.

The Islamic nation has an interest in not picking fights with China, India, or even Yugoslavia these days. Wherever Muslim minorities can live
safely, and practice their religious rites freely, independence is not necessary. In fact, the pursuit of independence could be deadly. Generally speaking, Muslim minorities are not requested to govern the countries they live
in by Islam, nor to think about independence, because this will lead to
their genocide and put the entire Islamic nation's interests in danger.

Sheikh Rashid al-Ghanuchi, "Islamic Movements: Self-Criticism and
Reconsideration," *Middle East Affairs Journal* (Annandale, Va.), Winter–
Spring 1997/1417, 13–15.

Fundamentalism Is Not Transitory

In traditional Islam (as in Judaism), laws apply to the individual, not (as in
the West) to the territory. It matters not whether a Muslim lives here or
there, in the homeland or in the diaspora; he must follow the *shariᶜa*. Con-
versely, a non-Muslim living in a Muslim country need not follow its directives. For example, a Muslim may not drink whisky whether he lives in
Tehran or Los Angeles; and a non-Muslim may imbibe in either place. This
leads to complex situations whereby one set of rules applies to a Muslim
thief who robs a Muslim, another to a Christian who robs a Christian, and
so forth. The key is who you are, not where you are.

In contrast, European notions of law are premised on jurisdictions. Commit a crime in this town or state and you get one punishment, another in
the next town over. Even highways have their own rules. Where you are,
not who you are, is what counts. Ignorant of the spirit underlying the *shariᶜa*,
fundamentalists enforce it along territorial, not personal lines; Turabi de-

clares that Islam "accepts territory as the basis of jurisdiction." As a result, national differences have emerged. The Libyan government lashes all adulterers. Pakistan lashes unmarried offenders and stones married ones. The Sudan imprisons some and hangs others. Iran has even more punishments, including head shaving and a year's banishment. In the hands of fundamentalists, the *shari*ᶜ*a* becomes just a variant of Western, territorial law. This new understanding most dramatically affects non-Muslims, whose millennium-old exclusion from the *shari*ᶜ*a* is over. Now they must live as virtual Muslims. Umar Abd al-Rahman, the Egyptian sheikh in an American jail, is adamant on this subject: "It is very well known that no minority in any country has its own laws." Abd al-Aziz ibn Baz, the Saudi religious leader, calls on non-Muslims to fast during Ramadan. In Iran, foreign women may not wear nail polish—on the grounds that this leaves them unclean for (Islamic) prayers. Entering the country, the authorities provide female visitors with petrol-soaked rags and insist they wipe clean their varnished nails. A fundamentalist party in Malaysia wants to regulate how much time unrelated Chinese men and women may spend alone together.

This new interpretation of Islamic law creates enormous problems. Rather than fairly much leaving non-Muslims to regulate their own conduct, as did traditional Islam, fundamentalism seeks to intrude into their lives, fomenting enormous resentment and sometimes leading to violence. Palestinian Christians who raise pigs find their animals mysteriously poisoned. The million or two Christians living in the northern, predominantly Muslim, region of the Sudan must comply with virtually all the *shari*ᶜ*a* regulations. In the southern Sudan, Islamic law prevails wherever the central government rules, although "certain" *shari*ᶜ*a* provisions are not applied there; should the government conquer the whole south, all the provisions would probably go into effect, an expectation that does much to keep alive a forty-year civil war. Fundamentalist Islam has adopted so many European legal notions that the details may be Islamic but the spirit is Western. . . .

Despite themselves, fundamentalists are Westernizers. Whichever direction they turn, they end up going west. Even in rejecting the West, they accept it. This has two implications. First, however reactionary in intent, fundamentalism imports not just modern but Western ideas and institutions. The fundamentalist dream of expunging Western ways from Muslim life, in short, cannot succeed.

Second, the resulting hybrid is more robust than it seems. Opponents of fundamentalist Islam often dismiss it as a regressive effort to avoid modern life and comfort themselves with the prediction that it is doomed to be left behind as modernization takes place. But this expectation seems mistaken. Because fundamentalism appeals most directly to Muslims contending with the challenges of modernity, its potential grows as does its numbers. Current trends suggest that fundamentalist Islam will remain a force for some time to come. That is not to say that fundamentalism will last, for it will wither just as surely as did the other radical utopian ideologies of this century, fascism and communism. But this process may take decades rather than years, and cause great damage in the process. Opponents of fundamentalism, Muslim or non-Muslim, cannot afford the luxury of sitting back and awaiting its collapse.

Daniel Pipes, "The Western Mind of Radical Islam," in *The Islamism Debate,* ed. Martin Kramer (Tel Aviv: Moshe Dayan Center for Middle Eastern and African Studies, 1998), 63–65.

Sources of Future Islamist Strength

The future of Islamist power obviously rests on the determinants of Islamist strength. What are the main preconditions for the emergence of strong Islamist movements in the Muslim world? Briefly, the most important preconditions start with the failure of the state and the state order. This means states and regimes dealing ineffectively with economic and social grievances—employment, food, housing, social infrastructure, and social services including health and education. Second, the state is usually vulnerable to charges of illegitimacy in never having met the test of popular support in elections, and to charges of corruption, favoritism, and moral weakness in Islamic terms. Third, political repression and authoritarianism are important preconditions for the emergence of strong Islamist movements. Fourth, implicit in the authoritarian order is the absence of alternative political parties, forces and movements; the state has usually emasculated or eliminated alternative parties so that they enjoy only marginal support in certain narrow segments of society. The Islamists thus become the only viable alternative to regime power. Some regimes actually put the choice just that baldly: Mubarak in Egypt thus tells the public that the only choice is between him and the Islamists. Such tactics may work for a while, but invariably lead to the hollowing out of support for the regime, leaving street power to the Islamists in the end.

Fifth, Islamist regimes flourish when discredited regimes are in close proximity to non-Muslim power. Arafat's PLO has moved towards this danger. Saudi Arabia's legitimacy is under strong challenge due to its close security ties with Washington that are seen primarily to support the regime. Finally,

Islamist movements flourish when they are linked with struggles of Muslim peoples for separatism or national liberation. Here again the Palestine situation comes to mind, as does Bosnia, Kashmir, and Uighurs in Xinjiang, among others. Similar situations exist in Kazakstan and some other Central Asian states where the highly compromised character of regime cooperation with Moscow combines with the need to formulate a new national character (a character never forged in the sudden "gift" of unsought independence following the collapse of the Soviet empire). While Islamist movements are only slowly emerging where Islam has been all but destroyed under seventy years of communism, Islam almost surely is in the process of being integrated in the nationalist project by which Kazaks, Kyrgyz, and others are seeking to build a new national entity in which not only language, but also Islam helps distinguish them from the Russian "other."

Graham E. Fuller, "Islamism(s) in the Next Century," in Kramer, ed., *Islamism Debate*, 144–145.

Refocusing on Woman and the Family

One result of the contemporary revival of Islam has been a refocusing on the Muslim family, in particular, a reexamination of the status of women in Islam. Women and the family have traditionally been regarded as the heart of society; as wives and mothers, women have been regarded as the culture bearers, exemplars, and teachers of family values. Islamic law and practice provided a centuries-long tradition and institution that had been an operative nucleus for fostering an Islamically oriented society. However complicated and difficult it might be to define and implement specific models for modern Islamic states, since the early Islamic ideal soon gave way to usurpers and kingdoms, the traditional Muslim family offered a clear and easily identifiable starting point for implanting a strong sense of faith, identity, and values. In modern times, Muslim women had two distinct models before them: the relatively new, modern Westernized lifestyle common among a minority of women and the traditional "Islamic" lifestyle of the majority of women, living much the same as previous generations had. The social impact of revivalism has resulted in some Muslim women grappling anew with a desire to develop an alternative lifestyle that is both modern and compatible with their Islamic faith and identity (a lifestyle that integrates modern life and Islamic identity and values). The debate over Islamic identity and women's role in society has expressed itself most visibly in matters of dress and personal conduct. . . .

The return to some form of Islamic dress reflects the sense of concern for what is viewed as the social and moral decline in many Muslim societies as well as the tension between modernity and authenticity, a concern to subordinate social change to indigenous, Islamic values and ideals. For many women, it is an attempt to combine traditional values and ideals with contemporary levels of education and employment, and thus produce a more integrated lifestyle, one that is both modern and Islamic. More-over, in societies where it has become increasingly common to blame the ills and failures of society on Westernization and to associate Western dress and values with cultural imperialism, an undermining of Islamic life, license, and immorality, the donning of Islamic dress represents an attempt to make things right, to attain true progress and success, by returning to God's law. . . .

Such women are not critical of progress in education, technology, and science because many are professionals. They reject what they regard to be the false progress of uncritical acculturation, or Westernization, which is blamed for social disintegration and a loss of values. Islamic dress also has the practical advantage of enabling some women to assert their modesty, dignity, and self-esteem in a public manner in societies where Islamic dress represents female modesty and respectability, whereas Western dress often symbolizes a more modern (Westernized), permissive lifestyle. It [Islamic dress] creates a protected, private space of respectability in the midst of the permissive atmosphere and sexual harassment that many experience in crowded, urban settings.

For many women, the Western lifestyles of the upper class are both out of touch with the socioeconomic realities of life and often a new source of exploitation rather than emancipation.

John L. Esposito, *Islam: The Straight Path* (London: Oxford University Press, 1988), 188–189.

Muslim Women as Citizens?

One would have thought that Muslim women would unambiguously have fallen within the first [-class citizen] category as they constitute an integral part of the *umma,* and even reproduce it. Yet no such automatic inference follows in orthodox Muslim constitutional thinking. In the Islamic state as imagined in conventional sociopolitical theory, women are second-class citizens enjoying no right to self-determination. In historical *shari'a,* Muslim women are simply appendages to their men, first their fathers and brothers, later their husbands (and possibly, at the end of a long life, finally their sons). Within historical *shariʿa*, the situation is one where Muslim men exercise domination over women and enjoy a monopoly of political power and force.

In the historical process of their colonisation, the populations of many of what are today considered Muslim states were pluralised in terms of race and creed. This historical development has now brought out the latent tension that is inherent in a definition of citizenship according to faith. With their diverse populations—including Muslims of different origins and cultural identity as well as diverse types of non-Muslims—various Muslim states are now left to grapple with the postcolonial task of nation-building, on the foundation of the pluralised social order that was left as the legacy of colonialism. Amid this complexity and uncertainty, many Muslims in their confusion have looked to historical *shariʿa* for the constitutional basis of some new, encompassing and non-Western polity. But while Islam understood as historical *shariʿa* at first beckons brightly in these troubling circumstances, recourse to it as the basis of some new political order only yields greater, even more intractable problems.

Just as Dr. [Abdullahi Ahmed] An-Naʿim argued earlier that, under these dramatically transformed circumstances of ethnic and religious differentiation, historical *shariʿa* is no more tenable, in the same way it cannot now be appropriately implemented because of its inability to accommodate modern understandings of gender relations and the status of women. Because it is male biased, a new interpretation needs to be arrived at—which it readily can—through a new methodology of Qurʾanic interpretation. Such a methodology can provide modern Muslims, both men and women, together with their fellow citizens in a pluralistic world with a contemporary and appropriate understanding of *shariʿa*, distinct from historical *shariʿa*. That new understanding must rest upon, and give expression to, a more egalitarian concept of citizenry that can encompass all—regardless of differences of culture and gender—who are permanent residents within the boundaries of the nation.

New Methodologies of Qurʾanic Interpretation

How such a new methodology of Qurʾanic interpretation can be developed and applied I have outlined elsewhere. . . . But central to any effective challenge to the conservative character and effects of historical *shariʿa* must be a focus on Qurʾanic interpretation and the *Qurʾan* itself.

Reemphasising the centrality of the *Qurʾan* can break the popularly received image of women's role and status in the family. Their contributions, which are fast becoming more complex and which straddle both private and public space, should be given due recognition. A holistic reading of the *Qurʾan* will reflect these changes in women's contemporary circumstances and provide women with an enhanced economic status and expanded opportunities for productive, rewarding and challenging economic employment.

Such economic empowerment is fundamentally relevant to the question of women's citizenship within the *umma*. For citizenship is not simply an abstract, constitutional matter but must be made concrete if it is to be effective and meaningful. Economic participation cannot be separated from citizenship, not simply because it can transform women's dependence upon and social subordination to men. More than that, political citizenship remains an empty abstraction if those who on paper enjoy it have no economic autonomy; and the social empowerment that such an active and autonomous economic role may provide can enable women to give meaningful and independent content to the otherwise empty shell of formal citizenship within an Islamic polity.

None of this, it should be finally noted, is really terribly radical. It is all entirely consistent with Qurʾanic ethics and imperatives, if we understand the Qurʾanic text through appropriately modern methodologies, a modern hermeneutic. Such flexibility in devising new and newly appropriate forms for the realisation of enduring Qurʾanic and *shariʾa* principles can even be grounded in unimpeachably orthodox expositions of Islamic jurisprudential thinking, as Dr. Hashim Kamali's presentation showed.

[Dr. Kamali] might not accept all the details that others would like to insist upon; but he is in no doubt, as his presentation argued, that it is for the Muslims of every period to discover the form for the realisation of enduring Islamic principles that is most suitable to their times and needs. If, as he argues, the legal heritage of Islam is a flexible one with a rich capacity for adaptation, then we should intelligently avail ourselves of those interpretive possibilities—in our own interests and in the interest of Islam itself. [For Kamali's presentation, see "Umma, Dawla, and the Islamic State," Readings, chapter 5.]

Muslim women, in particular, have the right to avail themselves of those interpretive possibilities to redress the long-standing bias against them which has characterised orthodox Qurʾanic interpretation and the conventional understandings of *shariʾa* that have been based upon it. New interpretation, especially interpretation by modern Muslim women, can renew the strength and flexibility of Islam by reactivating its adaptive genius. In doing so, Muslim women will not be indulging in heretical innovation but simply recalling the true spirit and message of the *Qur'an.* They will be enlarging the social space within the actual world of contemporary Islam, making it coextensive with the moral breadth and spaciousness of the Qur'anic vision itself.

Amina Wadud-Muhsin, "The Qur'an, *Shari'a* and the Citizenship Rights of Muslim Women," in *Shari'a Law and the Modern Nation-State,* ed. Norani Othman (Kuala Lumpur: Sisters in Islam Forum [Malaysia] Berhad, 1994), 78–80.

9

A Last-Ditch Stand

What can be called the Turabi experiment, in Sudan, is not cited nearly often enough in discussions of the subject of Islamist movements. The facts are well known. Ja'afar Numeiri, Sudan's sole ruler throughout the 1970s and part of the 1980s, at some point decided that he wanted to see Sudan a wholly Islamic republic, obeying and practicing every tenet of Islam. Numeiri's efforts failed, and failed dismally—and they were pronounced impracticable by none other than the religious fundamentalists themselves.

This is not the place to go into the Sudanese experiment in detail. One example will suffice. One of the tenets of the shari'a decrees that a person who is convicted of theft should have his or her hand cut off. Numeiri in his zeal wanted to put this into practice, along with all the other rules of Islam. The Muslim fundamentalists in Sudan, who opposed Numeiri despite his proclamation of the country as an Islamic state, argued against this particular rule with vigor and aggressiveness. How, they asked—how can you punish a poor person for stealing in such a way when the whole social order allows a state of affairs in which people become hungry and destitute enough to resort to stealing? Can you reasonably cut off the hand of a man compelled to steal a loaf of bread in order to feed his family?

The implications of this line of argument are as clear as they are far-reaching: In order to establish the Islamic state on the principles and tenets of Islam you must first change the order of things—a change so radical and so extensive it would amount to a reordering of the universe. And this only where domestic policy and economics are concerned. Where foreign policy and international relations come in, the situation is far more critical. A truly Islamic state will have to be in a constant state of jihad against practically everybody and every other non-Muslim political entity in the world—until that time when they will all either embrace Islam or pay a poll tax, jizya, to their Muslim rulers. Plainly, not even Khomeini could have so much as fantasized in this dismal fashion.

The problem becomes even more acute where the position of the individual Muslims, especially those who actually practice, and claim to speak for, their religion are concerned. Lord Cromer, British resident-general and consul general in Egypt from 1883 to 1907, has been quoted earlier in this paper as reflecting that an upper-class Muslim must be "either a fanatic or a concealed infidel." Almost a century has passed since Cromer made this observation, yet the situation has changed very little. Indeed, in the controversy raging in the world of Islam between moderate and fundamentalist the modern, educated, believing Muslim is placed in a real dilemma.

On one plane, the fundamentalists' argument for a return to pristine Islam—the Islam of jihad, strict observance, separation between the sexes, and a theocracy that recognizes no distinction between religion and government, mosque and state—is well-nigh unanswerable. On another, the necessity to cope with the conditions of modern life, the justice of the call for the emancipation of Muslim women, the conduct of correct and productive international relations, and the crying need for some sort of representative democratic government are all becoming increasingly difficult to ignore.

What tends to make the educated, conscious Muslim believer vacillate between fanaticism and unbelief is the obvious discrepancy between the stupendous claims of Islam and the golden moments in its history on the one hand and its present deplorable state on the other. This was the case a hundred years ago and this is the case today—and the result is that the present-day Muslim intellectual finds himself trapped in a tricky, virtually untenable position. This is amply demonstrated in the writings of leading members of the Egyptian intelligentsia—from the academic world, the judiciary, literary culture, the religious establishment, and journalism—such leading lights of the Egyptian cultural scene as Justice Muhammad al-ʿAshmawi, Zaki Najib Mahmud, Fuad Zakariyya, Saʿdeddin Ibrahim, Naguib Mahfouz, Yusuf Idris, Ahmad Bahaeddine, and many others.

Surveying the background to the present state of affairs in Egypt, one realizes how the situation had gone so steadily from bad to worse in the space of eighty years or so. The Islamic reformists of the late nineteenth and first half of the twentieth centuries were religious leaders and men of letters who were fairly familiar with Western ways, and a large majority of them accepted the separation of church and state, as well as certain Western values in the spheres of legislation, education, politics, and science and technology.

Today, in contrast, Western-style liberalism is viewed by religious fanatics as hateful, corruptive, and anti-Islam, and educated Egyptian youth tend to steer clear of it. In the worlds of the prominent political commentator and novelist Fathi Ghanim, what attracts Egyptian youth today, youngsters who lose their respect for school, for their teachers and principals and all their elders, is the excitement and novelty provided by fanatical, underground movements—"the secrecy and the concealment, working together with other anonymous people, total obedience in orders and instructions from an unknown supreme command which issues holy orders that must be obeyed. . . . Tyranny and terrorism. Indeed. . . . But this is a situation that is clear, stable, black-and-white, with no two ways about it. That's what attracts youth."[1]

Attacking the problem from a wider vantage point, Zaki Najib Mahmud, the doyen of Egyptian philosophy professors and a prolific author (died 1995), writes in the course of his response to a loaded question asked by one of his readers ("Isn't Islam sufficient for us to forgo the West and everything in it?"):

> . . . The greatest lie in the present stage is the false claim propagated that one must choose either Islam or this age with all its arts and sciences—that if a Muslim wants the true Islam he must abandon this age and everything in it. If we see someone inclined toward the age and its values, we consider him an infidel to Islam. And I say that the true Muslim cannot acquire what is distinctive about this age through Islam alone. My question is: Does something in Islam drive you to acquire knowledge and science, or does something in it repel you from them? . . . What is in Islam that would deprive Muslims of the culture of our age in all its aspects? And where is the devil who whispered to us that spiritual life is limited to a reading stripped of action? . . . Ask me again if Islam is not enough for us to forgo the West and everything in it. I will reply that Islam is indeed enough if we live the life of Muslims, lives which do not reject any basis of present-day culture, but will add bases on top of those which exist from previous cultures.[2]

These are just two samples of the reactions of enlightened Egyptian intellectuals to the current upsurge of Islamic fanaticism, but they are fairly representative of all such reactions. The truly sad aspect of the present situation, and the deep irony of it, is that these responses and all the arguments on which they are based are almost identical both in tone and in content to those voiced by the original reformists in Egyptian Islam as far back as a century ago. The problems that faced the Islamist activists in both Sudan and Libya, again, proved insurmountable, making it clear that attempts at pairing pristine Islam and government in a modern state carry the seeds of their own failure.

The phenomenon is not new. Calls for the establishment of Islam and its precepts as the sole basis of their states were made periodically by wide sections of Muslim Arabs, not excluding a number of men in power. However, Muslim theologians are not of one mind on this subject. Insofar as it is a matter of interpretation and correct reading, the texts have shown, time and again, that there is more than one approach to the subject. Moreover, the overwhelming majority of these ʿulema, who in the contemporary Muslim-Arab world are mostly paid officials of their respective governments, are ready to endorse the policies and the rules and regulations laid down by their providers, and have never been at a loss to locate the right text and find the apt quotation.

This adaptability on the ʿulema's part was demonstrated—among many other occasions—in Egypt throughout the past five decades on the subject of Israel and of how Muslims ought to deal with it. When King Farouq and his cabinet decided to join in the war against the newly established Jewish state, the ʿulema duly issued numerous fatwas explaining why a jihad must be waged against the foreign "usurpers."

This went on for at least thirty years, with Nasser's revolutionary regime—which succeeded the monarchy in July 1952—adopting an increasingly militant stance against Israel and the ʿulema unanimously joining. However, when Nasser's heir and successor decided, toward the end of 1977, to make peace with the Jewish state, the selfsame religious leaders hastened to issue fatwas in support of their president, citing relevant passages from the Qurʾan and the hadith urging Muslims to seek peace and reconciliation if the adversary follows the same peaceful course.

Such manifestations of uncertainty and of seemingly opposing interpretations of the religious code increased in number and in intensity since the rise of the West and its ways and the apparent need for Muslims to adapt to the modern world. These manifestations, among many others, became evident in controversies that raged on such subjects as the status of women in Islam, religion and the state, relations with "the infidels," Islam and communism, modern banking practices, secular education, and the findings of modern science and technology.

Toeing the Line

On all these subjects, as well as others, the Muslim religious establishment was often of two minds, though invariably ending up toeing the line adopted by the secular regimes. The situation in Algeria following the sweeping victory of the Islamic Salvation Front (FIS) in the first round of the first free parliamentary elections to be held in that country follows the same pattern. Not only are almost all the other Islamic groups and parties in the land—and they are numerous—in sharp disagreement with the front's fundamentalists, the leaders of the FIS themselves appear to be divided on the basic issues confronted by the organization should it finally secure a parliamentary majority to form a government and establish an Islamic republic. While what can be termed the hard-liners among these leaders were talking of a government and a polity based exclusively on the teachings of pristine Islam, the established leadership was giving assurances that no drastic changes were contemplated.

ʿAbd el-Qader Hashani, the man who assumed leadership of the FIS while its two leaders, Abbasi Madani and Ali Belhaj, were in prison, made a number of assurances to an evidently concerned public: That the FIS will cooperate with the incumbent president and seek "coexistence" with him provided he refrains from taking measures restricting the powers and prerogatives of the elected parliament; that the government which the front was hoping to form after securing an absolute parliamentary majority will seek reconciliation with its opponents, and pledges not to revoke Algeria's present constitution; that the FIS hopes the armed forces will refrain from interfering in the political process; and that the new Islamic regime will respect Algeria's commitments in the international sphere and honor all obligations, agreements, and treaties already concluded with other states. Algeria, Hashani pledged, "will not live in isolation from the outside world."[3]

It is interesting to note, though, that while making all these sweeping commitments Hashani still spoke of his future government as one based on the precepts of the shariʿa, adding however that this religious code "did not forbid relations with others," meaning non-Muslims. This, however, is a version of the shariʿa to which many Muslim fundamentalists will take great exception—and with good theological reasons. But an Islamic regime anywhere in today's world cannot afford to ignore the basic facts of life. In Algeria's case, for one, it is sufficient to point out that the country's foreign debt amounts to $25 billion, of which about $18 billion and half of its export earnings are spent on servicing the debt. And this in a country where three out of four young people have no jobs, and where residents of the capital, Algiers Qasbah, live seven to a room.

With hundreds dead and billions of dollars lost by the tourism industry in the past few years, Egypt became second only to Algeria in the heavy toll inflicted by Islamist militants anywhere in the Arab world. The material losses suffered by the economy resulted from a sudden 40 percent drop in revenue from tourism, Egypt's main source of foreign currency, while victims of Islamist-related violence included militants, Copts, security personnel, and tourists. In an attempt to stem the violence, tens of thousands of suspected activists were detained and many more homes and mosques searched.

The war against the Islamists is being waged on other fronts. So far, three measures have been taken by the Egyptian government to curb Islamist activities and restrict the influence that the so-called Islamic Group— al-jama'a al-Islamiyya—wields in a multitude of ways. The government's first action came when an amendment was introduced to the political parties law, prohibiting any activity by a party or group still in the process of formation. The move was plainly directed at the Muslim Brotherhood, which, though outlawed since 1954, has been increasingly active, contesting elections to the People's Assembly and local government by aligning itself to the Socialist Labor Party, thus gaining seats both in the assembly and in local councils throughout the country.

Then came the professional syndicates law, making 50 percent participation of the total membership mandatory for elections to a syndicate's governing bodies. The move came after the brotherhood managed to gain control of a number of leading professional syndicates, including those of doctors, lawyers, engineers, and pharmacists, by mobilizing its supporters for the voting—again under the umbrella of the Socialist Labor Party.

The government's third move against the Islamists came when the Ministry of Religious Endowments (awqaf) decided to place all privately run mosques under its control. These mosques, built and financed by the neighborhoods themselves, had hitherto been run and controlled by the local inhabitants, while the ministry exercised control only over government-built mosques, which make up a mere 12 percent of an estimated 170,000 mosques nationwide.

This last action serves to show how deeply and how thoroughly the authorities intend to be involved in the fight against the extremists. In gaining control of the mosques, the Awqaf Ministry plans to determine the subjects which their respective imams may address in their sermons at the Friday noon prayers. Defending the government's move, the head of the ministry's Mosques Administration Department said it was a means of "protecting the Houses of God," by seeing to it that the sermons delivered there are "in strict compliance with true Islamic teachings."

Concern about the growing influence of the Islamists in Egypt goes all the way to the top. Responding to a proposal made by a leading intellectual of the Egyptian left, Muhammad Sid Ahmad, that religious parties be allowed "to serve as an early warning system to avoid things getting out of hand," President Mubarak said that, while Sid Ahmad could afford the luxury of alternative solutions which, as the Algerian experience proved, are fraught with danger, he, as the supreme decision maker, could not take such risks. The reference to Algeria is instructive in that, as with that country's disastrous first experiment in democracy and parliamentary elections, the Egyptians themselves can one day be confronted by the prospect of a democratically elected Islamist regime.[4]

Of the various verbal battles sparked off by Iraq's invasion of Kuwait in 1990, the fiercest was fought not by state organs or policymakers but by opposing camps of ʿulema. The points at issue were whether a Muslim state is permitted to wage war, invade, or take over another Muslim state; whether Islam allows its followers to seek and accept help from "the infidels" in times of need or for purposes of self-defense; and whether forceful annexation by one Muslim political entity of another constitutes an act of aggression or religious rebellion, *baghi*.

The debate raged mainly between Muslim religious dignitaries in Egypt, Jordan, and Saudi Arabia, with active participation by the Palestinians. Not surprisingly, the division followed strictly state-national lines, and the rules and opinions laid down by these theologians faithfully reflected the positions taken by their respective governments. The Egyptians, along with the Saudis, issued a number of fatwas and statements vociferously advocating Arab and foreign military intervention to put an end to Saddam Hussein's act of aggression, while their Jordanian and Palestinian counterparts insisted with equal conviction and eloquence that Islam forbids the faithful from seeking help from the infidel or allowing him to "desecrate" Muslim soil—in this case Saudi Arabia, which houses Islam's two most cherished holy places, the Kaʿba in Mecca and the tomb of the Prophet Muhammad in Medina.

The opinions and the verdicts were worded in extremely strong language. Sheikh Jad el-Haq ʿAli Jad el-Haq, the sheikh of al-Azhar, called the Iraqi ruler the Iraqi baghi, and called on the Arab nation "to hasten to dispatch its armies for the containment of [his] act of rebellion even as a fire ought to be contained."

Speaking of "the inhuman acts" perpetrated by Iraqi soldiers in Kuwait, Jad el-Haq added that "the peoples adjoining Kuwait asked for help from Arab and Islamic states, and others that possess weapons that match those used by the Iraqi forces. . . ." Coming closer to the point, the sheikh asserted that "no harm accrues" from this call for help, since these states are entitled to defend themselves "against this treacherous brother." Another leading ʿalim, the grand mufti of Egypt, Muhammad Sayyid Tantawi, in a separate fatwa urged the believers to take up arms against the Iraqi aggressor, couching his edict in terms almost identical to those used by the sheikh of al-Azhar and the various edicts issued by the ʿulema in Saudi Arabia.

Rejoinders from Jordanian and Palestinian ʿulema were not late in coming, and were worded in far stronger language. Especially outspoken were statements made by the Jordanian Minister of Waqf and Islamic Affairs, ʿAli al-Faqir, who in an interview in the Amman daily *Al-Dustour* dubbed Sheikh Tantawi's fatwa "evil and erroneous and smell[ing] of oil," adding that it was issued "*after* American troops entered the sacred land." Elaborating, the minister said that those who invited these troops were "sinners," and called on Muslims "to evict the foreign forces from the Arabian Peninsula and to contribute to every possible military measure aimed at cleansing our soil from their filth."

The Palestinians, for their part, were even more stringent. A fatwa issued by "the mufti of the Palestinian Armed Forces" referred to the Qurʾanic decree that if two groups of believers fight each other, Muslims are duty bound to make peace between them. The Palestinian ʿalim argued, however, that the decree—cited by his Egyptian counterparts in advocating a peaceful resolution of the crisis—did not apply to the situation at hand, since here we have a dispute not between two groups of believers but between patient and long-suffering believers on the one hand and "a sinful, aggressive and tyrannical" coalition represented by the United States and its allies, on the other. Again Dr. Nader al-Tamimi, the PLO's mufti, decreed that what Iraq did in annexing Kuwait was a religious duty, "since it is forbidden for [the Arab] nation to have boundaries between its lands; it should be one state with one ruler." Elaborating, al-Tamimi added: "Unification is a duty even if it is to be attained only by force. . . . We ask President Saddam Hussein to unify the rest of the Islamic world even as Saladin did in the wars of the Crusades."

Dismissing his Egyptian and Saudi counterparts as "the Sultans' ʿulema," al-Tamimi said it was not surprising that they should release "their ready-made fatwas." Did they not issue such edicts in support of Sadat's "Camp David conspiracy?" This of course was a reference to the famous fatwa issued by the then sheikh of al-Azhar in which relevant passages from the Koran were cited in support of peaceful settlements of armed conflicts generally and of the Arab-Israeli conflict itself.[5]

The Case of Saudi Arabia

In the ongoing war against radical Islam, in which practically every Arab country is now engaged, Saudi Arabia has until very recently seemed to be the least affected. This is because, unlike Egypt, Algeria, Tunisia, and Jordan, the Saudi regime styles itself as an Islamic one guided strictly by the rules of the shariʿa. However, for many years now Islamist groups have been forming in the kingdom, attacking the regime in various minor ways such as the distribution of recorded sermons and scarcely veiled anti-regime propaganda in mosques. By the mid-1990s, however, the rules of the game radically changed, with the establishment of a human rights organization by six prominent Muslims known to be supporters of the ruling establishment or part thereof. The announcement bearing their signatures spoke of the task of the new committee as being "to defend the legitimate rights of citizens."[6]

The announcement took the regime completely by surprise. The sight of members of the Muslim establishment challenging the government in so open a manner was so unfamiliar that the regime somewhat overreacted, condemning the step and going directly on the defensive, with the interior minister boasting that the Saudi kingdom "respects and implements human rights more than do the European and Western regimes that criticize us."

"Where are the human rights of the Palestinians?" he asked—and what about human rights in Bosnia where they are trod upon day by day? "And why does the Western media omit to deal with such cases? . . . We by virtue of our commitment to the Islamic shariʿa most certainly respect human rights."

In a sense, the fact that members of the Muslim establishment should thus be openly challenging the Saudi regime is not surprising. King Fahd repeatedly promised reform—not exactly an elected parliament but some substitute that would help solve two pressing problems. On the one hand, it would serve as an answer to growing demands for an end to the autocratic system of government that uses Islam and its precepts in an ongoing attempt to entrench itself. On the other hand, it may help stem the danger posed by the fundamentalists, who in Saudi Arabia have the advantage of invoking and speaking freely in the name of Islam, to which the regime itself claims to adhere.

It was this two-pronged danger that led the Saudi regime—many years ago—to think up the idea of a consultative (shura) council, depicting it as the nearest approximation to a representative assembly of the kind known in democratic regimes. Throughout the years, indeed, a fitting building was planned and completed to house the council, overlooking a hill in the capital. Instead of going ahead with his plans for the council, however, Fahd found himself turning his attention to his Muslim extremists. In December 1996 he dismissed seven elderly members from the country's highest clerical body, the Supreme Authority of Senior ʿUlema. The dismissals came amid reports that the seven religious dignitaries involved—government officials to a man—had failed to join the other ten members of the authority in denouncing 107 Muslim fundamentalists from the country's top religious institutes and universities who had submitted an ultimatum to the king voicing objections to various government policies.

The fundamentalists were outspoken. In what was described as "a memorandum of advice"—itself considered a challenging terminology in the context of Saudi concepts—these fundamentalists demanded rigorous application of Islamic rules to every aspect of Saudi life. Going even farther, the self-styled advisers—who mostly belonged to a younger generation of Muslim scholars—counseled the repudiation of relations with all non-Islamic governments and with the West as a whole.

It was then that the king decided to act. Apart from dismissing almost half the members of the country's supreme Islamic authority, he went out of his way to denounce the Islamist agitators publicly and in no uncertain terms. Among other things, he accused the hard-liners of being inspired by "foreign trends" in a campaign to destabilize the kingdom. In what was taken as a reference to Iran and Sudan, he complained that "somebody who comes to us from outside our country" was trying to tell the Saudis what to do. "Has it come to the point," he added, "where we depend on criticism and cassette tapes and talk that does not lead to any good?"

In a reference to the growing use of mosques by religious extremists to air their antigovernment views, Fahd said, "the pulpit was made only for certain limited things," decrying the circulation of tens of thousands of tapes containing harsh criticism of the regime and of certain members of the royal family accused of pro-Western leanings. All this, it has to be borne in mind, directed at the ruling establishment of a country that is widely viewed to be one of the very few truly Islamic states in the world.[7]

The standard criticism made by the fundamentalists against the Muslim religious establishment is that its representatives are mere paid servants of the secular governments of the day. Some of these militants have indeed called the ʿulema and other religious leaders and teachers of Islam "stooges," "spies," even "heretics"—and in private papers seized by the Egyptian police, one such Muslim militant vowed that these sheikhs will be allotted menial jobs to do when the day of reckoning comes and pristine Islam reigns supreme again.

In this unsparing verbal contest the Muslim establishment in Egypt finds itself at a distinct disadvantage. To start with, its two leading representatives—the grand mufti of Egypt and the grand imam of al-Azhar—are, together with their many aides and subordinates, virtually paid officials of the government. Second—largely as a result of this dependence—the religious establishment has seldom been consistent about any of its orders or edicts. Whenever some change or reform in the society is contemplated— like the schooling of girls, mixed classes at the universities, bank interest on personal savings, and a host of others—the Muslim divines declare themselves adamantly against it, citing copiously from the Qurʾan and the Hadith in support of their stand. As change becomes pressing, however, and as the situation on the ground renders it an accomplished fact, these dignitaries hasten to support it, arguing that it is part and parcel of what Islam teaches— and citing equally copious supporting evidence from the Sources.

No less damaging to the religious establishment have been its shifting attitudes toward the Jews, toward Israel, and toward peace between the Arabs and Israel. Up to the late 1970s, the successive sheikhs of al-Azhar— the highest juridical authority in contemporary Islam—laid it down that peace with the Jewish state was a heresy, an unforgivable sin, in the words of the edict issued by Sheikh Mahmoud Shaltout in the 1960s.

Less than fifteen years later, however, Dr. Abdel Halim Mahmoud, Shaltout's successor as grand imam, cabled the late president Anwar Sadat in 1979 from the United States, where he was visiting, congratulating him on the signing of the peace treaty with Israel and pledging his own and his establishment's support. Other dignitaries were equally supportive of the daring move, duly citing relevant Qurʾanic verses.

With such a record of shifts and turns, it is no wonder the religious establishment in Egypt has become an easy object of disdain and mockery among the extremists, who as far as reading and interpreting the Scripture are concerned, have a one-track, uncompromising mind. Hence the difficulty official Islam has been having in repudiating the fundamentalists, especially on the sensitive and much-disputed issue of Islamic government and how it ought to be run.

Numerous instances can be given here of the ways in which official Islam has responded to the challenge of its fundamentalist critics; but one will suffice as an illustration. One of the hottest religious controversies raging in Egypt constantly concerns the country's Copts. Citing the "right" dicta and commands from the Qurʾan and the traditions, the extremists have perpetrated some of the ugliest physical assaults against Copts living in the many mixed villages and townlets of Upper Egypt. This gave the Muslim establishment a relatively easy task of repudiation—and so far it has made excellent use of it. For the fact is that both the Qurʾan and the Hadith are rich with references to non-Muslims and how they ought to be treated by their Muslim rulers—especially with regard to followers of the two revealed religions that preceded Islam—Judaism and Christianity.

It is interesting to note, in this connection, that some of the more telling of these responses came in the form of repudiations, not of the extremists' stand itself but of certain Western publicists and "Orientalists," quite often unnamed, who are accused of distorting the teachings of Islam on the subject of ahl al-kitab (people of the Book) as well as the record of their actual treatment at the hands of Muslim rulers. One of these is a work published in Cairo by the prominent Muslim divine Sheikh Muhammad al-Ghazzali. The book, *History and Tolerance in Christianity and Islam*, purports to be a rejoinder to a book about Muslims and Copts from the Arab invasion to 1923, published in France by one Dr. Jacques Tajer, described as "an Orientalist who obtained his Ph.D. in France."

Islam, al-Ghazzali argues, has always been against all ethnic, tribal, and family zeal and fanaticism (ʿasabiyya). The ethnic-tribal fanaticism that informed the terror and the violence perpetrated by the fundamentalists against the Copts are condemned by him in no uncertain terms. He even reminisces about his sojourn in the Gaza Strip before 1967. "I witnessed with a sinking heart the warring tribal loyalties there—and then, observing the Jews, I found no competing solidarities, no boastfulness abut pedigree and titles, nothing except personal ability and aptitude brought to these parts by the persecuted [Jew] who relies only on his effort and his toil."

Far more emphatic condemnations have come from other ʿulema, both from the ranks of the establishment and outside them. Al-Azhar's grand imam declared in an interview with the Cairo daily *Al-Akhbar* that the perpetrators of murderous acts against the Copts "must not be called Muslims." Nor should they be called "extremists." To the extremes of what [faith] had they gone to deserve that appellation? he protested. Certainly not to those of Islam, since Islam disowns them in the first place. The sheikh also dwelt briefly on what he called "the religious vacuum among the youths," who he said should be protected from the mischief of the fundamentalists now that they are showing signs of returning to the faith.

These words, coming from a man of such status, amount to more than mere lip service and conformity with the regime's declared policies. They seem also to point to a more general trend. Writing in *Newsweek* recently, Carla Power reaches the conclusion that the challenge for the Islamic world "is navigating a middle path between radicalisms." "Iran, of all places," she adds, "provides the most recent cause for hope." She goes on to quote Iran's newly elected president, Mohammed Khatami, who, speaking at celebrations marking the eighth anniversary of Khomeini's death, talked to a group of visiting students about Plato, freedom, and Huntington. "The clash-of-civilizations theory advanced by [Samuel P.] Huntington," he is quoted as saying, "is of no use. . . . The concept that must prevail is the meeting of civilizations." At times, Power comments, "moderation can prove to be the most radical innovation of all."

In the course of her article, Power makes some extremely apt observations on the subject of Islamic radicalism. Pointing out that the image of the Muslim as Kalashnikov-and-Qurʾan-toting extremist was a stock composite even during the eighties, she says such distortions seem more suspect today. In the seventies and eighties, she explains, political Islam was viewed predominantly as a magnet for dispossessed rural migrants or anti-Western reactionaries; now it increasingly attracts the educated middle class. Citing recent developments in Algeria since 1992, when the likely victory of the Islamic Salvation Front in parliamentary elections led the government to cancel elections, outlaw the FIS, and throw its leaders in jail, she describes the regime's use of the threat of Islamic radicalism to justify repression as "a self-fulfilling prophecy." Free and fair elections in Algeria in 1992, she adds, "may indeed have produced an Islamic state. But the alternative has proved far more terrible. Algeria's lesson is this: it may be dangerous to let democracy work freely, but it's a lot more dangerous to stifle it."[8]

Readings

The Ideological Worldview of Revivalism

While there are distinctive differences of interpretation, the general or common ideological framework of Islamic revivalism includes the following beliefs:

1. Islam is a total and comprehensive way of life. Religion is integral to politics, law, and society.
2. The failure of Muslim societies is due to their departure from the straight path of Islam and their following a Western secular path, with its secular, materialistic ideologies and values.
3. The renewal of society requires a return to Islam, an Islamic religiopolitical and social reformation or revolution, that draws its inspiration from the Quran and from the first great Islamic movement led by the Prophet Muhammad.
4. Although the Westernization of society is condemned, modernization as such is not. Science and technology are accepted, but they are to be subordinated to Islamic belief and values. . . .
5. The process of Islamization . . . requires organizations or associations of dedicated and trained Muslims, who . . . are willing to struggle (*jihad*) against corruption and social injustice. Radical activists go beyond these precepts and operate on the following assumptions, believing that theological doctrine and political realism necessitate violent revolution.
6. A Crusader mentality, Western (in particular, the United States) and Eastern (the Soviet Union) neocolonialism, and the power of Zionism pit the West against the Islamic world.
7. Establishment of an Islamic system of government is not simply an alternative but an Islamic imperative, based on God's command or will. Therefore, all Muslims must obey and follow this divine mandate by struggling to implement and follow God's law.
8. Since the legitimacy of Muslim governments is based on the Sharia, those governments that do not follow it are illegitimate. Those who fail to follow Islamic law, governments and individuals, are guilty of unbelief. They are no longer Muslim, but are atheists whose unbelief demands holy war.
9. Opposition to illegitimate governments extends to the official *ulama,* the religious establishment, and state-supported mosques and

preachers who are considered to have been co-opted by the government.

10. Jihad against unbelief and unbelievers is a religious duty. Therefore, all true believers are obliged to combat such governments and their supporters, whether individuals or foreign governments. Like the Kharijites in early Islam, radicals demand total commitment and obedience. One is either a true believer or an infidel, saved or damned, a friend or an enemy of God. The army of God is locked in battle or holy war with the followers of Satan.

11. Christians and Jews are generally regarded as unbelievers rather than "People of the Book" because of their connections with Western (Christian) colonialism and Zionism. They are seen as partners in a Judeo-Christian conspiracy against Islam and the Muslim world. Thus, non-Muslim minorities are often subjected to persecution.

John L. Esposito, *Islam: The Straight Path* (London: Oxford University Press, 1988), 169–171.

Problems of Islamism in Power

It would seem evident . . . that if regional Islamists enjoy considerable national support and power, the most auspicious and "safest" way for Islamists to attain power is within procedural frameworks that set automatic limits (in principle) to the range of their conduct. (This promises little by way of the possible wisdom of their policies.) The pessimist will argue that the Iranian and Sudanese cases so far prove the very worst about Islamist regimes—how many more do we need to get the point? The optimist might reply that the problems of the Islamists in power reflect the problems of that state's political culture in general. But one depressing conclusion may be that Islamists who gain power in the future are likely indeed to come on the heels of fairly authoritarian regimes—Egypt, Algeria, Tunisia, Saudi Arabia, Bahrain, etc. Such a situation bodes ill for the prospects that Islamists in those states will suddenly honor moderate and democratic norms that have scarcely existed under the previous regime. The major hope, then, is that these states will open up the political order to permit more moderate political evolution that in turn encourages greater adherence to new political rules on the part of the Islamists as well. "One man, one vote, one time" is not a risk limited to the Islamists but is rather a nearly universal dilemma of these states. . . .

This paper posits that Islamist forces are here to stay and that so far no rival political movements exist in most states to challenge them—sometimes as a result of short-sighted state repression of all parties. The question then becomes one of managing the transition of Islamists into power (or partial power) in ways that will be the least destabilizing, radicalizing, or damaging to Western interests in the region as well. The first true test of whether the Islamists are inherently dedicated to ineffective, radical anti-Western policies will be their performance in power in more democratic or pluralistic institutions of governance, including the local level. Absolute power corrupts absolutely in any society, including Islamist ones; absolute power for Islamists is just as undesirable in principle as it is for any party. Democratic process suggests important constitutional limits on behavior. The Refah party in Turkey, for example, so far shows no signs of playing outside the game at all, and now shares power constitutionally. Turkey may be "different," but every country is different.

Islamists faced with the problem of retaining power over the longer run also face certain challenges. It is my supposition that while Islamists ask very good questions about what is wrong with Middle Eastern governance in general, they have very few answers. (I do not rule out that Islamists in power may bring certain positive features—elimination of corruption at least initially, a sense of how to run social programs, an eye to the grass roots and people's needs, and some satisfaction of nativist impulses as opposed to internationalist ones.) But the demands for success will be overwhelming. If they begin to fail in answering the momentous questions of the day—as have most of their predecessors since the problems are truly daunting—they may rationalize that they need more time, or more power, to attain their political goals. They will be strongly tempted to turn to populism, or to accuse the opposition of underhanded tactics and destructive criticism. These are all well-known phenomena in large numbers of societies the world over. The temptation of turning to authoritarian means might then grow.

Graham E. Fuller, "Islamism(s) in the Next Century," in *The Islamism Debate,* ed. Martin Kramer (Tel Aviv: Moshe Dayan Center for Middle Eastern and African Studies, 1998), 153, 155.

The Islamist Contradiction

The duality of state law and *shariʿa* is still the predicament of the elusive Islamic state. By definition, *shariʿa* defines a private space (*haram*) which the state cannot penetrate. Family as such should not be touched. And how can a state be totalitarian if it recognizes the family's untouchable status? The question arose in revolutionary Iran during the 1980s. How could a house search be made religiously legal, if it resulted in a young man seeing a *haram* woman? This question is surely rhetorical in terms of police practices, but not in terms of legitimacy. In this instance, coercive action from the state appears as outright illegitimate. Khomeini himself had to regularly address the question, and house searches are rather limited nowadays.

Compared with communism, Islamism has less leverage to change the society from above. There is the basic fact of social acceptance or resistance to Islamization. Conservative societies (like Morocco and Afghanistan) more readily accept a very Islamic family law, even when it is not imposed by the state in the name of Islamization, while more modern and sophisticated societies, like Iran, oblige the state to water down its commitment or issue for flexible rulings, as we saw in the case of divorce. It is easier to ban driving for women, as well as music, in Saudi Arabia than in Iran. When it comes to law and family status, radical political Islamists are not necessarily more "Islamic" than traditional and pro-Western elites.

The dualist approach ("bad Islamists" against "good secularists") misses the point about the real changes in contemporary Muslim societies. Islamization cannot work as an abstract practice that ignores actual society. The need to achieve some consensus and to play on nationalism obliges the Islamists to accept a certain degree of cultural specificity. Cultural and sociological factors (the role of women, urbanization, passage from extended to nuclear families, education) are more important than the explicit ideology of the rulers. For instance, it is not by chance that the issue of the veil is pivotal in societies which experienced a brutal modernization with the coming of women into the labor market (Iran, Algeria, France for immigrants), while it remains secondary in more traditional societies (Afghanistan, Pakistan, Morocco).

I will not enter here into the question whether the Islamist movement is a backlash against modernization, or any agent of modernization. But it should be stressed that Islamism is helpless against long-term sociological evolutions—urbanization, Westernization, expanded role of women—which will undermine the basic tenets of its ideology. Whatever judgement we pass on Islamism, it will not survive the test of actual rule—and it will fail faster than communism. . . .

The paradox of political Islam is that if the role of Islam is defined by the state, it means that political power is above any independent religious authority, and thus that Islam is subordinated to politics. And if independent religious authorities control state decisions, that means that there is no such thing as Islamists who exercise absolute power. The paradox disappears only if the highest religious authority is also the highest political leader, something likely to happen only briefly in a revolutionary period. In a word, the distinction between two different levels, religious and political, cannot be bypassed, making impossible an "Islamic totalitarianism" in the true sense of the word.

Plus la même chose

Islamists in power do change many basic aspects of society, in a short span of time and by using spectacular or even violent means (such as destruction of liquor stores, enforcing of the veiling of women, executions of opponents). But, violence apart, the final results are not very different from what we see in more conservative Muslim countries. The Islamists do not create a new kind of totalitarian system. Their main mark on the society is Islamization according to patterns similar to those of conservative and pro-Western states like Saudi Arabia (veil, ban on alcohol, restriction on co-education and entertainments, and so on). They are even rather more "democratic" than many other conservative Middle Eastern regimes. (Most notably, there are elections in Iran, although restricted to "Islamic" groups.) What really separates them, in Western eyes, from the Saudi establishment, is their foreign policy: they are anti-Western, they oppose the Arab-Israeli peace process, and they support radical groups abroad. In fact, radicalism remains a constant in foreign policy, not in domestic policy.

But even in foreign policy, the Islamists in power are limited by strategic and national constraints. They simply express in ideological terms what is clearly a nationalist policy: the Iranian regime, the Algerian FIS and the Refah party in Turkey, as well as the Palestinian Hamas and even the Lebanese Hizbullah, increasingly cast their strategy in terms of national interests. They became "Islamo-nationalists," giving up any idea of building up the *umma* beyond their own nation.

In some aspects of law and society, Islamists in power might even be less "Islamic" than conservative states. For example, family law is less restrictive against women in Iran than in Morocco, and the penal code is less "Islamic" than in Saudi Arabia. Religious practices, like prayers, are not enforced by a special police in Iran as they are in Saudi Arabia. In all these aspects, Saudi Arabia is more "Islamic" than Iran or even Afghanistan (where there are films, music, and dance). Paradoxically, Islamization does not characterize Islamists in power. What is new is the call for an overall Islamic society, including politics and economy—in a word, the ideologization of Islam. This ideologization is visible in the systematic use of Islamic symbols (slogans, pictures, Qur'anic verses, *bismillah* to introduce any official statements). But when one goes to the basic tenets of the society (politics, economy, and social relations), the picture changes.

In politics, Islam is, for Islamists, an ideological tool to maintain their power. Islam, once turned into an ideology, can be bent at will to legitimize state policy. Hence the different colors of Islamization: it might be statist or it might favor a private economy; it might exclude women from public life (the Taliban in Afghanistan) or promote a kind of "Islamic freedom" for them (Iran); it might strike a deal with the Christians (Iran), or call for their expulsion. There is no one "Islamic ideology," but there are different "Islamic" readings of different social and political attitudes—readings shaped by power politics. Reference to Islam also provides a criterion to dismiss political opponents. The myth of the *umma* works to disqualify those who would "divide" the community. This leverage can be easily manipulated because the Islamists are always the first to dismiss the legitimacy of any independent religious authority, in order to be the only ones to speak in the name of "true Islam." . . .

This flexibility looks like opportunism. One of the consequences is that Islam loses its power of mobilization as soon as it is identified with a specific group. Society then either heads towards a kind of secularization by disillusion, or towards the restoration of an independent, apolitical Islamic pole, which challenges the pretension of the regime to embody Islam. Both trends are obvious in Iran: on the one hand religious practice is decreasing, on the other hand some clerics (Montazeri) or lay thinkers (Abdolkarim Sorush) call for a distinction between Islam and state.

Ultimately, Islamists in power do not meet the expectations of the population. Corruption returns, the economic situation worsens, politics is little more than a factional struggle for power, women are unhappy about the limitations on social life and job opportunity, young people are left with few entertainments. The answer cannot be the mere suppression of any opposition.

Olivier Roy, "Islamists in Power," in Kramer, ed., *Islamism Debate*, 82–83.

Islam on the Defensive

. . . When, in March 1975, Prince Faisal ibn Musaʿid assassinated his uncle King Faisal of Saudi Arabia, it was revealed that the assassin's brother, Prince Khalid ibn Musaʿid, had been killed by Saudi police some nine years previously while heading a demonstration by Muslim zealots. The demonstration, it transpired, had been staged in protest against the setting up of a television station in Riyadh—on the ground that Islamic law forbids the representation of a human image in any form.

Something of the same religious zeal was the motive force behind two plots to overthrow the Sadat regime during the first half of 1975. The plotters, who planned to set up a government in Cairo that would adhere to the teachings of pristine Islam, appear to have represented a totally new breed of Muslim fundamentalist, one whose zeal surpasses anything Arabic Islam had known in modern times. According to information gathered from the Egyptian press at the time, the plotters were a small group of fanatics with no backing whatsoever from either the masses or the acknowledged religious leadership of the day. For the existing religious establishment, indeed, the group had nothing but scorn, if not worse. They considered their direct ideological precursors and ancestors, the Muslim Brethren, inept failures who shied away from violence and engaged in endless pontifications about *shura* (consultation), *ijma'* (consensus), and similar theoretical questions. Members of such groups—which included the one responsible for Sadat's assassination on October 6, 1981—were said to have avoided these "fellow zealots with past experience" like the plague. The motto of the group was: Recruit three and avoid three! "Recruit the young, the poor, and the conscript. Avoid the argumentative, those with past experience among the advocates of Islamic practice, and married men."

The revulsion these groups of zealots felt toward Muslim believers "with past experience" extended to the 'ulema of Al-Azhar. Their members were cautioned not to attend mosques where such men preached at prayers. One of them—who died shortly after being wounded in the course of the attack on the Technical Military Academy in Cairo in April 1974—expressed disapproval of those Azharites who visited him at his deathbed. The leader of the Alexandria ring of the group went so far as to declare that in the new Islamic state he and his comrades would set up, the sheiks of Al-Azhar would be employed as street cleaners. He assured his police interrogator that they (the 'ulema) would not object, and that then the country's street cleaners' crisis would be solved. "They are cowards and fear-stricken," he said about these religious savants. "Al-Azhar never was an honorable institution throughout all of its history," he added for good measure. . . .

Especially revealing were the notes seized in the room of one of the accused, a student at the Agricultural College born three months before the free officers' revolt of July 1952. "On the one hand," he wrote in one of these notes, "I attended prayers; on the other hand, I went to beaches and the movies. In the end I decided to put an end to these contradictions, and ever since I was enrolled in college I took the path of Islam and stopped frequenting beaches and cinemas." However, the contradictions kept pursuing him, this time in the society as a whole. "We are," he explains, "an Islamic state and we have the Koran—and yet we follow the Charter [of National Action, Nasser's program based on the ideology of Arab socialism] rather than practice the Koran." His analysis of the current state of affairs in Egypt, what he terms "the five fingers of the hand of oppression," is summed up in these "definitions":

Politics: "Intellectual and political tyranny."

Religion: "Backwardness, stagnation, and negativism."

Media: "Freedom of speech and information provided they voice no dissent."

Society: "The overwhelming majority follows outworn customs and traditions, while the others are devoid of all values."

Science: "They masquerade as adherents of science, attribute to it more than it can bear, and manipulate it according to their whims and caprices."

Another university student, Muhammad, objects to the regime's adherence to the doctrine of nationalism. "Islam," he noted, "does not recognize the concept of nationality. This doctrine implies that people are defined according to a certain geographical location, a concept which negates Islam and its principles."

Nissim Rejwan, *Arabs Face the Modern World: Religious, Cultural, and Political Responses to the West* (Gainesville: University Press of Florida, 1998), 187–189.

Hamas: Strategy and Tactics

The eruption of the Intifadhah in December 1987 led to the formation of a new political organization called Hamas—an acronym for the Arabic *Harakat al-Muqawama al-Islamiyya*, or the Islamic Resistance Movement. The term *Islamic* was indicative of Hamas's orientation. It also reflected the reassertion of political Islam as an organized force in Gaza and the West Bank. Hamas's main goal, as articulated in its charter of August 18,

1988, was the uprooting of Israel and its replacement with an Islamic state to be established over the entire territory of Mandatory Palestine. With specific reference to the status of Palestine, article 11 of the charter asserted that the land is an "Islamic trust (*waqf*) upon all Muslim generations until the Day of Resurrection" and that it is not right to give up any part of it.

The charter also rejected peace negotiations and initiatives and considered territorial compromise as being equivalent to "giving up part of the religious faith itself" (art. 13). Finally, the charter asserted that jihad (struggle) is the only solution to the Palestine problem because "when an enemy occupies part of the Muslim lands, jihad becomes obligatory on every Muslim" (art. 16, sec. 5).

Although Hamas was born during the Intifadhah, its roots can be traced to the Muslim Brotherhood, the largest Islamic movement in Gaza and the West Bank since the 1948 Palestine war. The Muslim Brotherhood was founded in March 1928 in Isma'iliyya, Egypt. Its founder, Hasan al-Banna, stressed the principle of an Islamic state. . . . The Brotherhood carried out propaganda activities on behalf of the Palestine cause in Egypt. It also participated in the Palestine revolt of 1936–39. After World War II the Brotherhood became more actively involved in the Palestinian cause, not only spreading the call to Islam but also training Palestinian scouts, sending Egyptian volunteers, helping Palestinian paramilitary organizations, and actively participating in the Palestine war of 1948.

All these activities enhanced the Brotherhood's popularity in Palestine. By the end of the Mandate period there were about twenty-five Brotherhood branches in Palestine with a membership of up to 20,000 activists and with all branches under the Cairo-based leadership of the Brotherhood. Links between the Brotherhood and the Palestinians were particularly strong in Gaza, a 140-square-mile area of Palestine that adjoined Egypt and which passed to Egyptian rule in 1949. For the Brotherhood in Gaza and the West Bank, the first priority was reforming the Muslim individual. The group maintained that true Islam, as a system of politics and social life, was the only solution to the Palestine problem, as well as for other problems in Arab societies. . . .

After the Arab-Israeli war of June 1967, the Brotherhood faced the problems of how to preserve and expand its base in the face of the emerging Palestinian resistance movement, whose dynamism in confronting the Israeli occupation had far greater appeal for the overwhelming majority of Palestinians. A few general observations concerning the strategy of the Brotherhood during the first two decades of Israeli occupation are worth under-scoring for their bearing on the growth of the movement.

Despite the fact that the Brotherhood had significant differences with the Palestine Liberation Organization (PLO), particularly differences over the secular nationalism of the PLO and the PLO's search for a diplomatic settlement with Israel, the leadership of the Brotherhood refrained from declaring their movement as an alternative to the PLO. This was the case because the Brotherhood was conscious that an open challenge to the PLO was hopeless in view of the PLO's dominant influence in Palestinian politics. . . .

Less than a decade after its emergence, Hamas was thrust into the center of Palestinian politics. In the relatively brief span between 1987 and 1997, the political and social profile of the movement was transformed and its leadership could not afford to watch the unfolding events in the Arab-Israeli theater from the sidelines. Hamas was too much of a spoiler of the peace process to be ignored by others, including the Palestinian mainstream, the Israeli government, and U.S. administration. One suicide bombing was potent enough to obstruct the peace process or even to undermine it alto-gether.

The record of Hamas also demonstrated the fundamental limitations of its strategic position. In the first place, it underscored the extent to which Hamas was a prisoner of its own limited resources. Although the move-ment had its own agenda, and sabotaging the Oslo process was at the top of this agenda, the Hamas leadership could not avoid being drawn into relations of accommodation with the Palestine Authority (PA), and even into situations of alliance building with the Palestinian left. True, Hamas was bold enough to challenge other actors, but it also was too weak and cautious to ignore them.

The limitations of Hamas's strategic position had other implications. The position of the movement peaked sometime in the early years of the Intifadhah and then took a dive after Oslo from which it never fully recov-ered. Three interrelated fundamental reasons underlay this reversal. The first had to do with the absence of a national leader for Hamas. The series of challenges around the entire perimeter of Gaza and the West Bank re-quired a leader who could manage to maneuver the movement through them all to a sustainable degree of stability and growth. An effective Hamas leader on the national level was better able to pursue a coherent policy in the second stage of Hamas development, keep the movement's objectives and priorities steadily in view even while making necessary tactical detours, and respond with carefully crafted policies to the changes in the environment. This task was left to the collective leadership based in Amman and elsewhere outside the Palestinian territories and, in some instances, to local leaders on the town and neighborhood levels.

The second reason was the effects of a collective leadership, which were indecisiveness, slowness, and ambiguity, especially in the 1996–97 period. It is important in this respect to note the different orientations within Hamas. The resort of the Qassam Brigades to more radical measures in the winter of 1996 was an indication that politicians inside Hamas were losing ground to the military wing. Also, Arafat's ability to co-opt some prominent Hamas members illustrated the contending trends inside the movement.

A third reason was the Palestinian environment itself. A majority of Palestinians in Gaza and the West Bank consistently supported Oslo despite the ups and downs in the negotiations with Israel and delays in the implementation of whatever was agreed upon between Israel and the PA. The persistence of support for the peace process seriously limited Hamas's ability to challenge the PA from a position of strength.

These factors suggest the following observations about Hamas's mode of operation.

1. Hamas's policy, even its most radical aspects, had been over the past years essentially defensive, stemming more from a sense of weakness than from an ideological drive. Hamas has shown that it is not averse to striking a modus vivendi both with the PA and with Israel. When the PA responded with firmness to Hamas military escalation against Israel, Hamas has used the slogan of reconciliation to dissuade the PA from taking undesired action against the movement.

2. In situations involving a choice between incurring short-term danger to advance long-term interests or seeking to avoid the former at a risk to the latter, Hamas did not always opt for the second course. This was illustrated in the early 1996 decision to escalate military attacks inside Israel. Yet at the same time, when Hamas was pressured by the PA, it deliberately maintained a low profile and played for time. This tendency was illustrated in the military quietism of Hamas since the summer of 1996.

3. As a corollary of the general disposition of Hamas, the leadership of the movement has pursued over 1996 a political style characterized by a preference for caution over maximization of potential gains if the price of gains was a confrontation with the PA; a tendency to issue contradictory statements simultaneously from Gaza, Amman,

Damascus, and Beirut; a willingness to make sharp tactical reversals; and a limited concern with the principle of consistency.

In view of the above, more Hamas voices probably will be raised to stress the need for a policy of adaptation to Oslo. These probably will be countered by reiterations of the traditional Hamas argument that the movement's natural place is on the side of opposition to Oslo. Whether Hamas will find a third way remains an open question. Israel's release of Hamas's leader, Shaykh Yasin, in September 1997 has not meant that the field for military activism has become wider. On the contrary, the field has become much narrower.

Author's note: This essay is largely based on field research in Gaza and the West Bank, including interviews with Hamas members.

Muhammad Muslih, "Hamas: Strategy and Tactics," in *Ethnic Conflict and International Politics in the Middle East,* ed. Leonard Binder (Gainesville: University Press of Florida, 1999), 309–309, 329–331.

In Israel: "Islamization from Below"

A number of theories have been put forward for explaining the return to Islam. The "crisis theory" claims that the Islamic awakening is a result of political or military crises, internal political crises such as unsuccessful leadership, or severe political and economic crises. The psychological need to "find an absolute and simple solution to all these crises turned many believers to religion." However, this theory was severely criticized because the return to Islam was not confined only to crises. Indeed, the "success theory" developed in reaction to the "crisis theory." According to this view, success in the Islamic arena (mainly political) brought about massive support to Islamic groups (i.e., the perceived Arab victory in the 1973 October War and the success of the 1979 Iranian revolution). This theory was criticized on the grounds that the roots of Islamic fundamentalism are deeper and go back further into history than the 1970s. A third theory was the "evolution theory." According to this theory, the present Islamic revival is another stage of Islamic reaction to the modernization processes that have occurred in Muslim societies during the last two centuries. Though sophisticated in comparison with the other two theories, it is difficult to see the connection between Islamic trends in various parts of the world such as Indonesia, Yugoslavia, Iran or the former Soviet Union Muslim republics, owing to the huge historical, cultural, social and geographic differences among them.

Therefore, it is too simplistic to adopt only one theory to explain the complex and multi-faceted phenomenon of Islamic fundamentalism all over the world. . . .

The aim of this article is to examine the nature of Islamic fundamentalism in Israel by looking at two major issues: the attitude of the Islamic movement toward the Israeli-Palestinian conflict and the extent of its integration into Israeli political life. . . . The Islamic fundamentalist movement in Israel was established in 1983 after the release of Shaykh ʿAbdallah Nimer Darwish, the spiritual leader of the movement, from an Israeli prison (he had been convicted for inciting violence against the State of Israel). Initially, the activities of Islamic activists followed the pattern of "Islamization from above." The movement was organized in small militant groups with the aim of toppling the dominant Israeli-Jewish order and destroying Jewish dominance and turning Israel into a Muslim state with the Jews relegated to minority status. The group comprised between 60 and 100 male activists who had returned to Islam, most of them under the age of 25 and all from the area known as the Little Triangle. . . . Most of the activists from this area came from lower middle class backgrounds and lacked higher education. . . . However, the early arrest of its members in January and February 1981 brought drastic change to the activities of the movement. After his release from prison in 1983, Darwish declared that the movement's members would act within Israeli law and avoid any public calls to establish an Islamic state. Since 1983, we have witnessed a process of "Islamization from below," whereby the Islamic movement concentrates on socio-cultural, religious and educational projects.

Muhammad Hasan Amora, "The Nature of Islamic Fundamentalism in Israel," in *Religious Radicalism in the Greater Middle East,* ed. Bruce Maddy-Weitzman and Efraim Inbar (London: Frank Cass, 1997), 155–157.

The Case of Faraj Fouda

In the ideological lexicon of religious fanatics, the word *secularist* is almost always equated with *atheist* or *apostate*. As far as one can judge from his own writings, Faraj ʿAli Fouda, the Egyptian author and columnist who was gunned down in a Cairo suburb on June 7, 1992, was no apostate. He was certainly not an atheist, and not only because as a child and youth he was given a strictly traditional Islamic education.

Fouda was, however, an advocate of a modern, Western-style secular state, as opposed to the religious state Muslim fundamentalists demanded. Strictly speaking, Egypt is effectively a secular state, though along with almost all other Arab states—with the exception of Syria and Iraq, where the Pan-Arab Baʿth Party rules—its constitution declares that Islam "is the religion of the state."

This, of course, is far short of what is envisioned by the Islamists, whose spokesmen consider the present Arab regimes, with the possible exception of Saudi Arabia—and more recently Sudan—heretical. The fundamentalists advocate a state run strictly according to the laws and commands of the Koran, the kind of state the Islamic Republic of Iran claims—or aspires—to be.

It was against this fundamentalist "tide" that Fouda set himself and his sharp, pithy pen. While by no means the only one among the Egyptian intelligentsia to see the danger and sound the alarm, he was undoubtedly the most outspoken of all those who fought what he perceived as a threatening avalanche. Consistently and mercilessly, Fouda exposed the leaders and the ideologues of the Islamist groups known in Egypt as *al-gamaʿat* and all boasting the name jihad (holy war). He showed them to be forces of darkness—lawless bigots, anti-progress, anti-women, xenophobes, and, above all, incurable hypocrites, to use his own terminology. . . .

Fouda's most serious charge against the fundamentalists was that they had "abandoned the true teachings of Islam." He also thought that the authorities should adopt tougher measures to stem "the tide." In the course of a meeting that Egypt's President Hosni Mubarak held in May 1992 with a group of journalists and editors, Fouda asked him to initiate anti-terror legislation to curb the extremists.

Fouda—who was by profession an economic consultant—devoted all his political and intellectual energies to fighting Islamic fundamentalism. All his books had two main themes—curbing the Islamic tide and promoting Muslim-Coptic reconciliation and coexistence. Their titles faithfully reflect their contents: *The Terror, The Absent Truth, Before the Fall, The Omen.*

In *The Omen,* Fouda lists most of the fundamentalists' main stands:

1. They do not recognize Egyptian nationalism and national unity.
2. They disown the acts of violence and terror they themselves commit.
3. They are ignorant of Islamic history and distort its true character.
4. They teach that woman's place is in the home.
5. They distort modern civilization and depict it as one of permissiveness, sexual perversion, and AIDS.
6. They portray the Islamist state as a veritable Garden of Eden, ignoring the shameful record of torture and summary executions in the Islamic Republic of Iran.

Fouda's style was pithy and unsparing, and at times perhaps too biting and too personal. Muhammad Sid-Ahmad, a fellow political intellectual and a friend, said after the assassination that, while Fouda's erudition was not in question, his style was characterized by sarcasm—"and, perhaps, there was in it a certain measure of innocence, of naivete."

Nissim Rejwan, *Arabs Face the Modern World*, 231–233.

What Future the Islamist Movement?

[A] bird's eye view of the fate of the Islamist movement in the three paradigmatic cases of Iran, Egypt, and Algeria might allow us to set up a model for analyzing its developments worldwide in the last quarter of the twentieth century. Because the movement toppled the ruling regime in one of the three countries, had been in existence for so long in another, and fell a bit short of seizing power in the third, its characteristics and features became particularly manifest—enabling us to construct the Young Urban Poor, the Intellectual Counterelite, and the Pious Bourgeoisie ideal-types, and to study how their interplay determined, in our understanding, political success or failure of the movement as a whole in given circumstances. [In chapter 8, see the reading by Giles Kepel.] But such a model will prove operative—provided it shed some light on the three aforementioned cases—on the condition that it can be applied to the fate of Islamist movements in other countries as well, where political antagonisms did not reach the climaxes of Iran, Egypt, or Algeria. Can it allow the analyst to construct an interpretive framework that gives significance to otherwise blurred political action of social actors? For instance, how can the peculiar nature and interplay of our three components of the Islamist cluster in Turkey explain the political fortunes and misfortunes of Refah Partisi? How did the political systems of countries as different as Jordan, Malaysia, and Indonesia manage to defuse the Islamist challenge through an early co-option of the Pious Bourgeoisie at the expense of the Young Urban Poor?

Another dimension has to be taken into account: the transnational level. Though we focused on issues of domestic policies in our survey, access to international networks of funding, media, charity, etc., is a powerful means to gain support and fuel mobilization. It can provide standards to emulate for some groups or social threats to others.

This social analysis of the Islamist movements of today is nothing but an attempt at putting such movements in perspective, some twenty-five years after they first appeared in postcolonial states. I tried to point out that their reference to Islam was in effect the sole means through which two social groups with altogether diverging agendas—the Pious Bourgeoisie and the Young Urban Poor—could mobilize side by side. I also attempted to show that the function of the Intellectual Counterelites was to produce the Islamist ideology that would make them coalesce in order to seize power.

Though any ideology tends to portray itself as the core truth or the essence of social relations, the historical and comparative perspective that we used helped us perceive that neither this coalition nor this ideology are eternal. They are but the product of peculiar social conditions, determined by such variables as demography, social mobility, type of state power, availability and distribution of wealth, etc. When some of those variables are subject to significant change, social conditions get modified, and this may have a destabilizing effect on the Islamist cluster. When state power fell into Islamist hands, as happened in Iran, Islamist ideology changed from a revolutionary tool to a means to freeze the new social order topped by the Pious Bourgeoisie. Such a phenomenon was well documented all along history and was particularly blatant in the case of twentieth-century communism. In this regard, the landslide victory of antiestablishment candidate Mohammad Khatami in the Iranian presidential election of 1997, brought to office by a majority of the very youth that had no other political experience than the seventeen-year-old Islamic republic, may call into question the future of Islamist ideology in this country. Some other variables have changed over the elapsed quarter of a century: population increase has slowed down; migrations from the countryside to large cities is less widespread; and Islamism, which looked like a Utopia two decades ago, now has a record of twenty years—a mixed record of success and failure, which on the one hand makes it more established, but on the other hand may also break its spell.

Giles Kepel, "Toward a Social Analysis of Islamic Movements," in Binder, ed., *Ethnic Conflict*, 204–205.

10

Unity in Islamic Diversity

Early in 1995, Britain's Prince Charles—of all unlikely commentators, one might add—spoke thus at the Oxford Centre for Islamic Studies: "We must not be tempted to believe that extremism is in some way the hallmark of and essence of the Muslim. The Prophet [Muhammad] himself disliked and feared extremism."

As an introduction to this piece of advice the prince said, among other things:

> Many people in the Islamic world genuinely fear Western materialism and mass culture as a deadly challenge to their Islamic culture and way of life. We fall into the trap of dreadful arrogance if we confuse "modernity" in other countries with their becoming more like us. Our form of materialism can be offensive to devout Muslims. We must understand that reaction. This would help us understand what we have come to see as the threat of Islamic fundamentalism. We need to be careful of that emotive label, "fundamentalism," and distinguish, as Muslims do, between revivalists, who choose to take the practice of their religion most devoutly, and fanatics or extremists, who use this devotion for political ends."[1]

Some four months later, Anthony Lake, President Clinton's top foreign policy adviser, was quoted by *Newsweek* as saying roughly the same thing put somewhat differently. In a speech at the Washington Institute for Near Eastern Policy "meant to define a shift in U.S. attitudes," according to the weekly, Lake asserted, "Islam is not the issue. . . . Our foe is oppression and extremism," not "a renewed emphasis on traditional values in the Islamic world."

These are important, novel sentiments the likes of which are not heard very often, even in the stately seats of academe. Of the books surveyed in these concluding remarks, in fact, only three—Akbar S. Ahmed's *Living Islam* and F. E. Peters's *The Hajj* and *Mecca*, can be said to present a sober, well-balanced, and fair-minded idea of what Islam is—Islam as a faith as against political Islamic extremism.

Ahmed goes to the root of the problem. Western commentators, he writes, "often use—or misuse—terms taken from Christianity and apply them to Islam. One of the most commonly used is fundamentalism. As we know, in its original application it means someone who believes in the fundamentals of religion, that is, the Bible and the Scriptures. In that sense every Muslim is a fundamentalist believing in the Quran and the Prophet. However, in the manner it is used in the media, to mean a fanatic or extremist, it does not illuminate either Muslim thought or Muslim society. In the Christian context it is a useful concept. In the Muslim context it simply confuses because by definition every Muslim believes in the fundamentals of Islam. . . . A Muslim even talking of Islam will be quickly slapped with the label fundamentalist in the Western media." Elsewhere in his account Ahmed speaks of the phenomenon as "the Western bogeyman."[2]

In an earlier work, *Postmodernism and Islam: Predicament and Promise,* Ahmed tackles the problem of Islam and its perception in the West. "On the threshold of the twenty-first century," he writes, "confrontation between Islam and the West poses terrible internal dilemmas for both. The test for Muslims is how to preserve the essence of the Quranic message . . . without it being reduced to an ancient and empty chant in our times; how to participate in the global civilization without their identity being obliterated." He calls the text "apocalyptic," and a most severe examination. "Muslims stand at the crossroads," he explains. "If they take one route they can harness their vitality and commitment in order to fulfill their destiny on the world stage, if the other, they can dissipate their energy through internecine strife and petty bickering: harmony and hope versus disunity and disorder."

The challenge for those in the West, on the other side, is "how to expand the Western idealistic notions of justice, equality, freedom and liberty beyond their borders to include all humanity and without appearing like 19th-century imperialists; to reach out to those not of their civilization in friendship and sincerity." In both cases a mutual understanding and working relationship are essential, he asserts. "The logic of the argument demands that the West uses its great power . . . to assist in solving the long-festering problems that plague Muslim society. . . . There is the need to push unwilling rulers, who subsist on Western arms and aid, towards conceding democracy and a fairer distribution of wealth, of ensuring the rights and dignity of women and children, the less privileged and those in the minority. These problems are interwoven, binding Muslims and non-Muslims together. There can be no just and viable world order—let alone a New World Order—if these wrongs are not redressed."

It is crucial, Ahmed argues, that the potential points of conflict are identified if continued confrontation is to be avoided, and he believes this is not only necessary but also possible. "Into the predicament that postmodernism plunges us there is also promise," he writes, adding that, while this conclusion may appear illogically optimistic, it is understandable in the context of the Islamic vision, which is rooted firmly in history and belief. Islam, he explains, "has much to offer a world saturated with disintegration, cynicism and loss of faith." However, this will only be possible if there is a universal tolerance of others among Muslims and non-Muslims alike, an appreciation of their uniqueness and a willingness to understand them. "It will only be possible if this sentiment becomes both personal philosophy and national foreign policy, if it is placed on top of the agenda in preparation for the next millennium," he concludes.[3]

A different and rather more outspoken approach to the subject is followed in *The Failure of Political Islam,* by Olivier Roy. Islamism (what is generally termed Islamic fundamentalism), Roy asserts, being above all "a sociocultural movement embodying the protest and frustration of a generation of youth that has not been integrated socially or politically," will never unify the Muslim world nor change the balance of power in the Middle East.

"Today's Islamist movements . . . do not offer a new model of society; far from consecrating the return of a conquering self-assured Islam, they reflect first and foremost the failure of the Western-style state model, which was imported and commandeered by single parties and patronage networks. They assemble the outcasts of a failed modernism."

"Any Islamist victory will be a mirage. But the illusion it creates will not be without effects. . . . What the Islamists advocate is not the return to an incomparably rich classical age, but the establishment of an empty stage on which the believer strives to realize with each gesture the ethical model of the Prophet."

The Islamist view of the world is defensive; it represents the movement's inability to incorporate modernity. "It has been a long time since Christianity was Islam's other. Even if there is a religious revival among Christians and Jews, it is in no way parallel to that of the [Muslim] fundamentalists. The culture that threatens Muslim society is neither Jewish nor Christian; it is a world culture of consumption and communication, a culture that is secular, atheist, and ultimately empty; it has no values or strategies, but it is already here, in the cassette and the transistor, present in the most remote village. This culture can withstand any reappropriation and rereading. It is a code and not a civilization."[4]

These are but a few of the seemingly habitual obiter dicta pronounced by Roy in *The Failure of Political Islam*, a closely argued, sweeping assault on the movement he alternately calls Islamism and neofundamentalism. Roy takes what is called "the Islamic threat" very lightly indeed, derisively almost. "A strange Islamic threat indeed," he mocks, "which waged war only against other Muslims (Iran/Iraq) or against the Soviets (Afghanistan) and caused less terrorist damage than the Baader-Meinhof gang, the Red Brigade, the Irish Republican Army. . . . "

On closer examination, however, these judgments—pleasing though they may be to Western ears—turn out to be too sweeping and sorely lacking in both factual and theoretical supporting evidence. For while Islamism may well have failed intellectually and historically—and while it is true that the various Islamist movements "never coalesced into an Islamic International"—the danger they pose is always there. Moreover, these movements are bound to inflict a great deal of loss and destruction in the societies in which they are active before their core leaderships even begin to realize that they were pursuing an inaccessible dream, a mirage—if they ever do so, that is.

Muhammad Arkoun's *Rethinking Islam* is an almost haphazard collection of twenty-four loosely connected "chapters" given in the form of answers dubbed "uncommon" to questions dubbed "common." Most of the chapters are two or three pages long and deal with such aspects of Islam as the Qur'an, exegesis, Muhammad, Hadith, dogma, women, authority—as well as topics like secularism, nationalism, church and state, Sufism, "the Person," ethics and politics, and human rights.

One of the most intriguing of the "common" questions Arkoun answers is the last, number 24, bearing the title "Mediterranean Culture." The question is every bit as "uncommon" as the ten-page answer: "How can scholars most effectively give greater currency in today's most dynamic societies, those bearing most of the burden of change and innovation, to the notion of Mediterranean culture?"[5]

The nearest thing to a coherent answer to this weird query is to be found in an answer to one of the many questions Arkoun himself incorporates in his lengthy answer: "Will the refusal issued by political Islam to the aggressive aspects of the conquering West contribute to the reaffirmation of a reassembled, active Mediterranean, or will it hasten the breakup of the world and the end of the region's mission?" His answer: "The quality of civilization in gestation rides on that question. The current confrontation between Islam and the West must be perceived, conducted, and lived in the perspective of this fight for the meaning of human existence begun by the prophets and pursued by the saints, heroes, thinkers, and creators at the heights of Mediterranean culture."[6]

Rethinking Islam was widely praised for the sheer daring and provocativeness of what its very title implicitly suggests—in that Islamists dismiss any "rethinking" of Islam as heresy. This may well be so. The point is that the results signally fail to match the expectations.

Islam and Democracy

"Seen today as the culture most capable of channeling popular frustrations, Islam gives the believer enormous expectations of social solidarity. The sacred, after long being utilized to pacify the masses and keep them quiet, is today taking its revenge on those who have manipulated it. It has become, as at the time of its birth, a force for the destabilization of privilege, whether regional or global." This is only one of the many impressive and useful insights scattered in Fatima Mernissi's *Islam and Democracy,* a rare mix of personal reflections and scholarly writing interspersed with fascinating fragments of autobiography. The book, which offers much more than an answer to the question as to why democracy has generally failed to take root in the Arab world, is written in a rather discursive, fairly disorganized manner, and is not addressed to academic-oriented, deductive minds. But what it lacks in organization it amply compensates for by the courage and the thoughtfulness of its contents.

Mernissi, who teaches sociology at Muhammad the Fifth University in Rabat, hails from an observant Muslim family. Though she would rightly appear to many as a thoroughly Westernized person—especially to those who have read her work on the subject of women in Islam—Mernissi nevertheless has some rather scathing things to say about the West. In a chapter entitled "Fear of the Present," to give one example, she writes: "The feeling of absurdity that pervades our lives today stems from the fact that modernity reminds us every minute that it is Western."

Since the night of July 20, 1969, she remarks, "when a tall blond man planted the flag of his nation on it, the moon is not universal. . . . " Following the planting of the American flag, what is more, non-Western spectators were treated to a quotation from the first chapter of Genesis. "It is," Mernissi comments, "a given that the West, which flaunts before us the dream of one world, bears responsibility for the future of humanity. Its responsibility is heavy because it . . . alone decides if satellites will be used to educate Arabs or to drop bombs on them. It is understandable and even excusable that the Third World, off course and unable to participate in the celebration of science, seeks to find its way by drawing on myths and historical memory. But when the West, which is opening the way toward the galactic era, trots out tribal flags and bibles to inaugurate man's exploration of the moon, it does not help the excluded, among them Arab youth, feel they are partners in this universality."

Having said all this Mernissi adds that it is "obvious" that the powerful monolithic West that haunts Arab and Third World imagination "is more fiction that fact, especially in the decade of the nineties, since the fall of the Berlin Wall." Nevertheless, "seen from the Arab side of the Mediterranean, the West (more exactly, Europe), however splintered and divided it may be, is a power that crushes us, besieges our markets, and controls our interest resources, initiatives, and potentialities."

In a chapter entitled "Fear of the Foreign West," Mernissi explains that the word *gharb,* which is Arabic for west, is also the place of darkness and the incomprehensible, always frightening. It is "the territory of the strange, the foreign (*gharib*)," and foreignness in Arabic has a very strong spatial connotation, *gharb* being the place where the sun sets and where darkness awaits. "It is in the West that the night snaps up the sun and swallows it; then all terrors are possible. . . ."[7]

As the title he chose for his book indicates, Aziz al-Azmeh perceives more than one kind of Islam. As he points out in a long and discursive prologue, the essays and papers assembled in *Islams and Modernities* "derive from the contention that there are as many Islams as there are situations that sustain it [Islam]." The conflict between fundamentalist Islam and the West—highlighted, among others, by the famous fatwa on Salman Rushdie—is not as impossible to resolve as it is usually made out to be, the reason being that behind both positions lie "similarly romantic and ahistorical notions of Islamic culture and of the West itself. . . . Both sides speak the same language of ancestral authenticity and identity."[8]

The result of these symmetrical world views, al-Azmeh asserts, is a culturist essentialism which he considers "a postmodern form of racism." The history of Islam, he argues, and the complexity of the modern world systems, belie both the homogenizing claims of Islamic radicalism and the Western discourse of Orientalism. In support of this position, al-Azmeh highlights the plurality and historicity of both Islam and the West.

Turning to the thorny subject of Islamic fundamentalism, and the various ways in which contemporary Muslims have tried to meet the challenges of the West, al-Azmeh writes that, in terms of the rules governing their respective discourses, the difference between the Muslim modernists and their fundamentalist counterparts "resides in their attitudes to the translatability of traditional texts." "The hallmark of Islamic modernism," he explains, "is its admission of the possibility, even the necessity, [of such translation]; thus *shura* [counsel] becomes democracy, even parliamentary democracy; Islam becomes a charter for socialism; and the cosmic calamities indicated in the early, apocalyptic chapters of the Koran become premonitions of modern scientific discoveries."

For the fundamentalists, on the other hand, "Islam is *sui generis,* and is utterly distinctive; it is therefore totally unrelated to democracy, especially parliamentary democracy, and any talk of relating it to socialism is polluting by implication, for the term 'socialism' is contiguous with communism, and communism is atheistic, and neither socialism nor democracy occurs in the Koran or the salutary tradition." Translation is thus totally ruled out, and the paradise that the fundamentalists desire "is a literalist one whose institutions have already been fully established."

Thus the present becomes "no more than a shadow of unreality in comparison with the full ontological weight of the salutary example," and in the discourse of fundamentalism it is hardly ever referred to, being considered somehow as "a register running parallel to itself." In the discourse of Islamic fundamentalism, indeed, discussion of matters that happened in the time of the Prophet "takes the form of a metonymic representation of present realities."[9]

Fundamentalism as a "Modernist Phenomenon"

While it is difficult to summarize the rich variety of topics discussed and conclusions drawn by the author of *Islams and Modernities,* the thrust of al-Azmeh's argument is fairly clear. For him, Islamic fundamentalism represents a break with some crucial aspects of Muslim tradition and should

246 / The Many Faces of Islam

be seen as a characteristically modernist phenomenon, drawing on themes commonly encountered in the discourse of romantic populism and subaltern nationalism.

In a way, al-Azmeh's approach can be perceived from the counsel he gives to Western students of Islam. Any proper writing of Islamic history, he writes in his concluding essay, "has to rest on the dissolution of Islam as an orientalist category." European Islamic scholarship, he adds, "will have to start with putting into question the very notion of objectivity itself—or rather, to regard it as a historical category and as a historical and discursive problem." It has, what is more, "to liberate itself from Islam, and scrutinize Islamic histories, societies, economies, temporalities, sociology, critical theory and anthropology." Only then will Islam be reconstituted "as historical categories amenable to historical study."[10]

The contents of Bernard Lewis's *Islam and the West* are so variegated, its texture so rich, and its substance so dense that to impart any meaningful summary of its themes would probably take another volume. Reading it and pondering its many offerings, one cannot but repeat what must have been said again and again about the author: Only a scholar of Bernard Lewis's caliber, his depth of knowledge, keen interest, endless curiosity and—not least—the lucidity of his style can provide so much instruction and so much food for thought in such a relatively modest number of pages.

Take the subject of relations between Islam and Christianity, for example. We have been habitually taught, all along, that these two faiths have little if anything in common. Not quite so, it transpires. As Lewis puts it, compared with the remoter cults of Asia and Africa, "Islam and Christianity are sister religions, with an immense shared heritage and a shared—or more often disputed—domain." For one thing, "each saw itself as the bearer of God's final revelation to humankind, with the duty of bringing that revelation to the rest of the world. For another, each recognized the other "as its principal, indeed, its only, rival in this claim and in this task."

Again, referring to the difference in perception of "the religious other" in Judaism on one hand and in Islam and Christianity on the other, Lewis notes that, "while Jews claim that the truths of their faith are universal, they do not claim that they are exclusive." Judaism is for Jews and those who care to join them, it is true. "But, according to a well-known Talmudic dictum, the righteous of all peoples and faiths have their place in paradise."

Not so with the other two revealed religions. "Traditional Christianity and Islam differed from Judaism and agreed with each other in that both claimed to possess not only universal but exclusive truths. . . . Neither admitted salvation outside its own creed. In the fourteen-centuries-long encounter between Islam and Christendom, the profoundest conflict between the two religions, the most irreconcilable disagreements between their followers, arose not from their differences but from their resemblances."[11]

Except by historians, though, the term *Christendom* is rarely used today. The civilization formerly designated by that name "has undergone a process of secularization and has come to be known, in various contexts, as Europe, as the free world, and, nowadays, principally as the West." In contrast, the Islamic world, or as Muslims call it, the House of Islam, is still known, "both at home and abroad, by that name, albeit with regional, national, and—rarely—sectarian subdivisions." It is with the relations between these two civilizations that the eleven studies and essays in *Islam and the West* are concerned.

Charles Krauthammer, the noted *Washington Post* columnist, once dubbed the Islamic Republic of Iran "the center of the world's new Comintern," adding that the new threat it constituted was "as evil as the old Evil Empire." Another well-known American commentator, who writes from Europe, William Pfaff, reported early in 1991: "There are a good many people who think that the war between communism and the West is about to be replaced by a war between the West and Muslims."

John Esposito, one of America's foremost authorities and interpreters of Islam, cites both these quotations in *The Islamic Threat: Myth or Reality?* with learned disapproval. "There are," he writes, "lessons to be learned from a past in which fear of a monolithic Soviet threat often blinded us to the humanity, values and aspirations and diversity of the majority; led to uncritical support for regimes as long as they remained allies in the Cold War; enabled an easy acceptance of authoritarianism and the suppression of the legitimate dissent of any whose governments and security forces labeled them communists or socialists."

However, "If we are to understand and respond to the challenge of political Islam, its diverse manifestations must be seen within the multiplicity of the intellectual and political contexts in which it occurs. While the threats of extremism and violence must be countered forcefully and effectively, the long-term relations of the West with the Muslim world . . . will hinge on its response to the emergence of new social and political forces and its respect for their legitimate aspirations for greater political participation, social justice, and human rights."

How this is to be accomplished is not made entirely clear. However, more than a hint can be detected from Esposito's general criticism of the West's attitude toward Islam as a whole. To give one of the more explicit reservations: "Monolithic Islam," he writes in the chapter entitled "'Islamic Fundamentalism' and the West," "has been a recurrent Western myth which has never been borne out by the reality of Muslim history. When convenient, Western commentators waste little time on the divisions and fratricidal relations of the Arab and Muslim world so as to underscore its intractable instability. . . . Yet when equally convenient, Islam, the Arabs, and the Muslim world are presented as a unified bloc poised against the West."

"Our challenge," Esposito writes in his concluding remarks, "is to better understand the history and realities of the Muslim world. Recognizing the diversity and many faces of Islam counters our image of a unified Islamic threat. It lessens the risk of creating self-fulfilling prophecies about the battle of the West against radical Islam."[12]

Ervand Abrahamian, another Islamic scholar living and teaching in America, is even more critical than Esposito of the Western media's habitual equation of political Islam with the Islamic revival and what is called Islamic fundamentalism. The central thesis of *Khomeinism: Essays on the Islamic Republic* is that *populism* is a more apt term than *fundamentalism* for describing Khomeini, his ideas, and his movement. The reason Abrahamian advances for this preference is that, while *fundamentalism* implies intellectual purity, political traditionalism, even social conservatism, *populism* is associated with ideological adaptability and intellectual flexibility, and with political protest against the established order.

There is more at issue here than semantics, Abrahamian explains. "On the one hand," he writes, "if Khomeinism is a form of fundamentalism, then the whole movement is inherently incapable of adapting to the modern age and is trapped in an ideological closed circuit. On the other hand, if Khomeinism is a form of populism, it contains the potential for change and acceptance of modernity—even eventually of political pluralism, gender equality, individual rights, and social democracy."[13]

Readings

Four Orthodox Schools

The Muslim system of law grew largely from two roots: the Koran and the traditions. At an early date, however, three other sources—analogy, consensus, and opinion—had a profound effect upon the *Shariah*. Caliphs and their judges . . . discovered that the Koran and the traditions were not explicit with respect to many situations with which they had to deal. In the absence of a definite statement, judges and lawyers resorted to the use of analogy (*kiyas*) to some instance in the Koran or the traditions in deciding a case brought before them. Although the strictest judges did not practice analogy on the grounds that it allowed too much to human judgment, it was, nevertheless, adopted widely in the eighth century as a legal aid and from precedent to precedent became an integral part of the *Shariah*.

In the same century Malik ibn Anas, a jurist-theologian of Medina, compiled a book of traditions which incorporated many of the local juridical customs and practices. This procedure introduced the element of public consensus (*ijma*). At first it was reserved to Medina, but in the following century it was widened by al-Shafii to include the consensus of the Muslim community at large. Although criticized by many who believed that it was too difficult to secure unanimity among widely scattered Muslim scholars, consensus enabled Islam through the centuries to adapt its institutions to a changing world.

A third additional source of Muslim law has been private opinion (*ray*). Private opinion was never quite accepted as the fifth principle of the *Shariah*, but it was widely practiced. Early caliphs employed it extensively until bitter complaints that legislation by man corrupted divine law forced its abandonment. Nevertheless, most caliphs and later rulers were compelled by administrative necessity to issue laws and decrees which were sanctioned almost wholly by opinion. Such laws and regulations were later termed *Kanuns,* from the Greek and Latin word. Thus, Muslim canon law meant civil and secular law, whereas Islamic divine law was the equivalent of Western canon law.

The orthodox jurists accepted the five roots of the *Shariah* but differed as to which traditions were genuine and as to the weight which ought to be allowed to analogy, consensus, and opinion in establishing a viable Muslim code of law. At the time of al-Mansur it was suggested that he codify and enforce the diverse laws in the empire. Local particularism, however, won the day, and numerous systems prevailed among the Muslims. Since the eleventh century four principal schools of legal practice have been recognized as permissible by the orthodox, and law schools such as al-Azhar in Cairo have carried instruction in all four of the rites.

In point of development the earliest school was the Hanafite. Abu-Hanifah, legal scholar of Kufah and Baghdad, held a tolerant view on the use of analogy and consensus and particularly emphasized the value and necessity of private opinion and judgment on the part of those administering the law. By the eleventh century, however, a strong conservative movement closed the door on further innovations in the matter of juridical opinions. Judges, henceforth, could allow only opinions previously rendered and were required to adhere closely to the Hanafite teachings. The Hanafite rite was the established procedure followed in the Ottoman empire, parts of India, and central Asia.

Historically, the second orthodox school was the Malikite. Malik ibn Anas of Medina, who died in 795, codified the traditions of Islam and acknowledged the authority of the consensus of the Medina community. Malikite jurists, however, never equivocated in their stand against general consensus, private opinion, and the broad use of analogy. The Malikite school was accepted in Spain, and still prevails in North Africa and eastern Arabia.

Next to the Hanafite school in general acceptance has been that of the Shafiite. The jurist al-Shafii studied under Malik in Medina and taught in Baghdad and Fustat (Cairo), where he died in 820. The Shafiite rites permitted wider use of consensus than did those of the Malikites, and al-Shafii asserted that consensus was the safest and highest legislative authority in Islam. The Shafiite school dominates legal practice in Palestine, Lower Egypt, eastern Africa, western and southern Arabia, parts of India, and the East Indies.

The Hanbalite school was the fourth and smallest among the orthodox schools. Its founder, Ahmad ibn Hanbal, a student of al-Shafii, rebelled against the teachings of his master. The Hanbalites accepted neither private opinion nor analogy and scorned the use of consensus. The only valid basis of Muslim law, besides the Koran, were the traditions. They would not accept public office, and Ibn Hanbal was beaten and persecuted by al-Mamun and al-Mutasim. Although more than 500,000 attended Hanbal's funeral when he died in Baghdad in 855, Hanbalism was too rigid to be popular or practical over the centuries and had only scattered followers in Syria and Iraq. After the Ottoman conquest the doctrine perished, to be revived in the eighteenth century by the Wahhabis in central Arabia, where the Hanbalite rites are still observed.

In addition to the four principal codes of law, another body of law evolved from a court practice of submitting the summary of involved and important cases to a learned jurist, as a consultant, for an opinion. Such a consultant was called a *mufti;* and his reply, which presented the legal issues and indicated the proper decision, was a *fatwa. Fatwa*s were later collected and served as guides to the courts in rendering judgments. Until the advent of the Ottoman empire *mufti*s more or less remained free from control or restraint by the government.

W. Montgomery Watt, *Islamic Philosophy and Theology* (Edinburgh: Edinburgh University Press, 1962), 100–101.

The Wahhabi Movement

The movement led by Muhammad ibn Abd al-Wahhab in the middle of the eighteenth century was not, in principle, an Arabian movement. Its inspiration lay in the puritanical Hanbalite school, the school which recognized *ijma* only within the narrowest limits and produced Ibn Taimiya and which still, though much reduced in numbers, lived on in the Hijaz, Iraq, and Palestine. Muhammad Ibn Abd al-Wahhab, in selecting his native central Arabia as the scene of his mission, was (whether consciously or unconsciously) adopting the same course as was taken by the leaders of similar reformist movements both before and after his time. This course was to seek out some region which was out of reach of an organized political authority, where there was, therefore, an open field for the propagation of his teaching and where, if he were successful, he might be able to build up a strong theocratic organization by the aid of warlike tribesmen. It was by such means that the early Shiʿites and the Berber empires of the Almoravids and the Almohads had gained their first successes; and so, too, Ibn Abd al-Wahhab achieved his initial purpose by alliance with the house of Saud in the fastnesses of Nejd.

The results of this first Wahhabi movement were, and still are, far reaching. In its original phase it shocked the conscience of the Muslim community by the violence and intolerance which it displayed not only toward saint-worship but also toward the accepted orthodox rites and schools. By holding them all guilty of infidelity to the pure transcendental ideal and excluding them from the status of true believers, the first Wahhabis repeated the error of the Kharijites (the uncompromising idealists of the first century of Islam), alienated the sympathy and support of the orthodox, and made themselves heretics. Ultimately, therefore, like all fighting minorities who reject any kind of co-operation with more powerful majorities, their opposition was, in a political sense, crushed. But in its ideal aspect, in the challenge which it flung out to the contamination of pure Islamic monotheism by the infiltration of animistic practices and pantheistic notions, Wahhabism had a salutary and revitalizing effect, which spread little by little over the whole Muslim world.

During the greater part of the nineteenth century, however, the revitalizing element in Wahhabism was obscured by its revolutionary theocratic aspect. It set an example of revolt against an "apostate" Muslim government; and its example was the more eagerly followed in other countries as their Muslim governments fell more and more patently under European influence and control.

H. A. R. Gibb, *Modern Trends in Islam* (Chicago: University of Chicago Press, 1947), 23–24.

A Mosaic of Cultures

Starting with no cultural asset other than poetry, to which religion was later added, Arabians could claim no developed literature, fine art, philosophy or science. They had to wait to acquire such assets from the peoples they conquered. In this their experience paralleled that of the Teutonic tribes vis-à-vis the Roman Empire and differed from that of Mongols and Tartars under Chingiz Khan, Hulagu and Attila. Gradually Moslem Arabians adopted and adapted what did not conflict with their religious tenets, identified themselves with their subjects and ultimately were absorbed by them. Theirs was another case of conquerors led captive by the conquered.

What we call Islamic culture, therefore, was Islamic only in the sense that it evolved under Moslem aegis. A better designation would be Arabic, Arabic being the medium through which that culture was expressed. The first conquest . . . was that of the arms, the state; the second that of religion; now we come to the third, the conquest of language. The linguistic victory was not achieved until Persians, Syrians, Egyptians, Berbers and Andalusians—Moslems, Christians and Jews—began to use the language of the Koran for expressing their thoughts and feelings. As the lingua franca Arabic did not necessarily supersede the vernaculars in home use. In general, linguistic loyalty outlived religious loyalty. In northern Mount Lebanon, Syriac (Aramaic, the language of Christ) survived till the seventeenth century and is still used in the ritual of the Maronite Church. In Anti-Lebanon Aramaic has survived to the present day in three villages. Prior to Islam the term Arabs, in the sense of Arabic-speaking people, and Arabians, in the sense of natives of Arabia proper, could be used interchangeably, but now no more. The area covered by the linguistic term became by virtue of the conquest no more coterminous with the geographic term.

Philip K. Hitti, *Islam and the West* (Princeton: Van Nostrand, 1962), 33, 34.

Three Concepts of Islam

. . . The word "Islam" is used in at least three distinct ways, to refer to three related but different things. First, there is Islam, the self-commitment, the *taslim kardan,* of an individual Muslim: his own personal submission to God, the act of dedication wherein he as a specific and live person in his concrete situation is deliberately and numinously related to a transcendent divine reality which he recognizes and to a cosmos imperative which he accepts.

Secondly and thirdly there are the Platonic ideal and the empirical actuality of the total system of Islam as an institutionalized entity. This is a generalized pattern, of the religion in the one case as it ideally is, at its conceivable best, in the other case as tangible reality, a mundane phenomenon historical and sociological.

We may designate these three as Islam the active personal faith, Islam the religious system as transcendent ideal, and Islam the religious system as historical phenomenon. In the first case, the term "Islam" is a *masdar,* a verbal noun, the name of an action rather than of an institution; it is the response of a particular person to a challenge. That person's whole being is involved, in a transaction, as it were, between his soul and the universe; and, according to his conviction, his eternal destiny is at stake. It involves a decision, private and inalienable. His personal submittingness—if we may use such a term—is, of course, quite distinct from any other person's. Between this action *(Islam)* and the fact of his personal faith *(iman)* the relation is not altogether straightforward and has been much discussed; yet in general the two are of the same order of ideas. "Islam" here may not mean exactly what "faith" means (and no one, Muslim, Christian, or philosopher, has ever been able satisfactorily to translate religious faith into words); but it means something comparable.

In the second and third cases, "Islam" is the name of a religion. On the whole, there is a tendency here for believing Muslims to use the term in the second sense, as an ideal, and for outside observers to use it in the third, as an historical-sociological actuality. This is because men generally tend to talk about other people's religions as they are and about their own as it ought to be. If they have no faith of their own they usually think of all religion as observably practised. As a result, insiders and outsiders may use the same words but be talking of different things.

However, this distribution of meanings is not absolute. Believers also recognize that their religion has in fact had a history, a mundane application, an objectively institutionalized development; and although they may regard this as perhaps but a sorry reflection of the transcendent ideal, yet they may still call it Islam, in its earthly version as it were. Similarly non-believers, although they cannot share with the faithful the notion that ideal Islam is eternal and universal, a pre-existent idea in the mind of God, a final truth, yet may and often do postulate an ideal entity, Islam, which transcends the practice of the community and transcends perhaps even the concepts of individual Muslims.

Wilfred Cantwell Smith, "The Concept of Islam as an Historical Development," in *Historians of the Middle East,* ed. Bernard Lewis and P. M. Holt (Oxford: Oxford University Press, 1962), 485.

Distorting the Teachings of Islam

Islam's history shows a clear demarcation between that group of jurists and thinkers who—contrary to the teachings of the Quran and the Prophet—provided religious justification for oppression by despotic rulers, and the philosophers, scientists, and movements which resisted this distortion of Islam. Between the eleventh and fourteenth centuries, for instance, the Sunni clergy demonstrated more flexibility than their Shiʿite counterparts in adapting their views to those of ruling regimes. But once Shiʿism was established as the official religion in Iran by the Safavid dynasty (sixteenth century), many Shiʿite clerics also legitimized the despot in power. There was a readiness, even among distinguished Muslim scholars, to accept the most tyrannical rule, as long as it could to some degree guarantee the community's security and peace. In the eleventh century, Abu Hamid Muhammad al-Ghazzali, one of the most revered philosophers in the history of Islam, wrote: "These days, the government is completely dependent on military power. The (rightful) caliph is whomever the holders of military power vow allegiance to."

The tolerance of despotism finally reached a point where security alone took precedence, not freedom and justice. Many jurists paid more heed to a ruler's ability to keep law and order than to his honesty or piety. Ibn

Taymiyah, another famous Islamic scholar (thirteenth century), wrote: "It is far better even that an oppressive sultan seize power than that no man take charge. As is said, sixty years under an oppressive ruler is better than one night without a ruler." To that effect, "tyranny is better than anarchy" became a favorite theme of the Jurists. . . .

Judge Abu Bakr Al-Baghlani, a tenth-century statesman and the Abbasid caliph's ambassador to Constantinople, wrote in his book *Al-Tamheed:* "The Caliph cannot be deposed and it is not permissible to revolt against him even if he were corrupt and oppressive, or plundered the *umma*'s [nation's] wealth, or crushed the people under the blows of his whip, or violated all divine laws. He should only be given counsel."

Ten centuries later, in presenting the theory of the "absolute sovereignty of the jurist," Khomeini virtually repeated the words of Judge Abu Bakr Al-Baghlani. The only, yet very important, difference was that Judge Abu Bakr and others endorsed the rule of someone else, while Khomeini was himself in power.

Numerous cases exist of arbitrary distortions of the teachings of Islam throughout its history. Hafiz Yahya Al-Nawawi, a jurist and chief of the Syrian *Dar Al-Hadith* (center for the collection of narrated traditions of the Prophet), for example, wrote in the thirteenth century: "Muslims concur that despite the corruption and oppression of a caliph or a ruler, rebellion and waging war on him are forbidden."

The Prophet's traditions have disappeared altogether from the words of such jurists. The Prophet is quoted as saying: "The most precious martyr in my *ummah* is he who rebels against a tyrannical leader, enjoins him to good, forbids him from evil and is killed by him." The Prophet's own grandson, Hussein bin Ali, rebelled along with his family and disciples against the corrupt ruler of his time, Yazid, and was slain in battle in the seventh century. The democratic and freedom-loving tradition of Prophet Muhammad was gradually distorted over time as despotic fundamentalists (or "traditionalists") veiled their backward views in the guise of Islam. The Umayyad (661–750) and Abbasid (750–1258) dynasties issued orders for the torture, pursuit and inquisition of their opponents, primarily the Prophet's descendants and their supporters. A few centuries later, Shah Ismaʿil, founder of Iran's Safavid dynasty, ordered the harshest punishment inflicted on anyone who refused to insult Abu Bakr and Umar (the two caliphs who succeeded the Prophet), resulting in the massacre of numerous Sunni sheikhs.

Mohammad Mohaddessin, *Islamic Fundamentalism: The New Global Threat* (Washington, D.C.: Seven Locks Press, 1993), 5–6.

Islam and Political Theory

It has often been stressed that Islam is like a vast mansion containing many rooms, not all of which are interconnected. There is good reason to assume that Muslim theology and law developed long after Muhammad, and that his immediate successors, the first four caliphs, were idealized by later generations of Muslim theologians, jurists and historians. This applies particularly to the *Sunni* theory of the *Khilafa,* and it is well known what a gulf separates this ideal theory from political reality. But it should be emphasized that this book is concerned with political theory only, which was worked out at a time when the actual caliphate little resembled the ideal picture drawn by writers on constitutional law. But it is precisely this picture of the *Khilafa,* as demanded by the (ideal) *Shariᶜa,* which is the centre of gravity and the point of reference for all Muslim writers who are concerned with political theory. Unless this is realized neither the religious philosophers of Islam, the *Falasifa,* nor Ibn Khaldun can be properly understood. . . . We must realize that no matter what modern research has established with regard to the origin and development of Muslim law and its threefold foundation in Qurʾan, Sunna and Hadith, it is, in a Muslim's consciousness, divine law, perfect and binding on all members of the Muslim community. Otherwise we cannot hope to understand what was in the minds of the Muslim writers whose political thought we consider. Our interpretation must take full account of their basic attitude.

A final observation concerns the character of Islam in relation to politics as understood by Western students. Unless we grasp this character we cannot appreciate the significance of the caliphate as it is presented in the theory of the *Khilafa,* which serves as introduction and background to this book.

The Status of Women

Ibn Rushd's application to contemporary states of Plato's ideas about the equality of women in respect of civic duties is a mark of political realism and shows a courageous willingness to go against established Muslim thought and practice. After reproducing Plato's arguments he draws this conclusion:

> In these states, however, the ability of women is not known, because they are only taken for procreation there. They are therefore placed at the service of their husbands and (relegated) to the business of procreation, for rearing and breast-feeding. But this undoes their (other) activities. Because women in these states are not being fitted for any of the human virtues it often happens that they resemble plants. That

they are a burden on the men in these states is one of the reasons for the poverty of these states. They are found there in twice the number of men, while at the same time they do not, through training, support any of the necessary activities; except for a few which they undertake mostly at a time when they are obliged to make up their want of funds, like spinning and weaving. All this is self-evident.

This outspoken criticism of the structure of Islamic society is the more astonishing in that it comes from an adherent of Almohad orthodoxy and from a man well versed in *Fiqh*. It shows that he boldly applied to Islamic civilization and life Platonic notions derived from an entirely different outlook and social organization. Plato's political principles, born of his philosophy, and based upon his experience of the Greek city-states, are considered valid, generally and in detail, and applicable to Muslim concepts and institutions. We cannot understand in any other sense his critical attitude to the Almoravid and Almohad states of the Maghreb, and his use of arguments against "false" philosophers (and especially against the *Mutakallimun*) taken from Plato's attack on the Sophists. In the rule of the *Mutakallimun* he saw the greatest danger to the state of his time. No doubt Ibn Rushd also had some personal stake in this matter; Berber fanaticism was not congenial to the flowering of philosophy, which could survive only under the personal protection of the Almohad caliphs.

E. I. J. Rosenthal, *Political Thought in Medieval Islam: An Introductory Outline* (Cambridge: Cambridge University Press, 1958), 7–8, 191–192.

Islam in the Mediterranean World

Born in one of the most primitive and backward regions of the ancient world, Islam soon overstepped its frontiers, developing from a local phenomenon and an internal factor in Arabian life into a universalist religion and a world force, in a process about which historians still dispute. For those who study the obscure dynamism of this process, it is neither Oriental nor Occidental, nor can it be given any other geographic or cultural specification; it is only the mysterious force radiating from the new faith, and of the state founded by it, which developed in every direction and produced a surprisingly united civilization despite the very diverse environments and cultural levels upon which it flourished. . . .

The contacts of conquest and penetration which . . . European lands had with Islam are divided chronologically into two main periods and aspects.

The first of these is the more important from our point of view; its "legacy" covers both the earlier and later Middle Ages and essentially concerns Islam in its origins, ethnically Arab with a strong Berber infiltration. The second, which concerns eastern Europe almost exclusively, falls within modern times, and the Islam which is the protagonist is that of the Ottoman Turks, representing the last wave of conquest under the symbol of the faith of Muhammad in the Mediterranean world. These two periods are, despite the identity of faith, profoundly different. In the first, Islamic civilization is still itself in the course of formation, absorbing elements of pre-existing Oriental cultures, of Hellenism and, generally speaking, the late classical period, and handing them on, after having assimilated and elaborated them to the countries and peoples with whom it came in contact. This is the most fruitful and glorious phase of the "legacy," in which as well as raids and invasions, the medieval West received from Muslim civilization the full benefit of its cultural inheritance, which was decisive for its own further development.

Rather different are the characteristics of the second and later period, contemporaneous with, or later than, our Renaissance. At that time the West had attained full consciousness of itself and was following, with vital energy, the path of modern civilization, whereas the Muslim East, which opposed it and in part also threatened it, had not progressed equally. A new power, that of the Ottoman Turks, conquered the less advanced parts of south-eastern Europe, but when it tried to penetrate into the European heartlands, it was repulsed. Turkish Islam brought with it a culture based largely on the older Arabo-Persian foundations, although it would be untrue to say that no individual and original cultural traits developed in the Ottoman Empire. Nevertheless, this second "legacy," even though like the first it lasted for centuries, was a poorer, less easily definable one. . . .

Francesco Gabrieli, "Islam in the Mediterranean World," in *The Legacy of Islam,* ed. Joseph Schacht and C. E. Bosworth (London: Orion Publishing Group, 1974), 63–65.

Literary Tendencies

Islam at its origin found a national poetic tradition that was already stabilized and blossoming. The Prophet's own rather slight inclination and competence for poetry, and the traces of polemic which as a result remained in the Koran itself and in Tradition, did not prevent him from recognizing the social value which poetry had long had for the Arabs and from utilizing it for his ends. But although recent studies have weakened the old thesis of the total impermeability of the ancient poetry to the Islamic message, there remains nonetheless the fundamental fact of the contrast, analyzed masterfully by [Ignaz] Goldziher, between *muruwwa* and *din*—between the pagan ideals, of which the antique poetry had become the vehicle, and Mohammed's Islamic ideal, which the first generations of Muslims developed. Islam's totalitarian character . . . should logically have led to the condemnation of poetry as a frivolous and even impious foe of revelation, a living witness to vanquished paganism, a diabolic inspiration of the jinns. If this did not happen at all, and if poetry continued undisturbed on its way (with sporadic concessions to the new faith but keeping its themes, motifs, and images intact, as well as its power to fascinate even the minds of the pious), this was due not only to the art's "charm"—a charm that Plato recognized when he banished the art from his Republic—but also to the unbroken continuity among the first Muslim generations of a specific national awareness and pride which the new religion never succeeded in removing completely from their souls. The "Muslim" never succeeded in killing the "Arab" in these men, for whom poetry had constituted the sole means of expression, the sole affirmation of spirituality, and, according to the well-known definition, the record of his pageantry, the living memento of his past. Thus it was that the old poetry survived the *metanoia* of Islam and was saved from oblivion, gathered into collections, and studied. It has been said that this was done because the ancient poetry contained documentary material for the exact understanding of the Holy Book, and this is partially true; but the whole archaic period of imitation of pre-Islamic poetry, which was pursued in the first century of Islam and which was to constitute one of the poles of the "ancients-moderns" quarrel under the Abbasids, proves that this poetry was nevertheless experienced not only as a means but as an end, with an artistic and historic dignity of its own. The Ancients par excellence, the *mutaqaddimun,* were the pagan poets, and the fact that two centuries after the end of the *jahiliyya* they could still be considered by erudite Muslims as an unparalleled model to imitate reveals in our opinion not only a nearsighted classicism—a narrow, archaic, and scholastic notion of poetry—but also a tenacious and perhaps unconscious survival of what we might, "with a grain of salt," call the "humanism" of the *jahiliyya*—a scale of values, a stylistic and poetic tradition which Islam might well have been able to eject and which yet maintained itself with an astonishing vitality.

During the first two centuries of the hegira (practically until the middle of the ninth century A.D.) Islam knew no literature other than the Arabic. The appearance about this time of neo-Persian literature is important not only for the history of Iran, which thus reaffirmed its national individuality, at least linguistically, but also for the whole Muslim civilization which with it begins to try out, alongside its mother-language, a new means of expression. The rapid and splendid blooming of this second Islamic literature is interesting, not only from a literary point of view, but also from the social and religious ones, for it breaks for the first time the close bond between Arabism and Islam and opens new possibilities of spiritual affirmation to non-Arabic Muslim peoples. The well-known fact that the religious, juridical, and philosophic sciences for a long time continued to be treated in Arabic in Persia here remains secondary; what count are the literary and artistic means of expression, suited to expressing a different ethos, a national characteristic, a more than linguistic "variety" within the common Muslim culture. According to the terms of our problem, we can then ask the following question: What did neo-Persian literature bring to Islamic civilization that was new, what did it borrow, what did it prolong, what did it modify in Arabic literature, and what did it add that was original from its own ethnic and cultural background?

Francesco Gabrieli, "Literary Tendencies," in *Unity and Variety in Islam,* ed. G. E. von Grunebaum (Chicago: University of Chicago Press, 1955), 90–91, 97–98.

Notes

1. The Uniqueness of Islam

1. P. J. Vatikiotis, *Islam and the State* (London: Croom Helm, 1987), 11.

2. Ibid., 5.

3. Ibid., 7–8, 10–11.

4. Ibid., 29–30, 31 (emphasis in original).

5. Joseph Schacht, "Islamic Religious Law," in *The Legacy of Islam,* ed. Joseph Schacht and C. E. Bosworth (Oxford: Clarendon Press, 1974), 397–398.

6. Ibid., 398.

7. Ibid., 400–401.

8. Duncan MacDonald, *Development of Muslim Theology, Jurisprudence and Constitutional Theory* (London, 1903; Beirut: Khayats, 1965), 3.

9. Ibid., 3–4.

10. Ibid., 6.

11. E. I. J. Rosenthal, *Islam in the Modern National State* (Cambridge: Cambridge University Press, 1965), 5.

12. Ibid., 61–62.

13. Ibid., 111, 112–113.

14. Ibid., 373.

15. Akbar S. Ahmed, *Postmodernism and Islam: Predicament and Promise* (London: Routledge, 1992), 36.

16. Ibid., 36–37.

17. Elie Kedourie, *Islam in the Modern World* (London: Mansel Publishers, 1980), vi.

18. Ibid., 2–3.

19. Ibid., 30.

20. Ibid., 69.

2. The Islamic Establishment in Decline

1. Bernard Lewis, "Politics and War," in Schacht and Bosworth, eds., *Legacy of Islam,* 156–157.

2. Quoted in Nissim Rejwan, "Islam Can Justify Anything," *Jerusalem Post,* November 2, 1990.

3. *Rose el-Yusuf,* Cairo, July 20, 1992, 20–22.

4. *Al-Ra°y,* Amman, August 2, 1992.

5. Quoted in Nissim Rejwan, "Political Reform According to the Saudis," *Jerusalem Post,* April 3, 1992.

6. Ibid.

7. Ibid.

8. John L. Esposito, *The Islamic Threat: Myth or Reality?* (New York: Oxford University Press, 1993), 204–205.

3. Islam and the Orientalists

1. Gustave E. von Grunebaum, *Medieval Islam: A Study in Cultural Orientation* (Chicago: University of Chicago Press, 1961), 345.

2. Ibid., 346–347.

3. Bryan S. Turner, "Gustave E. von Grunebaum and the Nemesis of Islam," in *Orientalism, Islam and Islamists,* ed. Asaf Hussain, Robert Olson, Jamil Qureshi (Jakarta, 1989), 193–194, 195.

4. Ibid., 199.

5. Quotes from Sam‘an's article are excerpted from Nissim Rejwan, "Attacking Orientalists," *Jerusalem Post,* March 25, 1991.

6. Khalla and Astiff are quoted in ibid.

7. Ibid.

8. Ibid.

9. Esposito, *Islamic Threat,* 47–48.

10. Ibid., 48–49.

11. Ahmed, *Postmodernism and Islam,* 94–95.

12. Ibid., 95, 96–97.

13. Ibid., 97.

4. The Anthropologist's Approach

1. Gustave E. von Grunebaum, *Islam: Essays in the Nature and Growth of a Cultural Tradition* (London: Routledge and Kegan Paul, 1955), 185.

2. Ibid.

3. H. A. R. Gibb, in *The Near East: Problems and Prospects,* ed. Philip W. Ireland and William E. Hocking (Chicago, 1942), 60.

4. Von Grunebaum, *Islam: Essays,* 185–186.

5. Raphael Patai, *The Arab Mind* (New York: Scribner, 1983), 143–144, 145.

6. Ibid., 147.

7. A. L. Kroeber, *The Nature of Culture* (Chicago: University of Chicago Press, 1952), 380–381.

8. Ibid., 381–382.

9. Ibid., 382–383.

10. Isma'il al-Faruqi, "Islam as Culture and Civilization," in *Islam and Contemporary Society,* ed. Salem Azzam (London: Longman, 1982), 162–163.

11. Ibid., 163, 164–165.

12. Ibid., 165–166.

13. Dale F. Eickelman, "Changing Interpretations of Islamic Movements," in *Islam and the Political Economy of Meaning: Comparative Studies of Muslim Discourse,* ed. William R. Roff (London: Croom Helm, 1991), 18.

14. Ibid., 19–20.

15. Ahmed, *Postmodernism and Islam,* 156–160.

5. Coping with Modernity

1. More on these groups and their teachings in Nissim Rejwan, "Islam on the Defensive," Readings, chapter 9.

2. Esposito, *Islamic Threat,* 49–50.

3. Maxime Rodinson, "The Western Image and Western Studies of Islam," in Schacht and Bosworth, eds., *Legacy,* 51–52.

4. Ahmed, *Postmodernism and Islam,* 185.

5. Ibid., 182, 188–189.

6. Hamilton Gibb, *Modern Trends in Islam* (Chicago: University of Chicago Press, 1947), 28–29.

7. Uriel Heyd, "The Ottoman 'Ulema and Westernization in the Time of Selim III and Mahmud II," in *Studies in Islamic History and Civilization,* ed. Uriel Heyd (Jerusalem: Magnes Press, Hebrew University, 1961), 95.

8. Ibid., 95–96.

9. Ibid., 96.

10. Bernard Lewis, "Religious Coexistence and Socialism," in *Islam and the West* (New York: Oxford University Press, 1993), 184–185.

11. Abdallah Laroui, "Western Orientalism and Liberal Islam: Mutual Distrust?" *Middle East Studies Association Bulletin,* July 1997, 9.

12. Ibid., 10.

13. Ibid., 10–11.

6. Islam Misunderstood

1. Arthur J. Arberry, *Oriental Essay: Portraits of Seven Scholars* (London: Allen and Unwin, 1960), 252–253.

2. Ahmed, *Postmodernism and Islam,* 189.

3. Vatikiotis, *Islam and the State,* 14.

4. Ali Rahnema and Farhad Nomani, *The Secular Miracle: Religion, Politics, and Economic Policy in Iran* (London: Zed Books, 1990), 16–18, 361–62.

5. Habib Boularès, *Islam: The Fear and the Hope* (London: Zed Books, 1990), ix, 136.

6. Ahmed, *Postmodernism and Islam*, 37–38.

7. Ibid., 41–42.

8. Edward Said, *Orientalism* (New York: Pantheon, 1978), 277; emphasis in original.

9. Ibid., 282; emphasis in original.

10. Ibid., 283.

11. Bernard Lewis, "Communism and Islam," in *The Middle East in Transition: Studies in Contemporary History,* ed. Walter Z. Laqueur (London: Routledge and Kegan Paul, 1958), 323.

12. Mustafa Mahmud, *Al-Marksiyya wal-Islam* (Marxism and Islam) (Cairo, 1975), 8, 79.

13. Bernard Lewis, "The West and the Middle East," *Foreign Affairs* (New York), January-February 1997, 127–128.

14. Quoted by Ahmed, *Postmodernism and Islam,* 85.

15. John Esposito, *Islamic Threat,* 205–207.

16. Ibid., 215.

17. Muhammad Mohaddessin, *Islamic Fundamentalism: The New Global Threat* (Washington, D.C.: Seven Locks Press, 1994), 1.

7. Islam and the Dhimmis

1. Esposito, *Islamic Threat,* 38–39.

2. Ahmed, *Postmodernism and Islam,* 62.

3. Ibid., 64–65.

4. Hamilton Gibb and Harold Bowen, *Islamic Society and the West* (London: Oxford University Press, 1957), 1:218.

5. Mohammed Arkoun, *Rethinking Islam: Common Questions, Uncommon Answers,* trans. and ed. Robert D. Lee (Boulder, Colo.: Westview, 1994), 44–45.

6. S. D. Goitein, *Interfaith Relations in Medieval Islam* (Tel Aviv, 1973), 28–29.

7. Norman Stillman, "The Commensality of Islamic and Jewish Civilizations," *Middle East Lectures* (Tel Aviv: Moshe Dayan Center for Middle Eastern and African Studies) 2 (1997): 104.

8. Fundamentalism Strikes Back

1. Quoted in *Jerusalem Post,* February 16, 1989.

2. John Esposito, *Islamic Threat,* 190–191.

3. Salim Mansur, "Muslims in the Year 2000 and Beyond," *Middle East Affairs Journal* (Annandale, Va.), Winter–Spring 1997/1417, 24–26.

4. Ibid., 28–29.

5. Sheikh Rashid al-Ghanuchi, "Islamic Movements: Self-Criticism and Reconsideration," *Middle East Affairs Journal* (Annandale, Va.), Winter–Spring 1997/1417, 12.

6. Ibid., 15–16.

7. Hasan Turabi, "The West and Islamic Revivalism," *Middle East Affairs Journal* (Annandale, Va.), Winter-Spring 1995, 24.

8. Ibid., 24–25.

9. Gabriel R. Warburg, "Turabi of the Sudan: Soft-Spoken Revolutionary," in *Middle Eastern Lectures* 1 (Tel Aviv, 1995): 92.

10. Quoted by Warburg, ibid., 93.

11. Ibid.

9. A Last-Ditch Stand

1. Fathi Ghanim, quoted in David Sagiv, *Fundamentalism and Intellectuals in Egypt, 1973–1993* (London: Frank Cass, 1995), 163–164.

2. Zaki Najib Mahmud, quoted in ibid., 142.

3. ʿAbd el-Qader Hashani, quoted in Nissim Rejwan, "The Case of Algeria," *Jerusalem Post,* January 10, 1992.

4. "Cairo Declares War on Militants," *Jerusalem Post,* March 17, 1993.

5. Excerpted from Nissim Rejwan, "Saddam Moslems vs. Fahd Moslems," *Jerusalem Post,* January 18, 1991 (emphasis in original).

6. Quoted in Nissim Rejwan, "Now Saudis Face the Fundamentalist Music," *Jerusalem Post,* July 4, 1993.

7. Ibid.

8. Carla Power, "Secular Radicalism," *Newsweek,* July 14, 1997, 2.

10. Unity in Islamic Diversity

1. From his lecture, "Islam and the West," delivered at the Oxford Centre for Islamic Studies, October 27, 1993.

2. Akbar S. Ahmed, *Living Islam: From Samarkand to Stornoway* (London: Penguin, 1993), 9.

3. Ahmed, *Postmodernism and Islam,* 264–265.

4. Olivier Roy, *The Failure of Political Islam,* trans. Carol Volk (Cambridge, Mass.: Harvard University Press, 1995), ix–x.

5. Arkoun, *Rethinking Islam,* 121.

6. Ibid., 129.

7. Fatima Mernissi, *Islam and Democracy: Fear of the Modern World* (Reading, Mass.: Addison-Wesley, 1993), 145–147.

8. Aziz al-Azmeh, *Islams and Modernities* (London: Verso, 1993), 1.

9. Ibid., 79–80.

10. Ibid., 141–142.

11. Lewis, *Islam and the West,* 175–176.

12. Esposito, *Islamic Threat,* 198–99, 215.

13. Ervand Abrahamian, *Khomeinism: Essays on the Islamic Republic* (Berkeley: University of California Press, 1993), 2–3.

Index

Index of Readings

Credits

1. The Uniqueness of Islam

"The Religious Foundation—Piety—Prayer," from Gustave E. von Grunebaum, *Medieval Islam*, is reprinted with the permission of the University of Chicago Press.

"Jurisprudence," from Gustave E. von Grunebaum, *Medieval Islam*, is reprinted with the permission of the University of Chicago Press.

2. The Islamic Establishment in Decline

"The Nature of Islamic Modernism," from Nissim Rejwan, *Arabs Face the Modern World: Religious, Cultural, and Political Responses to the West*, is reprinted with the permission of the University Press of Florida.

"The ʿUlama and Legal Reform," from John L. Esposito, *Islam: The Straight Path* (3d ed.), is used by permission of Oxford University Press.

"'Translating' Traditional Texts," from Aziz al-Azmeh, *Islams and Modernities*, is reprinted by permission of the publishers, Verso, Inc.

"Afghani's Legacy," from Nissim Rejwan, *Arabs Face the Modern World: Religious, Cultural, and Political Responses to the West*, is reprinted with the permission of the University Press of Florida.

"Two Views of Islamic Law," from Nomani Othman, "Hudud Law or Islamic Modernity?" in *Shariʿa Law and the Modern Nation- State*, ed. Nomani Othman, is reprinted with the permission of the author.

"The West's Inroads," from W. Montgomery Watt, *Islamic Philosophy and Theology*, is reprinted with the permission of Edinburgh University Press.

"The Travails of Modern Islam," from Daniel Pipes, *In the Path of God: Islam and Political Power*, is reprinted with the permission of the author.

"'Islamisation,'" from Muhammad Shukri Salleh, "Islamisation of State and Society: A Critical Comment," in *Shariʿa Law and the Modern Nation-State*, ed. Nomani Othman, is reprinted with the permission of the volume editor.

3. Islam and the Orientalists

"'Instrument of Patience,'" from Timothy Mitchell, *Colonizing Egypt*, is reprinted with the permission of University of California Press.

"The Critics Criticized," from Fred Halliday, "Orientalism and Its Critics," *British Journal of Middle Eastern Studies*, is reprinted with the permission of Taylor and Francis.

"The Middle East Is Not Unique," from Fred Halliday, "Orientalism and Its Critics," *British Journal of Middle Eastern Studies*, is reprinted with the permission of Taylor and Francis.

"Strong States, Weak Societies," from Yahya Sadowski, "The New Orientalism and the Democracy Debate," in *Political Islam: Essays from* Middle East Report, ed. Joel Beinin and Joe Stork, is reprinted with the permission of the University of California Press.

"Orientalists Old and New," from Yahya Sadowski, "The New Orientalism and the Democracy Debate," in *Political Islam: Essays from* Middle East Report, ed. Joel Beinin and Joe Stork, is reprinted with the permission of the University of California Press.

"Orientals, Orientals, Orientals," from Edward W. Said, *Orientalism* (copyright 1978 by Edward W. Said), is reprinted by permission of Pantheon Books, a division of Random House, Inc.

"The Matter of Arabic," from Morwan M. Obeidat, "Arabic and the West," *Muslim World* 88, 2 (1998), is reprinted with permission of *The Muslim World*. Copyright Hartford Seminary, 1992.

4. The Anthropologist's Approach

"The Nature of Muslim Civilization," from Robert Brunschvig, "Perspectives," in *Unity and Variety in Muslim Civilization*, ed. Gustave E. von Grunebaum, is reprinted with the permission of the University of Chicago Press.

"Unity in Diversity," from Gustave E. von Grunebaum, "The Problem: Unity in Diversity," in *Unity and Variety in Muslim Civilization*, ed. Gustave E. von Grunebaum, is reprinted with the permission of the University of Chicago Press.

"Government and Constitution," from Mohammad Hashim Kamali, "The Islamic State and Its Constitution," in *Shari>a Law and the Modern Nation-State*, ed. Nomani Othman, is reprinted with the permission of the volume editor.

"The Social Order," from Gustave E. von Grunebaum, *Medieval Islam*, is reprinted with the permission of the University of Chicago Press.

"Law and the State," from Gustave E. von Grunebaum, *Medieval Islam*, is reprinted with the permission of the University of Chicago Press.

"Adjustment," from Werner Caskel, "Western Impact and Muslim Civilization," in *Unity and Variety in Muslim Civilization*, ed. Gustave E. von Grunebaum, is reprinted with the permission of the University of Chicago Press.

"Political Organization," from Claude Cahen, "The Body Politic," in *Unity and*

Variety in Muslim Civilization, ed. Gustave E. von Grunebaum, is reprinted with the permission of the University of Chicago Press.

"The Body Politic," from Claude Cahen, "The Body Politic," in *Unity and Variety in Muslim Civilization,* ed. Gustave E. von Grunebaum, is reprinted with the permission of the University of Chicago Press.

5. Coping with Modernity

"Attitude to Arabism," from Nissim Rejwan, *Arabs Face the Modern World: Religious, Cultural, and Political Responses to the West,* is reprinted with the permission of the University Press of Florida.

"Islam and Nationalism," from P. J. Vatikiotis, *Islam and the State,* is reprinted with the permission of Routledge, Ltd.

"Nation, Nationality and Islamic Principles," from K. Haridas, "Islamization of State and Society," in *Shari>a Law and the Modern Nation-State,* ed. Nomani Othman, is reprinted with the permission of the volume editor.

"Umma, Dawla, and the Islamic State," from Mohammad Hashim Kamali, "The State and Its Constitution," in *Shari>a Law and the Modern Nation-State,* ed. Nomani Othman, is reprinted with the permission of the volume editor.

"Umma and Citizenry: A Modern Muslim Civil Society," from Norani Othman, "*Umma* and Citizenship," in *Shari>a Law and the Modern Nation-State,* ed. Nomani Othman, is reprinted with the permission of the author.

"Democracy and Shura," from Gudrun Kramer, "Islamist Notions of Democracy," in *Political Islam: Essays from* Middle East Report, ed. Joel Beinin and Joe Stork, is reprinted with the permission of the University of California Press.

"Adapting Democracy," from Shukri B. Abed, "Democracy and the Arab World," in *Democracy, Peace, and the Israeli- Palestinian Conflict,* ed. Edy Kaufman, Shukri B. Abed, Robert L. Rothstein, is reprinted with the permission of the author.

6. Islam Misunderstood

"Self-Image," from Gustave E. Von Grunebaum, *Medieval Islam,* is reprinted with the permission of the University of Chicago Press.

"Terminology and Precedent," from Muhammad Asad, *The Principles of State and Government in Islam,* is reprinted with the permission of the University of California Press.

"The Myth of Monolithic Islam," from John L. Esposito, *The Islamic Threat: Myth or Reality?* is used by permission of Oxford University Press, Inc.

"Anger, Powerlessness, Confrontation," from Akbar S. Ahmed, *Postmodernism and Islam: Predicament and Promise* (1992), is reprinted with the permission of Routledge.

"The Cultural Content," from Simon Bromley, *Rethinking Middle East Politics,* is reprinted with the permission of Blackwell Publishers.

7. Islam and the Dhimmis

"Muhammad and the Jews," from Barakat Ahmad, *Muhammad and the Jews: A Re-Examination*, is reprinted with the permission of Vikas Publishing House Pvt. Ltd., New Delhi.

"Non-Muslims under Muslim Rule: Qur<anic Imperatives," from K. Haridas, "Islamization of State and Society," in *Shari>a Law and the Modern Nation-State*, ed. Nomani Othman, is reprinted with the permission of the volume editor.

"*Ahl al-Kitab*," from Norman A. Stillman, "The Commensality of Jewish and Islamic Civilizations," in *Middle Eastern Lectures* 2 (1997), ed. Martin Kramer, is reprinted with the permission of the Moshe Dayan Center for Middle Eastern and African Studies.

"A Framework for the Coexistence of Judaism, Christianity, and Islam: Common Thread of Salvation," from Muhammad Sa>id al->Ashmawi, in *Against Islamic Extremism: The Writings of Muhammad Sa>id al->Ashmawi*, ed. Carolyn Fluehr-Lobban, is reprinted with the permission of the University Press of Florida.

"Muslim Anti-Semitism," from Bernard Lewis, *Semites and Anti- Semites: An Inquiry into Conflict and Prejudice*, is reprinted by permission of W. W. Norton and Company, Inc.

"'Muslim Anti-Semitism'?" from Abdelaleem El-Abyad, Press and Information Bureau, Embassy of the Arab Republic of Egypt, Washington, D.C., *Middle East Quarterly*, September 1998, is reprinted with the permission of *Middle East Quarterly*.

"The French King, the Muslim Ambassador, and the Blood Libel," from Mark R. Cohen, *Under Crescent and Cross: The Jews in the Middle Ages* (copyright 1994 by Princeton University Press), is reprinted by permission of Princeton University Press.

8. Fundamentalism Strikes Back

"The Muslim Brothers," from Nissim Rejwan, *Arabs Face the Modern World: Religious, Cultural, and Political Responses to the West*, is reprinted with the permission of the University Press of Florida.

"The Brotherhood's Political Theory," from Sayed Kotb, *Social Justice in Islam*, trans. John B. Hardie, is reprinted with the permission of the American Council of Learned Societies.

"Islamic Government: A Contemporary Muslim's Prognosis," from Muhammad Sa>id al->Ashmawi, in *Against Islamic Extremism: The Writings of Muhammad Sa>id al->Ashmawi*, ed. Carolyn Fluehr-Lobban, is reprinted with the permission of the University Press of Florida.

"The Three Components of Islamist Movements," from Giles Kepel, "Toward a Social Analysis of Islamist Movements," in *Ethnic Conflict and International Politics in the Middle East*, ed. Leonard Binder, is reprinted with the permission of the University Press of Florida.

"Fundamentalism Is Not Transitory," from Daniel Pipes, "The Western Mind of Radical Islam," in *The Islamism Debate,* ed. Martin Kramer, is reprinted with the permission of the Moshe Dayan Center for Middle Eastern and African Studies.

"Sources of Future Islamist Strength," from Graham E. Fuller, "Islamism(s) in the Next Century," in *The Islamism Debate,* ed. Martin Kramer, is reprinted with the permission of the Moshe Dayan Center for Middle Eastern and African Studies.

"Refocusing on Woman and the Family," from John L. Esposito, *Islam: The Straight Path* (3d ed.), is used by permission of Oxford University Press, Inc.

"Muslim Women as Citizens?" from Amina Wadud-Muhsin, "The Qur<an, *Shari>a* and the Citizenship Rights of Muslim Women," in *Shari>a Law and the Modern Nation-State,* ed. Nomani Othman, is reprinted with the permission of the volume editor.

9. A Last-Ditch Stand

"Ideological Worldview of Revivalism," from John L. Esposito, *Islam: The Straight Path* (3d ed.), is used by permission of Oxford University Press, Inc.

"Problems of Islamism in Power," from Graham E. Fuller, "Islamism(s) in the Next Century," in Martin Kramer, ed., *The Islamism Debate,* is reprinted with the permission of the Moshe Dayan Center for Middle Eastern and African Studies.

"The Islamist Contradiction," from Olivier Roy, "Islamists in Power," in *The Islamism Debate,* ed. Martin Kramer, isreprinted with the permission of the Moshe Dayan Center for Middle Eastern and African Studies.

"Islam on the Defensive," from Nissim Rejwan, *Arabs Face the Modern World: Religious, Cultural, and Political Responses to the West,* is reprinted with the permission of the University Press of Florida.

"Hamas: Strategy and Tactics," from Muhammad Muslih, "Hamas: Strategy and Tactics," in *Ethnic Conflict and International Politics in the Middle East,* ed. Leonard Binder, is reprinted with the permission of the University Press of Florida.

"In Israel: 'Islamization from Below,'" from Muhammad Hasan Amora, "The Nature of Islamic Fundamentalism in Israel," is reprinted by permission from *Religious Radicalism in the Greater Middle East,* ed. Bruce Maddy-Weitzman and Efraim Inbar, published by Frank Cass & Company, 900 Eastern Avenue, Ilford, Essex, England. Copyright Frank Cass & Co. Ltd.

"The Case of Faraj Fouda," from Nissim Rejwan, *Arabs Face the Modern World: Religious, Cultural, and Political Responses to the West,* is reprinted with the permission of the University Press of Florida.

"What Future the Islamist Movement?" from Giles Kepel, "Toward a Social Analysis of Islamic Movements," in *Ethnic Conflict and International Politics in the Middle East,* ed. Leonard Binder, is reprinted with the permission of the University Press of Florida.

10. Unity in Islamic Diversity

"Four Orthodox Schools," from W. Montgomery Watt, *Islamic Philosophy and Theology,* is reprinted with the permission of Edinburgh University Press.

"Distorting the Teachings of Islam," from Mohammad Mohaddessin, *Islamic Fundamentalism: The New Global Threat,* is reprinted with the permission of Seven Locks Press.

"Islam and Political Theory," from E. I. J. Rosenthal, *Political Thought in Medieval Islam: An Introductory Outline,* is reprinted with the permission of Cambridge University Press.

"Islam in the Mediterranean World," from Francesco Gabrieli, "Islam in the Mediterranean World," in *The Legacy of Islam,* ed. Joseph Schacht and C. E. Bosworth, is reprinted with the permission of the Orion Publishing Group.

"Literary Tendencies," from Francesco Gabrieli, "Literary Tendencies," in *Unity and Variety in Muslim Civilization,* ed. Gustave E. von Grunebaum, is reprinted with the permission of the University of Chicago Press.

Nissim Rejwan is a research fellow at the Harry S. Truman Research Institute for the Advancement of Peace at the Hebrew University of Jerusalem. He is the author of nine books, including *Arabs Face the Modern World: Religious, Cultural, and Political Responses to the West* (UPF, 1998) and *Israel's Place in the Middle East: A Pluralist Perspective* (UPF, 1998), winner of the 1998 National Jewish Book Award in Israel Studies. He is currently writing his memoirs of Baghdad, where he was born and grew up.